P9-CRH-778

Deregulating the Airlines

MIT Press Series on the Regulation of Economic Activity

General Editor
Richard Schmalensee, MIT Sloan School of Management

Deregulating the Airlines

Elizabeth E. Bailey
David R. Graham
Daniel P. Kaplan

DISCARDED

The MIT Press
Cambridge, Massachusetts
London, England

This book was set in Times New Roman by Asco Trade Typesetting Ltd., Hong Kong and printed and bound by Halliday Lithograph in the United States of America

Library of Congress Cataloging in Publication Data

Bailey, Elizabeth E.
  Deregulating the airlines.

  (MIT Press series on the regulation of economic activity; 10)
  Bibliography: p.
  Includes index.
  1. Aeronautics, Commercial—Government policy—United States. 2. Aeronautics, Commercial—Law and legislation—United States.   I. Graham, David R.   II. Kaplan, Daniel P.   III. Title.   IV. Series.
  HE9803.A4B32 1985   387.7′068   84-21816
  ISBN 0-262-02213-3

Contents

List of Tables

List of Figures

Series Foreword

Government regulation of economic activity in the United States has grown dramatically in this century, radically transforming government-business relations. Economic regulation of prices and conditions of service was first applied to transportation and public utilities and was later extended to energy, health care, and other sectors. In the early 1970s explosive growth occurred in social regulation, focusing on workplace safety, environmental preservation, consumer protection, and related goals. Though regulatory reform has occupied a prominent place on the agendas of recent administrations, and some important reforms have occurred, the aims, methods, and results of many regulatory programs remain controversial.

The purpose of the MIT Press series, Regulation of Economic Activity, is to inform the ongoing debate on regulatory policy by making significant and relevant research available to both scholars and decision makers. Books in this series present new insights into individual agencies, programs, and regulated sectors, as well as the important economic, political, and administrative aspects of the regulatory process that cut across these boundaries.

Airline deregulation is commonly treated by economists as a simple triumph of rationality over its foes: inefficient regulation was removed from a potentially competitive industry. In this important book Bailey, Graham, and Kaplan make it clear that the real story is both more complex and more interesting. They provide a valuable inside view of decision making at the Civil Aeronautics Board (CAB) during the critical transition to full deregulation. The CAB faced complex, unanticipated problems, which the intelligent application of economic theory helped it to solve. Further *Deregulating the Airlines* provides the first comprehensive analysis of the initial effects of deregulation and tests a number of hypotheses about the industry and its regulation that have been important in policy debates.

Although the airline industry has probably not yet reached equilibrium, this valuable study tells us a good deal about where it has come and where it is probably going. *Deregulating the Airlines* should be read by all concerned with the role of economic analysis in public policy formation as well as by specialists in regulation and transportation.

Preface

A common folklore in the economics profession is that the economist in Washington faces frustration at the level of ideology and policy though high satisfaction at the level of atmosphere and activity (see Stein 1984, 1). The three authors of this book enjoyed the high satisfaction but avoided most of the frustration. Each of us was at the Civil Aeronautics Board during at least a portion of the period during which the policy activity described in this book took place. Each of us found that our economics training provided us with a framework within which coherent policy could be formulated. The Congress and the Board were together able to achieve eregulation goals that were consistent with ideology. Reality impinged on the process to be sure. Transitional adjustments proved to be far more troublesome than anticipated. Many lessons were learned. It was an eventful period, and one that merits review and analysis.

Our roles in the process were not all the same. Daniel P. Kaplan has been the Director of the Office of Economic Analysis since 1980. David R. Graham was Chief of the Office's Policy Analysis Division and now is the Director of the Defense Economics Program at the Institute for Defense Analysis. These two authors were responsible for studying the effects of deregulation. Their collaboration resulted in a report "Competition and the Airlines: An Evaluation of Deregulation," completed in December 1982 that provides the analytical foundation of this book. The third author, Elizabeth E. Bailey, was a Civil Aeronautics Board member from mid-1977 to mid-1983 and is now Dean of the Graduate School of Industrial Administration at Carnegie-Mellon University. She contributed much of the focus on the policy perspective and much of the description of the process of change. As with all collaborations, however, it has become virtually impossible to unravel our various contributions as the book has evolved and been rewritten. For this reason we decided to list the authors' names alphabetically.

The views in the book are the authors and do not necessarily represent those of the people who assisted in its preparation, The Civil Aeronautics Board, or the Board's staff. Nevertheless, a number of people at the Civil Aeronautics Board played important roles in the preparation of this study. Tadas Osmolskis' contribution in coordinating data collection and programming was especially noteworthy. Other members who contributed to the report were Steve Cooperman, Steve Davis, Peter Belenky, Frank Lewis, Paul Bowser, and Jack Schmidt. The Data Processing Division of the Office of the Comptroller and most notably Richard Strite were extremely helpful in retrieving much of the data used in the report. A number of former employees including Anne Arvin, Julie Moll, Kathy Sharp and Ben Sobin also made valuable contributions. Anna Pegram, Regina Hughes, and Patricia Lazzaro diligently and patiently typed the first version of the manuscript. Betty Scarsella did the graphics. The Word Processing Group at the Graduate School of Industrial Administration, Carnegie-Mellon University, especially Janet Adamiak and Terri Jumper, were both responsive and careful in typing the final version of the manuscript. Eleanor Riess and Sally Rosemeyer were also extraordinarily responsive no matter what the unreasonableness of the deadlines imposed on them.

Extensive comments on the first version of the book were received from William J. Baumol, Robert J. Gordon, Theodore E. Keeler, Lester Lave, Richard L. Schmalensee, and an anonymous referee. These comments led to substantial revisions, which we feel have improved the book immensely.

The appendixes and other tables presented in this book rely extensively on the voluminous data the Board has compiled. Originally these information systems were designed for use in the Board's regulation of fares and routes. With the reduction in its regulatory authority, the Board eliminated some reporting requirements. Nevertheless, carriers continue to report substantial information on traffic patterns, fares, and finances. The *Origin and Destination Survey* is a quarterly sample of airline traffic on certificated airlines. The information contained on tickets of 10 percent of the passengers is reported to the Board. This yields information on where passengers traveled, their routings, the airlines they used, and, since the third quarter of 1978, the fares they paid. *Service Segment Data* (ER-586) provides monthly information on carrier flights. For each nonstop flight segment it indicates the kind of aircraft used, the number of seats available, and the number of passengers carried. Financial data are provided on *Form 41* and include detailed reports on carriers' costs of operations as well as balance sheet and income statement information. These three sources along with the airlines' schedules, published in the *Official Airline Guide*, constitute the principal data bases for our analyses.

The classification scheme of the trunks and the locals employed in the book is that used while the industry was regulated. With deregulation the Board decided to classify carriers solely on the basis of size. Currently the majors include all the former trunks as well as two former local service carriers. The nationals include the remaining former locals as well as the former intrastates and some new extrants. Commuter carriers are now termed regionals. Under regulation the trunk airlines differed in several notable respects from the locals; therefore throughout this book we continue to refer to the former regulated carriers as either trunks or locals.

Deregulating the Airlines

Introduction

In the mid 1970s deregulation became the rallying cry of observers of the federal government's regulatory agencies. They argued that regulation raised prices and limited the variety of goods and services available to consumers in many industries. Subsequently we have seen regulation liberalized in areas as diverse as banking and telephone service. But no industry has been affected as greatly as the airlines. After operating under strict regulation for nearly forty years, the air carriers have been given the freedom to choose the routes they serve and to set the prices they charge. Their experiences in the first years after deregulation provide a unique opportunity to see how an industry responds when regulation is removed. In this book we examine the theory and policy underlying the deregulation process and offer an interim assessment of the effects of deregulation on airline performance. Throughout, our focus is on economic regulation and domestic U.S. passengers transport.[1]

We provide a narrative of the decisions that the Civil Aeronautics Board (CAB) took during the transition to deregulation and the reasoning behind its decisions. At the same time we provide many comparisons of the industry before and after deregulation. In as comprehensive a manner as possible we use these comparative data to highlight the developments that have proved important in the initial post deregulation period. We also use these data to test various alternative hypotheses scholars and politicians have advanced about how markets would behave if regulation were removed. Our findings provide information about the characteristics on both the demand and the cost side that are proving to be important in molding the long-run equilibrium of the industry. They also give some insight into how quickly the industry is adjusting toward equilibrium.

The book is divided into three parts. The first part sets the stage for our analysis. Chapter 1 describes the legislation that mandated economic regulation of air transportation and offers an overview of the policies of the CAB while the industry was regulated. Chapter 2 provides a description of the regulatory reform movement and of the Airline Deregulation Act of 1978 (Public Law 95.504), which removed rate and route regulation.

Economic regulation of air transportation was established during the 1920s and 1930s and rested primarily on three pillars of belief: (1) it is necessary for a regulatory agency to design aviation route networks in order to ensure that an integrated service network develops; (2) it is desirable to provide subsidy in order to promote the development of the air service network; and (3) destructive competition might well characterize the industry absent regulatory intervention.

The key assumption underlying this view is that competition results in smaller and smaller pieces of a fixed demand pie being divided among carriers. Such competition requires duplication of services or facilities and therefore is wasteful. There are moreover economies of system integration. Thus monopoly or near monopoly right should be granted to carriers within particular regions or on certain parallel routes, thereby promoting better resource utilization. Because of the monopoly or near monopoly of route authority, it is in turn necessary to regulate rates so that consumers are protected from too high prices.

Subsidy was believed necessary to foster the development of the airline industry. In the early years the carriage of mail was used to provide a subsidy to encourage airline passenger services. Later, as larger routes became self-sufficient, subsidy was provided to expand the route system to include many smaller communities.

The faith in these theories justifying economic regulation was gradually undermined by a series of economic studies.[2] As early as 1951 Lucile Keyes could find no available evidence of any need for federal control over entry in aviation. Richard Caves (1962) found that the Big Four trunk carriers had average costs no lower than those of the smaller trunks. Thus he argued that economies of scale at a system level were minimal and competition would permit rational route choices.

Michael Levine (1965) and William Jordan (1970) chronicled the successful performance of the largely unregulated intrastate markets in California. There, services were offered at prices less than half those mandated by the CAB, and the carriers were profitable. George Douglas and James Miller (1974), among others, began to build more sophisticated models of airline competition. These models showed that the current regulatory regime, in which prices were set but carriers were free to determine frequency of flights, was resulting in excessive service competition. If prices were not regulated, a more efficient delivery of services (less empty seats) could ensue.

Finally, George Eads (1975) questioned the effectiveness of the regulated regime in fostering small community service. He found that, despite CAB subsidies, large numbers of small communities were being abandoned by the regulated carriers and were being serviced by a commuter carrier industry that had no rate or route regulation and received no subsidies. The scheduling of service at communities still on certificated carrier subsidized systems was based more on carrier convenience than consumer demand.

Thus the change in the regulatory framework stemmed from dramatic shifts in perceptions of the relative benefits from regulation versus those from reliance on market forces. Stephen Breyer marshaled the analysis of the economists and combined it with evidence responsive to the rhetoric of those who opposed reform. The detailed factual response appeared in a series of highly visible hearings held by Senator Edward Kennedy and was written up by Breyer in a U.S. Senate Report (1975). These hearings provided the political basis for reform.

The second part of the book describes the set of decisions made by the CAB during the transition to deregulation and the effects of these decisions between 1978 and 1981. In chapter 3 we examine how the airlines have changed their pricing policies. It is argued that service quality and price are now better matched to market demand and that the greatly expanded use of peak-load pricing has improved efficiency. In chapter 4 we explore how carriers have changed their route systems in response to increased freedom to enter and exit from markets. Chapter 5 examines the substantial cost advantages and growth of the new entrants. Chapter 6 analyzes the effect of deregulation and of changes in subsidy policies on the quality of service to small communities.

Just as economic theory was useful in laying the foundation for reform, so economics has played a large role in its implementation. But the role has been a different one than during the earlier period. Prior to regulatory reform, economic theory was ahead of policymakers in critiquing the existing system of regulation and was instrumental in providing the framework for change. However, once the Airline Deregulation Act (ADA) passed, rapid decisions by policymakers molded the new competitive environment. Many issues arose that simply had not yet been addressed in economics research, nor was there the luxury of taking the time to do such research. Because many of the decision makers at the Board were professional economists, the framework for change was not ad hoc. But there did not exist a fully developed theory for action. Instead, there was a practicum, a walking on the line where problems were systematically addressed, decisions were taken and lived with. Decision makers were aware of a number of theoretical strands that seemed to have relevance for the airline industry, but they had not come to a conclusion about whether, for example, a model of imperfect competition or one of contestability (in the sense of a new literature that was developing during the transition period) would eventually hold sway.[3] It was general principles of economic science rather than a detailed mathematical specification and analysis that provided the guide to action during the deregulatory period.

In its broadest terms the framework for deregulatory decisions was as follows. First, beginning in 1977, the Board adopted a conscious policy of questioning the desirability and need for every one of its regulatory activities. This view provided the starting place for decision making throughout Alfred Kahn's and Marvin Cohen's tenures as chairmen of the CAB. It was the basis of the strategy for an elimination of the CAB's regulatory programs.

Second, it was recognized that the success of deregulation would not be measured in terms of proliferation of carriers on routes. Economies in aircraft size meant that only one or two carriers would actually compete on many routes, even after restrictions on entry were dropped. Yet the decision makers agreed with the new statute's premise that price regulation would not be needed. Actual competition in the market along with potential competition for the market would be effective in guaranteeing that supranormal profit would not be achieved. Thus even in markets with substantial natural monopoly characteristics, the framers of deregulatory policy felt that carriers would not be able to set fares substantially above costs without inviting entry.

Third, entry by wholly new carriers (not just by existing carriers into each other's routes) was seen to be important if the benefits of new ways of doing business were to be obtained. Thus an early high priority was to provide for rapid conferral of operating authority to such new entrants and to carriers currently operating outside the traditional regulatory system.

Finally, small community service was to be guaranteed during a ten-year transition period. Such communities would receive rapid replacement service should the regulated carriers pull out, and a new method of subsidy ensured that the replacement service would be specifically tailored to their needs.

Throughout this period there was a strong awareness that the air transport industry was in transition and therefore formal models had limited usefulness in guiding policies. In addition it rapidly became apparent that several important disequilibria would persist for some time. Firms had specific endowments with respect to route rights, and it has taken time for them to realign their route systems, once granted the flexibility to do so. The initial endowment of labor work rules and pay scales differed substantially across different classes of carriers, and renegotiation of these provisions has been a lengthy process that is far from complete. Firms also had specific endowments with respect to aircraft. There has been substantial excess capacity for some types of equipment. To a considerable extent this excess supply stemmed from general economic conditions, such as fuel price increases and a recession. However, other types of equipment have been in short supply.

Moreover the conception of what the proper long-run economic model should look like has been changing as more is learned about the competitive behavior of the industry. Some elements of existing models have transferred readily to the deregulated environment. Other traditional elements are clearly inappropriate. Still other new elements have emerged. For example, because of pricing policies under regulation, preregulation demand models did not recognize heterogeneous passenger mixes, yet these have proved to be quite significant in pricing decisions after deregulation, and in many markets the ultimate structure of fares remains an open question. Preregulation demand models stressed service convenience in terms of passenger time sensitivity in nonstop markets. Such models ignored the value of single-carrier service to those traveling in markets without nonstop service. On the cost side, it appears that point-to-point cost models are inadequate to explain behavior, and instead cost models must be developed that focus on the airline's route network.

The analytic task we have chosen for this book is to provide a comprehensive review of the significant developments in the industry relating to entry, routes, prices, and small community service through comparative snapshots of key operating variables—once at the start of deregulation in 1978 and a second view several years into the process in 1981. We are not able to attribute the differences in 1981 over 1978 entirely to deregulation, however. In addition to dramatic changes in the regulatory framework in the late 1970s, the airline industry had to adjust to rapid increases in costs, most notably fuel prices, and to a prolonged economic slump. There are clearly problems in determining to what extent deregulation, rather than these exogenous events, influenced observed outcomes. Moreover we cannot know how the CAB would have reacted to the extraordinary developments in the economy if the industry had remained regulated. Because of these exogenous changes and the ongoing transition, it is impossible to provide precise quantitative measures of how the industry differs today from what it would have been had regulation continued. Therefore much of our analysis of the data focuses on qualitative issues such as whether the changes observed in the industry's performance indicate an increase in efficiency and competition and whether changes are consistent with predictions made prior to deregulation.

Much of our analyses is limited to the period ending in June 1981. We chose this cutoff date in order to avoid distortions caused by the air traffic controllers strike which severely disrupted airline operations in the third quarter of 1981. By 1983 the effects of the PATCO strike had diminished, and the national economy began to recover from the deep recession. As one would expect, these developments have been accompanied by improvements in traffic and airline earnings, as well as increases in service in many markets. Despite the change in the climate between 1981 and 1983, most of the qualitative conclusions drawn from our analysis continue to hold. Nevertheless, in several places we believed it helpful to refer to more recent information.

The Air Traffic Controllers' (PATCO) job action and its aftermath was not an economic shock similar to the economic recession and the fuel price increases. Rather, it effected the very core of the deregulation process. It prevented carriers from adding flights at every large airport within the United States, and at nonrestricted airports, because of the strains on the capacity of enroute control centers. When the strike began, the Federal Aviation Administration (FAA) required each airline to reduce operations proportionally at the affected airports, a move that clearly interfered with the route-restructuring plans of airlines. Carriers were simultaneously prevented from offering the flights they wished and inhibited from proceeding with the rationalization of their route systems. Moreover, since entry at these airports has become more difficult, the competitive discipline of entry and the threat of entry has been limited. New entrant carriers have in some cases been unable to begin operations and in other cases have been unable to compete in their preferred markets. In addition the PATCO strike has constituted a barrier to exit since FAA rules require a carrier to forfeit a landing or takeoff right if it is not used. During a downturn in demand, such as was experienced through 1982, carriers had the incentive to operate unprofitable flights to retain their valuable operating rights. Thus, at the same time when carriers were prevented from entering potentially profitable markets, they were deterred from exiting unprofitable ones.

The third part of the book continues to use comparative snapshots, but employs a more quantitative approach as well. Chapter 7 can be viewed as a test of the hypothesis that the integrated service network developed under CAB regulation would disintegrate without the guiding hand of government. It shows that, in general, there was no diminution in the availability of integrated services or the timing of their delivery. Convenience to passengers remained about the same as it was in preregulation days; in many small community markets it improved somewhat. Chapter 8 tests the hypothesis put forward by economists in the preregulation period that productivity would improve and discusses which cost factors in particular are displaying the greatest improvement. Chapter 9 tests the hypothesis that prices would move nearer to costs in all markets and that potential and actual competition would together serve as an effective check on pricing power in airline markets. Although we might like to find that airline markets are perfectly competitive, we can only find that they are reasonably so. Some of the results described in this chapter indicate that the initial endowments of the industry as it came into the deregulation era are still important, since we are unable to reject the hypothesis that market structure is exogenously determined. Since the equilibrium in a deregulated environment should display endogeneity, such equilibrium has clearly not held in the short run.

The remainder of the book consists of chapter 10 and a concluding section. Chapter 10 analyzes how the gradual removal of the traditional shield from antitrust law is progressing. It also considers the growing concern about maintenance of the airlines' freedom of access to airports and computer reservation systems. The concluding section draws together the various strands of our analysis and attempts to summarize the elements that have held in the short run and that are likely to be reflected in a postderegulation industry equilibrium.

Before leaving this introduction, we must say something about our own backgrounds. All three authors took part in the process of airline deregulation and firmly support it. Yet we recognize that deregulation has strong critics as well as fervent advocates. The experiences of airlines during the past five years have provided a range of results. Advocates from both sides of the issues are fond of marshaling data to support their point of view.

We attempt to consider both the pro's and the con's. Deregulation has placed substantial burdens on certain carriers and their employees. Several of the trunks in particular have suffered disproportionally in the early postderegulation period. They inherited large aircraft and high costs from the regulated environment, both of which have disadvantaged them relative to small airlines. But at the same time deregulation has given these airlines added flexibility in responding to the new competitive environment, both in realigning their route networks and in their pricing policies. As the distortions caused by regulation are removed, our analysis indicates that productivity and service convenience are improving and that over the long run consumers can expect to pay lower fares than they would have in a regulated regime.

In sum, we believe that competition, for all its imperfections, is proving itself superior to regulation as a means of serving the public interest.[4] In addition it offers the hope of being a persistently effective mechanism for holding costs and prices in check and for stimulating cost, price, and service innovation.[5] Attention can now be focused most directly on the appropriate remedies for the few remaining barriers that inhibit efficiency in this inherently competitive industry.

PART I

Economic Regulation and Its Reform

Chapter 1

Regulation of the Airline Industry

Congress adopted the Civil Aeronautics Act in 1938. The act created a five-member independent regulatory agency, the Civil Aeronautics Board, and gave it the authority to

1. control entry into the industry (both interstate and foreign commerce) and control entry of existing carriers into new or existing routes,
2. control exit by requiring approval before cessation of service to a point or on a route,
3. regulate fares on the basis of rate-making provisions adopted from the Interstate Commerce Act,
4. award direct subsidies to air carriers,
5. control mergers and intercarrier agreements, thus immunizing them from the antitrust laws,
6. investigate deceptive trade practices and unfair methods of competition,
7. exempt carriers from certain provisions of the act.

The act originally gave the CAB authority over safety as well. Two decades later, however, Congress separated safety regulation from economic regulation in the Federal Aviation Act of 1958.

The CAB was charged with promotion of adequate, economical, and efficient service by air carriers at reasonable rates. It was to foster competition to the extent necessary to ensure "sound development." Overall the powers and the objectives of the act reflected the general pessimism surrounding the workings of the marketplace that pervaded the United States at the end of the depression. They reflected too considerable faith in the effectiveness of government intervention.

Route Networks of the Regulated Carriers

The origins of the domestic route system can be traced back to the late 1920s when the Hoover administration granted to the predecessors of American, TWA, and United transcontinental mail contract authority over parallel routes and established Eastern as the north–south carrier on the East Coast and United as the north–south carrier on the West Coast. There was thus a presumption in favor of parallel services as distinct from directly competing services. The CAB policies continued this pattern of division of markets into systems. The Board never undertook any comprehensive consideration of how these route maps might be rationalized or made sufficiently flexible to adapt to changing airplane technology or changing patterns of demand. Instead, except when it established a broad plan for creating nonoverlapping routes served by local service airlines in the late 1940s and early 1950s, it focused on piecemeal efforts at correction through route extensions and mergers. These ad hoc increments were dependent largely on carrier applications.

These shortcomings were attributable to the specification and implementation of route regulation under the act.[1] First, the statute required that additions to the route system be undertaken on a case-by-case basis after notice and hearing. Evidentiary hearings were mandated in contested cases. To ensure due process to all affected parties, cumbersome procedures were established, so even those route award cases set for hearing often encountered delays of two years or more.

Second, the Board did not have the authority to reduce substantially, on the basis of economic considerations, the authority of any permanently certified carrier. The effect of this provision was that any increments to route authority became permanent features of the system.

The Board could not interfere with carriers' flight schedules or equipment, so it could not regulate capacity. However, the Board could and did impose restrictions on route authority, such as the requirement that a carrier must or must not operate beyond a named point or that a carrier make intermediate stops in serving a particular market. The carriers in turn had a great deal of discretion about how to serve a city-pair market, through nonstop service, connecting flights, or single-plane trips with one or more stops.

Entry into and Exit from the Industry and Markets

As a rule the CAB considered entry into the airline industry as part of the carrier selection phase of route proceedings. These proceedings normally considered cases involving new single-plane or nonstop service in a market or first competitive service in a market. The Board typically did not consider broad issues relating to the benefits of permitting new competitors; instead, carrier selection focused on the relative merits of the applicants for the specific route (or routes) to be awarded. A nonoperating airline could provide only promises of good service or lower fares. An established airline, on the other hand, had a proven track record as well as an existing route network that offered numerous connecting opportunities. Hence the incumbent had a significant advantage in pressing its case for new routes before the CAB—so significant in fact that the Board literally never awarded a major route to a new entrant. Over the years the Board rejected scores of applications to start new airlines. [2]

The Board took a broader view of the benefits of new entry when subsidized routes were involved. Following the second world war the Board decided to create a new class of airline to relieve the trunk carriers of the responsibility for providing subsidized service to smaller communities. In the late 1940s and early 1950s several airlines were granted temporary certificates for what was known as the "local service experiment." In 1955 permanent certificates were granted to fourteen local service airlines for service in largely nonoverlapping regions. By then these carriers were receiving nearly all of the federal subsidies for small community service. Subsequently a few commuter airlines were also given certificates so that they too could receive federal subsidies.

Because the local service airlines were intended to serve only small communities, the Board severely restricted their ability to compete against the trunks throughout the 1950s and much of the 1960s. For example, the route certificates of the local service airlines included explicit prohibitions against providing nonstop service in markets already served by trunk airlines. [3] Eventually, however, the Board allowed local service carriers to offer nonstop service to selected large markets within their regions in an effort to control growing subsidy costs.

Airlines were required to provide "adequate" service at the cities listed on their certificates. Thus a carrier could not stop serving a city without CAB approval either to suspend service or to delete the community from its certificate.

Exit from the industry occurred via merger. Given the Board's restrictive entry policies, a merger with a failing airline provided a relatively cheap and fast way for a successful carrier to acquire route authority. [4]

The Board's route award policies and procedures also restricted entry into markets by existing airlines. There were three reasons for this. First, the length and complexity of the CAB's route award proceedings limited the number of route applications the Board could process. [5] Second, the burden of proof was placed on applicants for routes to show that new entry was in the public interest and would not harm an incumbent airline. Consequently the CAB awarded competitive routes only when such awards would not significantly erode the profits of an incumbent airline, that is, when industry demand was growing rapidly. Third, it was an unofficial policy of the Board to limit the number of airlines serving any market. [6] Since most large markets had as many carriers as the Board deemed suitable, they were foreclosed to additional competition.

In the carrier selection phase of its route proceedings the Board considered many factors in addition to the relative merits of the applicant airlines' service proposals. Among the most significant was a carrier's financial need. The Board consciously strove to preserve all the existing carriers and to narrow the differences between the strong and the weak carriers. Carriers with financial problems were often granted new routes regardless of the merits of competitors' applications.[7]

The financial consideration not only influenced carrier selection decisions, it also influenced the Board's overall agenda for route awards. A good example of this was in the early 1970s, when the Board actively sought to limit competition in the industry. At the time substantial excess capacity had developed, and industry profitability was declining. In part, this was because of a cyclical downturn, and in part, the carriers had ordered many new aircraft in the mid-1960s, which sharply increased their capacity.

The CAB responded by extending its regulatory net wider. New route authority conferral came to a complete standstill in the first half of the 1970s in what came to be unofficially referred to as the route moratorium. In addition the CAB granted antitrust immunity to discussions between eight carriers who wished to reduce capacity on eighteen routes. Their attempts failed on most of the routes, but TWA, United, and American were able to reach such agreements in their transcontinental markets.[8] After an initial rejection (Order 70-11-35) the CAB began to sanction such agreements.[9]

Although the CAB strictly limited competition in the mainstream of airline markets, several categories of specialized passenger airlines developed to provide services that were not closely regulated by the Board. Two classes of carriers, commuter airlines and supplemental airlines, sprang up outside of the CAB regulatory structure following World War II. In 1952 the commuters were given a formal exemption to provide scheduled air service with small aircraft (15 to 20 seats maximum until 1972, and 30 seats until 1978 when it was raised to 60 seats). In 1962, after years of controversy, several supplemental airlines were granted specialized certificates to provide nonscheduled charter services. A third group of airlines, the intrastate airlines, operated beyond the jurisdiction of CAB regulation in a number of states, mainly California and Texas.

Industry Structure Prior to Deregulation
The status of each of the various carrier groups at the time of deregulation is summarized in table 1.1. Only the trunk airlines could operate in all kinds of markets with any kind of aircraft. Each of the other groups had restric-

Table 1.1 The structure of the airline industry under route regulation in 1978

Airline group[a]	Service permitted				Percent distribution of aircraft in use			Percent distribution of domestic RPMs
	Number of airlines	Scheduled service	Large jet permitted	Markets permitted	Wide-bodied jets	Narrow jets	Propeller aircraft	
Trunks	11	Yes	Yes	All	96.8	77.9	0.8	87.2
Local, Regional[b] and Other	12	Yes	Yes	Regional		17.0	11.0	9.2
Commuter[c]	258	Yes	No	All			86.0[d]	0.6
Supplemental[e]	5	No	Yes	All	3.2	1.8	1.7	0.6
Intrastates[f]	4	Yes	Yes	Within states		3.3	0.5	2.4
Totals:	290				100%	100%	100%	100%

a. There were additionally 4042 air taxi operators authorized to provide service during FY 1978. Air taxis did not utilize aircraft with a pay load capacity greater than 7,500 lbs. or 30 seats and operated under Part 298 of the Board's Economic Regulations. Commuters were air taxis: (1) operating five round trips per week between two or more points pursuant to a published schedule or (2) transported mail through a contract with the U.S. Postal Service. There are no reliable data showing the number of aircraft used by or RPMs flown by air taxis that were not also commuters.
b. Includes Air Midwest, Air New England, Aspen, and Wright.
c. Carriers reporting, CAB *Commuter Air Carrier Statistics*.
d. Year ending June 30, 1978.
e. Does not include supplemental cargo carriers or McCulloch which had suspended operations.
f. Only intrastate airlines operating in the lower, mainland 48 states are included.

tions on scheduling, markets, or aircraft. This policy lead to substantial concentration in the provision of domestic air services. Sixteen trunk carriers began operations in 1938. Forty years later these sixteen carriers were consolidated into eleven carriers through mergers, and they still accounted for slightly more than 87 percent of industry revenue passenger miles. In fact the Big Four that dominated the industry in 1939—United, American, TWA, and Eastern—were still the largest carriers in 1978.

Economists had cited evidence that such industry dominance was the result of regulatory fiat not of market forces. Keyes (1951) and Caves (1962) were both convinced that typical city-pair concentration would not differ much whatever the regulatory (or deregulatory) regime and that seller concentration at the national level would be much lower in an unregulated environment. Thus each advocated a removal of regulatory controls. Their work would lie largely untapped by public policymakers for a number of years.

Pricing Policies under Regulation

The Board's regulation of fare levels can be divided into four distinct phases: In the first, which was prior to World War II, the Board did not formally review rates; instead air fares were conventionally set at the prevailing first-class rail fare. In the second, after the first formal review of fares in 1942, the Board approved across-the-board fare increases but without any formal guidance as to the desired level of earnings for the industry. In the third, which is marked by the completion of the *General Passenger Fare Investigation* (Docket 8008) in 1960, the Board set fares to achieve an average 10.5 percent rate of return for the industry based on actual industry operating costs. In the fourth, which followed the *Domestic Passenger Fare Investigation* (U.S. CAB 1974), the Board set fares to yield a 12 percent return based on standard industry load factors and seating density, and standardized accounting conventions. In all four phases the Board's focus was on overall industry profitability rather than on the relationship between fares and costs in particular markets. Fare competition was not precluded by statute, but the CAB's procedures and policies strongly discouraged it. Proposals to change fares substantially were the subject of hearings; thus fares could not be changed quickly. Moreover an airline's competitors had ample opportunity to challenge any proposal or to introduce comparable fares. As a result fares in all markets were generally adjusted in unison, and in a large number of markets, fares differed substantially from costs. This disparity between fares and costs increased as new aircraft technologies were introduced.

Growing Disparity between Prices and Costs

At the time the Civil Aeronautics Board was created in 1938, passenger fares were proportional to distance since they were set at roughly the prevailing Pullman rates for train travel. Given the nature of airline operations, this structure of fares was probably not seriously out of line with the cost of providing air transportation. Air mail was an important factor in the growth of civil air transportation. Since initially aircraft were not designed for long journeys, air service was often provided by multistop flights over circuitous routings. Also these aircraft were not very fast and did not have long cruising ranges, so the economies of longer haul flights were much smaller than with later generations of aircraft.

After World War II the Douglas DC-6 and the Lockheed Constellation were introduced. Larger and cheaper to operate than the aircraft they replaced, these aircraft had substantially longer ranges and faster cruising speeds than their predecessors. At first, fares were not changed appreciably to reflect the cost savings of the new technology. However, a number of "irregular carriers" began offering service in a variety of heavily traveled markets. These carriers operated under exemptions from the Board and were permitted to operate as many as ten scheduled flights in a market per month. These large irregulars introduced coach service, which featured unrestricted fares at levels 30 to 35 percent below the prevailing first-class fares of the certificated carriers. These carriers wished to offer regularly scheduled, frequent service in these markets, but the CAB denied the large irregulars access to the markets they had developed. The success of the irregulars did, however, force the certificated carriers to introduce coach service in the early 1950s.[10]

The first off-peak fare, a night coach discount, was offered in the late 1950s. Other discounts were also available.[11] Consequently average fares declined as new more efficient aircraft were introduced. However, the fare reductions were largely achieved by introducing a new type of service and new classes of fares rather than by adjusting existing prices.

A more dramatic technological advance was the introduction of jet aircraft in the late 1950s and early 1960s. The jets further increased the convenience of air travel, while greatly reducing costs. Again the Board failed to force a realignment of fares but instead allowed carriers to expand their use of discounts. Some existing discounts were liberalized while others, such as youth fare and youth standby discounts, were introduced.

In 1966 "Discover America" excursion fares were introduced which offered discounts from prevailing fares in leisure markets and in the transcontinental markets in the off-season (February and March). The discounts were typically in the 20 to 30 percent range, although there were exceptions, especially in the Florida markets where the discounts tended to be greater. Other discounts available at that time were the youth standby (50 percent), youth reservation (20 percent), and the family plan (33.3 percent for children 12 to 21, and 50 percent for children 2 to 11).[12] These discounts widened the market for air travel by lowering fares for groups of travelers whose demand was most price sensitive. As the proportion of passengers traveling on discounts swelled, average fares declined.

The operating economies of the long-haul propeller aircraft and the jets over the planes they replaced increased with market distance. The Board's relatively minor adjustments in its pricing policies failed to reflect the falling costs of long-haul travel.[13] Moreover discounts offered only moderate flexibility for carriers to deviate from regulated fare levels. For example, between 1960 and 1969 the trunk's average seat-mile cost declined by 21 percent, whereas average fares declined by only 7 percent.

The growing disparity between fares and costs gave carriers in competitive markets strong incentives to engage in inefficient nonprice competition. The primary forms of nonprice competition were the scheduling of additional flights, thus increasing the proportion of unfilled seats per flight (i.e., reducing the load factors) and the offering of roomier seating. Through much of the postwar period, declining load factors offset some of the cost advantages of the new aircraft (see figure 1.1). This was especially the case in long-haul markets, where the new technology had the greatest impact on the cost of service. In these markets where price was well above cost, carriers provided more frequent service and lower load factors than consumers wished. Conversely, the Board's fares in many short-haul markets were actually below the cost of service. Since many of these markets could not be served profitably at Board-imposed fares, carriers often provided less frequent service with higher load factors than passengers demanded. Two economists, Douglas and Miller (1974), had the fundamental insight that instead of setting prices equal to costs, the Board's fare policy had the opposite effect—it tended to set costs equal to fares.[14]

These misincentives were reflected in labor contracts and in equipment decisions as well as in schedule frequency.[15] Moreover, by inhibiting price competition, the Board apparently encouraged airlines to engage in service competition involving aircraft type. An example is that of the Douglas DC-7 series and Lockheed Super Constellation aircraft (L-1049C though

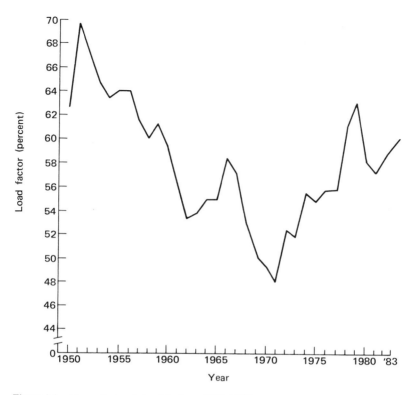

Figure 1.1   Domestic trunk load factors, 1950–1983

L-1649A) with new engines that enhanced nonstop distance. These planes were ordered in significant quantities by certificated carriers even though management was forewarned by the manufacturers that these aircraft would have higher unit costs associated with their operation than other available types, especially the L-1049 and DC-6B. Another piece of evidence is that California intrastate carriers (who could offer lower prices) adopted pressurized aircraft some thirteen years later than the trunks.[16] Even when carriers wished to offer lower prices by using less up-to-date equipment, the Board refused.[17]

The Domestic Passenger Fare Investigation
The shift to jet equipment, particulary turboprop and turbojet/fan aircraft, substantially reduced carrier costs. By the end of the 1960s the certificated carriers had completed their conversion to jet aircraft, and the cost reductions and the added convenience of the switch from propeller aircraft had largely been achieved. The carriers, however, had ordered substantial

additional capacity in the expectation that the rapid traffic growth of the mid-1960s would continue. It failed to materialize. In 1969 and 1970, with load factors at their lowest level since before World War II, and with profits deteriorating sharply, the airlines came to the Board for rate relief.

In early 1969 the Board approved rate increases in markets under 1,800 miles. Later in the year, after receiving a number of carrier filings, the Board approved fare increases that paralleled a distance-based fare formula proposed by American Airlines.[18] In addition the Board allowed reductions in the size of the discounts for a number of promotional fares. These steps were estimated to have raised fares by an average of 6 percent.

In reaching this decision, the Board had relied on informal contacts with carriers and failed to establish a standard by which the fare increases could be judged. Several congressmen challenged these procedures, arguing that in approving the fare increases the Board had violated due process and laws governing *ex parte* communications.[19] The courts upheld the challenge. The Board therefore suspended the fare increases it had approved and began a formal investigation, the *Domestic Passenger Fare Investigation* (*DPFI*), to determine the level and the structure of air fares.

The *DPFI* was the Board's first systematic analysis of its fare policies. Based on a voluminous record developed in the proceeding, the Board adopted regulations intended to bring fares more closely into line with costs and thereby encourage greater efficiency. The Board determined that fares should be related to the cost of service, which was assumed to be related to market distance. The Board established load factor and seating density standards in addition to a target rate of return. When carriers engaged in nonprice competition, and thereby decreased load factors, average costs increased. By judging the reasonableness of fares solely on the basis of industry profitability, carriers' incentives to minimize costs were reduced: lower load factors reduced profits and thereby warranted fare increases. By establishing standards on load factors and seating densities, the incentives to engage in cost increasing activities were reduced.[20]

The fare formula was more in line with costs than the prevailing fares, yet the Board deliberately set fares above costs in markets of more than 400 miles and less than the costs in shorter markets.[21] Because the local service carriers mostly had short-haul routes, they were permitted to set prices at 130 percent of *DPFI* fares. Moreover the *DPFI* did not consider other cost influences and factors aside from distance. In particular, the average cost of service falls as the number of people traveling in a market goes up, yet market density was not considered in establishing fares. Moreover in the *DPFI* the Board decided that the cost of providing service to a passenger traveling on a discount fare was no different than the cost of a passenger traveling on full fare; consequently the availability of discount fares was ordered sharply reduced.[22] Similarly, a concern about a cross-subsidy from coach to first class was addressed by increasing the markup of first class over coach fares.

The *DPFI* did not consider off-peak fares in any depth. The Board noted that several airlines, especially Delta, were offering service at 20 percent below prevailing fares for flights departing between 10 P.M. and 4 A.M. These night coach fares were essentially the only off-peak fares that received any widespread use while the industry was tightly regulated.[23] Although the Board did not address the reasonableness of these fares during the *DPFI*, it nevertheless decided that the use of off-peak fares should not be expanded. Greater use of off-peak fares, the Board ruled, would be confusing to the public and costly for the carriers to administer.[24]

The Board also did not particularly encourage other discount fares. Carriers were required to demonstrate that a proposed discount would be profitable, and the applicability of a given discount fare was limited to eighteen months.[25] In practice, the Board did not consistently apply these guidelines. The Board strictly reviewed the profit impact analyses of some fare proposals and ordered them suspended.[26] However, other discount proposals were approved despite an inadequate profit-impact analysis.[27] Generally, the Board was more receptive to proposals that extended existing fares than it was to new fare proposals. The mere existence of the *DPFI* evaluation criteria undoubtedly discouraged discount fare proposals.

Small Community Services

Subsidized air service extends back to the very beginning of the aviation industry. The basic philosophy of the subsidy program established as part of the Federal Aviation Act of 1938 was that subsidies were given in order to foster the financial health of air carriers by augmenting the airlines' passenger revenues through the payment of mail rates. Subsidy would provide an underpinning for a stable air transportation system and would encourage the completion of this system more rapidly than it might otherwise have been accomplished. The program was administered by the Postal Service until 1953, when the CAB assumed responsibility for it.

The Local Service Subsidy Program
The program began with subsidy provision to the trunk carriers. By the late 1940s and early 1950s the Board certificated several new local service

airlines to take over subsidized operations from the trunk airlines on an experimental basis. The Board's intention was to get the trunks off subsidy and create a new class of small aircraft operators who would specialize in serving small short-haul markets. In 1955 thirteen of the local service airlines were given permanent certificates.

The success of the local service subsidy program was substantially below expectations. In large part this resulted from conflicting forces that diverted the program from its fundamental purpose of providing air service for small communities at reasonable cost. As discussed in chapter 6, the local service airlines acquired aircraft that were too large for small subsidized routes, and they increasingly shifted operations into their large markets. As a result subsidy costs grew while the quality of service in the smallest subsidized cities declined.

A major problem with the local service subsidy was its orientation toward preserving the financial health of the airlines rather than ensuring adequate service for subsidized communities. In the earliest years the local service airlines were simply paid under individual fixed subsidy rates designed to cover their projected shortfalls for serving the communities listed on their certificates. After 1961 the airlines were placed on a system that determined the amount of subsidy according to a formula based on industry average performance. A particular carrier's subsidy was related to the number of flights provided and the number of cities served. This system was intended to provide greater incentives for efficiency by rewarding carriers whose performance was better than average.

However, in other ways proper incentives were not built into the subsidy system. The Board was prohibited from regulating schedules or aircraft types, and thus the subsidy program did not have adequate incentives to encourage convenient scheduling or economic equipment selection. For a carrier that provided service on both subsidy and nonsubsidy routes, there was an incentive to maximize revenues on the nonsubsidy routes through convenient peak-time scheduling and to fly the subsidy routes at inconvenient off-peak hours. For example, in 1975 North Central Airlines provided five daily flights from Pellston, Michigan. One flight departed at 1 : 16 A.M. and one at 6 : 03 A.M.; the remaining three flights were clustered between 12:58 P.M. and 2:35 P.M.[28] Moreover, because subsidy was paid for each departure, more subsidy could be earned by flying inconvenient multiple stop routings than if convenient nonstop or one-stop service were provided. Service quality was essentially beyond the Board's control.[29]

In sum, by the time regulatory reform of air transportation was being considered in the mid-1970s there was a great deal of dissatisfaction with the current subsidy program on the part of small communities. Studies by the Department of Transportation (DOT) and academics, such as that by Eads (1972), showed that local service carriers were rapidly withdrawing from small communities and that replacement service was being offered by the commuter carrier industry. The DOT study (1976) found that certificated air carriers dropped service to 173 points between 1960 and 1975, reducing the number of points served by certificated carriers by about 30 percent. In almost every instance the initiative for these withdrawals came from the carriers, with the Board granting approval.[30] In other instances the Board disapproved withdrawal and used a combination of "moral suasion" and linkage of decisions under its regulatory control to encourage airlines to remain in sensitive small communities. Over this period only a handful of small communities was added to the systems of the local service carriers. In addition carriers cut back departures at the small communities they continued to serve. Between 1970 and 1975 certificated airlines reduced small community flights by nearly 25 percent.[31]

Overall Growth and Profitability of Industry

Despite the many shortcomings of CAB route and pricing policies the airline industry grew rapidly during the nearly forty years of CAB regulation (see figure 1.2; also see appendix tables A and B). This growth was largely fueled by technological improvements that increased travel convenience and reduced fares. During the first wave of growth in the late 1940s and 1950s with the introduction of long-haul propeller aircraft and during the second wave spurred by the jet aircraft of the 1960s, the Board encouraged carriers to expand their scheduled service to every city of appreciable size in the United States. In addition the Board authorized competitive services in most of the densest routes. It also permitted carriers to offer selective discounts to expand their customer base to include price sensitive vacation and family travelers. Between 1949 and 1969 air traffic grew more than 14 percent per year.

Average air fares during this twenty-year period fell significantly in real dollar terms. The lower portion of figure 1.2 displays average air fares in terms of yield (passenger revenues divided by revenue passenger miles, RPM). Average fares fell by 2 percent in nominal dollars, while the Consumer Price Index increased by 50 percent. Thus there was a substantial decline in air fares relative to other goods and services.

Although the industry grew at a healthy pace, airline profits as a per-

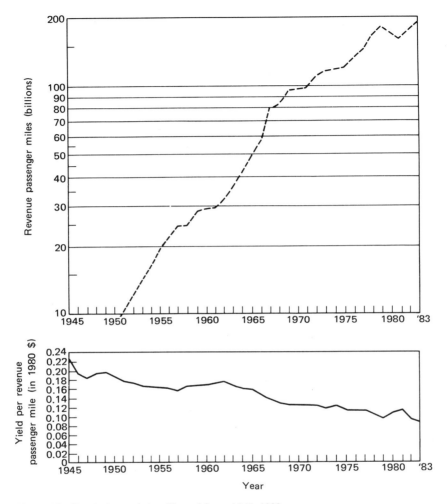

Figure 1.2   Domestic trunks' traffic and fares, 1945–1983

Table 1.2   Industry profitability

	Trunks—domestic operations		Locals		All manufacturing
	Operating profit margin	Rate of return on stockholder's equity	Operating profit margin	Rate of return on stockholder's equity	Rate of return on stockholder's equity
1957	3.0	4.8	−0.9	−11.4	10.9
1958	6.3	7.7	1.7	10.7	8.6
1959	5.9	9.6	0.5	0.5	10.4
1960	1.8	0.0	1.5	14.8	9.2
1961	−0.5	−5.2	5.3	21.1	8.9
1962	3.3	1.3	6.5	19.3	9.8
1963	5.3	1.9	5.3	13.1	10.3
1964	10.6	17.1	6.7	16.3	11.6
1965	12.8	21.6	8.3	19.3	13.0
1966	12.4	17.2	6.7	12.7	13.4
1967	9.3	13.3	0.2	−4.4	11.7
1968	6.4	6.3	−1.8	−28.8	12.1
1969	5.6	4.7	−2.9	−71.3	11.5
1970	0.3	−4.5	−1.2	−63.3	9.3
1971	3.4	1.6	3.5	−7.4	9.8
1972	5.8	6.6	5.6	8.5	10.6
1973	4.9	5.0	6.0	12.8	12.9
1974	6.5	10.5	7.7	18.1	14.9
1975	0.8	−2.1	2.3	0.5	11.2
1976	4.0	8.5	5.6	16.0	13.9
1977	3.8	11.2	6.8	22.4	14.2
1978	5.5	17.7	6.3	20.2	15.1
1979	−0.4	3.4	4.6	4.3	16.4
1980	−1.1	4.2	4.5	9.3	13.9
1981	−2.2	−3.7	4.8	6.7	13.6
1982[a]	−4.0	−15.8	3.7	8.0	9.3
1983	−1.7	−7.8	2.9	0.3	10.6

Source: *Form 41* and *FTC Quarterly Financial Report*.
a. Texas International, a former local service carrier, merged with Continental, a trunk carrier, in 1982

centage of stockholder equity exceeded the return for all manufacturing only in the periods immediately following the introduction of new aircraft technologies (see table 1.2). The Board's profit targets were established at roughly the levels earned by the manufacturing sector, that is, 10.5 percent for the 1960s and 12 percent for the 1970s. Yet the industry attained rates of profitability lower than the targets despite the Board's continual focus on the financial health of the industry in formulating its policies.[32]

Conclusion

Although Congress gave the Board authority to regulate entry and pricing, it did not grant it the authority to regulate schedules or equipment. By regulating some, but not all, of the economic variables in a structurally competitive industry, forces were set in motion that would undermine many of the intended effects of the regulatory policies. Moreover it seems unlikely that power to control all other factors would have been effective. Regulators had not shown an ability to select prices or network route maps in a way that kept up with a rapidly changing and dynamic industry.

Chapter 2

Deregulation of the Airline Industry

There was substantial empirical support for the view that the airline industry's economic performance under regulation was deficient. But political forces had to join economic evidence in order for major change to take place. These political forces were marshaled in the mid-1970s and reached full flower in the Kennedy hearings in 1975. Their most dramatic evidence concerned intrastate carriers. Such carriers, operating outside the Board's economic regulations, offered consumers substantially lower prices, while maintaining high profitability.

The Intrastate Carriers and Their Role in Deregulation

The inability of the CAB to cope successfully with the problems in the industry provided a stimulus for reform. So did its protectionist policies, for they provided egregious examples indicating that reform was needed. But perhaps the major stimulus was provided by intrastate carriers operating outside of the CAB regulatory framework. The activities of these carriers were studied by Levine (1965), Jordan (1970), and Keeler (1972).

The California Experience
The CAB had no jurisdiction over purely local transportation within a state, provided that the transportation could be conducted without overflying either another state or international waters. In 1949 a group of small carriers were formed in California to serve intrastate markets. These carriers operated at rates that were less than half those offered by the CAB certificated airlines. One of the smallest, Pacific Southwest Airlines (PSA), grew to become the dominant intrastate carrier, and by 1962 was carrying 28 percent of the total traffic between Los Angeles and San Francisco, up from 13 percent the year before.

Competitive service responses by the certificated carriers included Western's establishment of a fighting-ship airline, WAL of California, in 1949, but Western quickly abandoned this effort. Further competitive price responses by trunks did not begin until 1962.[1] The certificated carriers eventually competed vigorously and obtained CAB approval to match fares for persons buying tickets within California. Even in the late 1970s, however, tickets sold outside California for intrastate service were sold at the much higher CAB fare level.

The California experience suggested that low-fare carriers were capable of successfully competing with established airlines. The experience also made clear that there could be a substantial traffic response to significant price reductions. In the Los Angeles–San Francisco market traffic grew from 1.5 million in 1960 to 3.2 million in 1965, an increase of 117 percent. In smaller markets, such as Fresno–Los Angeles, traffic grew by 72 percent after 12 months of low-fare service.

The Texas Experience
The California experience was repeated with some new twists in Texas. After four years of regulatory and court challenges by incumbent carriers to prevent the start-up of Southwest Airlines, a Supreme Court decision permitted this new airline to begin operations. In mid-1971 it began scheduled service between Dallas, Houston, and San Antonio. Southwest priced its services to be competitive with out-of-pocket costs of the automobile. It had the flexibility to institute service at the downtown Hobby Airport rather than from Houston's outlying Intercontinental Airport. It introduced a number of innovative pricing strategies including two-tier pricing and half-price sales.[2] The two-tier pricing structure contained two classes of fares, one during peak periods and a lower fare during off-peak periods.

Southwest's basic formula was to offer frequent flights on short out-and-back routes, to encourage high labor productivity through profit sharing and highly flexible work rules, to provide minimal services, to serve airports close to the state's major business districts, and to offer fares sharply lower than existing ones. As was the case in California, these intrastate fares were lower than the Board-mandated levels for markets of similar distance. This was true not only for high density markets such as Dallas–Houston (39.5 percent lower during peak and 63.7 percent during off-peak) but for thinner markets such as Harlingen–Houston (47.5 percent lower during peak and 68.5 percent during off-peak) and Austin–Lubbock (22.4 percent lower during peak and 51.5 percent during off-peak). The traffic growth experienced in Texas also paralleled the California experience, with Dallas–Houston traffic growing 127.5 percent from 1970 to 1974 while ten similar high-density CAB regulated markets experienced an average growth of only 9.8 percent (see figure 2.1).

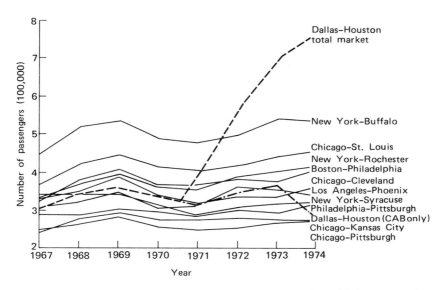

Figure 2.1   Comparative traffic growth of Dallas–Houston Market, with the average of the ten most similar markets under 500 miles served by CAB carriers exclusively

Financial Health of Intrastate Airlines

Most important, the low-priced intrastate carriers were generally profitable (see table 2.1). Air California and Southwest Airlines were extremely profitable, earning rates of return substantially in excess of most of the trunk and local service carriers throughout the period. Although PSA was very successful financially throughout the 1960s, by the mid-1970s a number of poor investment decisions in aircraft and in other subsidiaries such as hotels and automobile rentals held down their corporate rate of return.[3]

The intrastate airlines demonstrated that efficient and responsive carriers were able to evolve using different service patterns and fares than those that evolved under CAB regulation. It began to seem irresponsible for government officials to deny consumers the choice of the low-fare mass transit option.

Political Economy of Deregulation

By the mid-1970s economists had marshaled evidence that regulation was not needed and that the nearly continuous flow of regulatory rule adjustments had left much to be desired. A large change toward a new economic arrangement was in order.

Table 2.1 Estimated rate of return on investment

Year	Air California	PSA (consolidated including airline and other activities)	Southwest	Trunks (system)	Locals	Trunks (system) and locals combined
1973	52.56[a]	2.93	9.63	5.62	9.30	5.87
1974	31.91[b]	5.14	22.81	6.79	12.19	7.19
1975	16.51	(7.32)	23.44	2.79	4.88	2.95
1976	16.71	6.64	19.80	8.50	9.78	8.61
1977	16.25	5.40	18.29	9.97	13.57	10.31

Source: Calculated from data in carriers' annual reports and using CAB methodology (modified).
a. Would have been 19.33 if tax benefit of loss carry forward and accounting change excluded.
b. Would have been 22.50 if tax benefit of loss carry forward excluded.

The Ford Years

In 1974, at the start of President Gerald Ford's administration, the nation's leaders were having to face a severe inflation coupled with sluggish economic growth. Ford called an economic summit in August to solicit a wide spectrum of views on how to improve economic conditions. One area of agreement was the desirability of cutting back on federal regulation as a means of lowering the costs, and hence the prices charged by regulated firms. In October Ford asked Congress to establish a National Commission on Regulatory Reform to undertake a reexamination of federal regulatory agencies, with the aim of identifying and eliminating federal regulations that increased costs to the consumer. This was the first action in which political figures displayed their belief that government regulation was interfering with productivity.

Senator Edward Kennedy also saw the heavy hand of government as a significant political issue. He asked Stephen Breyer (formally of Harvard Law School and then Counsel to the Administrative Practices Subcommittee of the Senate Judiciary Committee) to investigate government economic regulations by federal regulatory agencies. The CAB was chosen as the prime target of regulatory reform. The choice was logical because of the ready pool of recognized experts who supported the case for reform and the large body of literature and evidence that facilitated the analysis. Planning for these hearings began in the summer of 1974; the hearings themselves were scheduled for February 1975. Breyer's own descriptions of these hearings (U.S. Senate Report 1975, Breyer and Stein 1981) are unsurpassed pieces of political economy. We give only a brief outline here.

The Kennedy oversight hearings dramatized the issues in a way that dealt carefully but visibly with the economic factors. The hearings used research and evidence to examine the fears aroused by the proposed reform and to convince others in the government of the benefits of reform. An example will suffice to illustrate this point. Opponents of reform felt that lower prices would be ruinous and that price competition, if permitted, would be destructive and would bankrupt small carriers. Even with the extensive economic studies analyzing the intrastate services, the certificated airlines maintained that the California and Texas experiences were attributable to unique operating conditions, such as good California weather. The Kennedy staff investigated the merits of these arguments. For example, they found that there were 228 hours of poor visibility in Los Angeles in 1974 and 233 hours in Boston; thus weather delay differences were insubstantial. Similary the cost of providing connecting services between airlines (interline costs), which were not incurred in intrastate operations, were shown to add about $3 to a ticket price, which would make a San Francisco to Los Angeles ticket cost $21.74 in 1974 instead of $18.75, still well below the $41.67 charged at that time between Boston and Washington. The two major variables explaining the cost differences were found to be load factor and seating capacity, with American Airlines configuring its Boeing 727-200 jet aircraft for 121 seats flown 55 percent full, as contrasted with a PSA configuration of 158 seats flown 60 percent full. This fact alone was shown to account for more than half the fare difference. As more allegations were introduced by those carriers wishing to maintain the status quo, careful analysis served to dispel the rhetoric. The value of specific evidence in counteracting opponents views was enormous. The dramatic newspaper coverage of the hearings created a political base of support and permitted the movement for reform to gather momentum. The evidence showed that consumer benefits were being withheld by the regulatory process, and a different regime was needed to bring the possibility of lower fares to the U.S. public.

At the Department of Transportation, Deputy Under Secretary John Snow and other officials were simultaneously engaged in drafting a reform bill for President Ford. This bill, supported by the Department of Justice, the Council of Economic Advisors and the Council on Wage and Price Stability, called for flexible pricing as well as for three forms of automatic market entry. It was submitted to the Congress early in the fall of 1975, and many of its ideas would form the basis for the later reform bills.

Meanwhile a CAB task force, under the leadership of Roy Pulsifer, issued a report in July 1975 supporting reform and offering specific blueprints for the process. This report supported the idea of deregulation rather than reform, by proposing that the control of entry and exit as well as rate regulation of the public utility type be relaxed over a three- to five-year period. In April 1976, at Senator Howard Cannon's Aviation Subcommittee Hearings, John Robson, chairman of the CAB, testified that the Board now endorsed reform legislation. The Board unanimously supported substantial reduction in the CAB's control over pricing and entry.

The Carter Years
The next significant event facilitating the reform of regulatory policy in aviation was the endorsement of deregulation by President Jimmy Carter. A key element in the strategy for deregulation was the appointment of economist Alfred Kahn as chairman of the CAB.[4]

While many groups in the government supported reform, most of the industry opposed it. The opponents early in 1977 included the ten major trunk carriers (although United was reportedly considering changing its position), and with varying degrees of fervor, eight of the ten local service carriers. Among the most vehement opponents were the less financially strong trunk airlines—TWA, Eastern, and American—who feared entry into their most profitable routes and hence a worsening of their already poor financial picture. The local service carriers opposing deregulation feared that the trunk carriers would squeeze them out of their densest routes, while their small markets would be raided by the commuter airlines.

Pan American wanted domestic route authority, which the CAB had refused to grant for thirty years, and therefore mildly favored deregulation. Other carriers supporting reform included the intrastate carriers, particularly Southwest, which wanted to expand beyond its Texas markets. Frontier and Hughes Airwest were the two local service carriers favoring deregulation. Many commuter airlines were sympathetic to new legislation because they wanted relief from the CAB restriction that limited them to 30-seat aircraft. The industry lineup pro and con, clearly reflected each airline's idea on whether it would gain or lose from regulatory reform.[5]

The same was true for labor groups and the financial community. Labor unions feared that new airlines entering the industry would employ, at least at first, nonunion workers, which would bring wages down. They also feared that increased competition would reduce job security. Under regulation no carrier had been permitted to go bankrupt, and CAB merger guidelines included labor protective provisions highly favorable to airline employees. Similarly commercial banks and insurance companies were concerned that competition would increase the risks of loan defaults and bankruptcies, and they did not support major legislative changes.

Another concern of the framers of reform legislation was that freedom of entry and exit would result in a withdrawal of service from small communities. The Board had been seeking ways to improve the subsidy program to such communities since the early 1970s. It was convinced that reform should include explicit determination by the federal government of exactly what level and kind of services should be subsidized and should include direct payment of the requisite subsidy to carriers selected as best able to provide them at minimum cost. It was convinced that commuter carriers were the key to providing high-quality service to the nation's smaller cities at an acceptable cost. This was naturally opposed by the local service airlines, who saw the system of subsidies they had been receiving threatened.

In the spring of 1977 there were nearly two weeks of legislative hearings before Senator Howard Cannon's Aviation Subcommittee. These hearings were designed to formulate a bill acceptable to Congress. It was at this time that the major domestic trunk carriers split for the first time on the need for aviation regulatory reform. United Airlines, accounting for some 22 percent of domestic air traffic, became the first major trunk to endorse reform. Its decision was undoubtedly influenced by its lack of success in gaining new route rights; it had received authority to serve only one new market in the prior seventeen years. United also felt that reform was required for the financial health of the industry generally, as well as to permit it to raise substantial capital in future years. With United changing its position, the industry trade association, the Air Transport Association (ATA), did not testify against reform as it had in 1975.

Starting shortly before the arrival of Alfred Kahn in 1977, and accelerating when he became chairman, the CAB began to deregulate administratively. In 1976, under Chairman John Robson, the Board substantially relaxed its restrictions on charter operations and then the following spring approved two innovative discount fare proposals: Texas International's Peanuts fare and American Airline's Supersaver fare. Under Kahn the Board offered nearly *pro forma* approval of discount fares. In December 1977 the CAB made low fares a decision variable in route awards and began to grant permissive route authority, which would allow a carrier to enter and exit from a route without CAB intervention. It also proposed to give carriers authority to reduce fares without CAB approval and to eliminate restrictions on charter operations. These moves toward reduced regulatory intervention took place in a very good year for the airline industry. In 1978, despite an increasing rate of inflation throughout the economy, air fares (in current dollars) declined for the first time since 1966, and air traffic (in revenue passenger miles) expanded faster than it had in more than ten years. Meanwhile carrier profitability was higher than it had been since the mid-1960s (see table 1.2).

The timing and confluence of events made it an ideal time for passage of reform legislation. The Senate passed a compromise bill by a vote of 83 to 9 on April 19, 1978. The House was considering a similar bill. Elliot Levitas, a congressman from Georgia, attached to the House bill provisions that would close the CAB. The idea caught on. The Levitas amendment passed the subcommittee. House passage came on September 21, 1978 by a vote of 363 to 8. The opposition had been minimal as congressmen surveyed the financial results for the industry over the spring and summer months of 1978. There was minimal political risk in supporting reform if it could simultaneously reduce fares for the public and increase profits for the industry. Moreover Chairman Kahn was ebullient about the merits of reform and had made a persuasive case both to Congress and the American public. Thus President Jimmy Carter was able to sign the Airline Deregulation Act into law on October 28, 1978.[6]

The Deregulation Act
The Airline Deregulation Act (ADA) proposed a gradual relaxation of the CAB's regulation of the industry, with full rate and route authority to phase out over a four-year period. The Board's authority over routes was to end on December 31, 1981, and its authority over fares on January 1, 1983. Its authority over domestic mergers, intercarrier agreements, and interlocking directorates would transfer to the Department of Justice on January 1, 1983. The Board would cease operations entirely on January 1, 1985. The remaining tasks of international negotiation and small community air service would shift to the Department of Transportation on that date (see table 2.2). The policy of setting fixed dates for the elimination or transfer of protective controls was designed to permit effective planning by both carriers and the Board. The setting of an earlier date for the removal of route regulations then for rate authority was supported on economic grounds. In its major provisions that took immediate effect, the ADA

1. shifted the burden of proof in route authority cases from the need for a positive showing that entry is required by public convenience and necessity to a showing by opponents that entry is inconsistent with public convenience and necessity;

2. provided for a limited degree of automatic market entry, which required no Board review of approval;

Table 2.2 Time phasing of major provisions of Airline Deregulation Act of 1978

CAB	1979	1980	1981	1982	1983	1984	1985	1986
Fares	July 1: upper limit of reasonableness becomes operative				January 1: domestic fares authority expires	January 1: Board review of deregulation to be submitted to Congress	January 1: sunset of CAB. authority over foreign transport transferred to DOT	
Subsidy	October 24: eligibility for essential air service determined	January 1: criteria for eligibility under Section 419(a) must be established		January 1: criteria for eligibility under Section 419(b) must be established	January 1: bumping rule takes effect		January 1: subsidy program transferred to DOT	January 1: section 406 subsidy program terminates
Routes	January–April: automatic market entry applications	January–April: AME program	January–April: AME program December 31: most domestic route authority expires					
Agreements							January 1: domestic merger, agreements, and interlock authority transferred to DOT	January 1: agreements, foreign mergers, foreign interlocks transferred to DOT

3. allowed carriers to obtain dormant route authority (i.e., authority for routes that were not being flown by the carriers that had been certificated to fly them);

4. set a statutory zone of reasonableness for fares, which was to be adjusted as airline costs changed and within which airlines could vary fares without permission by the CAB;

5. provided for a reform of Board procedures, setting tight procedural deadlines in route and merger cases;

6. established notice procedures for airlines wishing to terminate service at a community; and

7. provided for a ten-year Essential Air Service Program to ensure air service to small communities, with local service subsidies to be phased out within six years;

8. provided employee protective measures for dislocated workers.

The fare flexibility provisions of the ADA, particularly with respect to discount fares, were less broad than the fare policies the Board had already adopted. The ADA substantially liberalized the provisions on entry, however, allowing the Board to adopt a permissive route award policy as its standard procedure a few months after the ADA was passed. In actual fact, as we will discuss later, the Board's liberal administration of the act reduced the importance of the ADA's automatic entry and dormant route authority provisions, which had been expected to be the substantial vehicles for new entry. Instead, the Board, under the leadership of its new Chairman Marvin Cohen, began to confer new authority at such a rapid pace that within a year after passage of the act, carriers were able to serve virtually any route they wanted. Thus the transition in route policy was much quicker than that anticipated under the act. New entry into the industry also began to occur, with new low-fare entrants joining the former intrastate carriers in the provision of interstate services.

The Board's actions with respect to pricing were dominated by the doubling of jet fuel prices between the latter part of 1979 and the early part of 1980. Average fares failed to keep pace with increased costs, and coach fares in many markets were set at the Board ceiling. Carriers had been raising fares in unison as the Board adjusted its fare formula to reflect cost increases. In May 1980 the Board took a major step to stop such unified pricing behavior and to encourage independent pricing by substantially broadening the zone of fare flexibility. As described in chapter 3 carriers increasingly moved away from setting prices according to the formula fare under this policy.

In the small community arena, following the act, the Board held a series of meetings throughout the United States in an effort to set up a program responsive to the needs of these communities. Subsequently the Board established several small field offices in various regions of the country, to help smooth the transition from the local service subsidy program to the new essential air service program.

In the labor arena the act provided temporary federal assistance payments and hiring rights to protected former employees in cases where deregulation was found to be the major cause of a significant air carrier contraction. In practice, the compensation provisions have never been funded and the attribution of major cause has been mired in the difficulty of separating out the near simultaneity of deregulation, fuel-price increases and the recession.

In the merger area the Board adopted the policy of relying on potential (as opposed to actual) competition in judging the merits of mergers. Hence the Board approved mergers even when carriers were actual competitors on some routes. This made the Board more liberal than the Department of Justice, which tended to support only end-to-end mergers. The Board began to review its traditional conferral of antitrust immunity to collusive agreements recognizing that a deregulated airline industry should be subject to the same antitrust scrutiny as other unregulated industries.

Conclusion

Once the stage was set for deregulation, policy changes followed one another with dazzling rapidity. Those in charge at the CAB from 1977 on had the determination to exercise its regulatory authority in a pro-reform manner, and had some initial success in terms of industry response to a lessening of regulation. By 1978 they had the mandate to deregulate fully.

PART II

The Implementation of Deregulation and Its Effects

Chapter 3

Airline Pricing Policies

Airline deregulation stemmed from a growing recognition that increased competition would lower air fares, permit more innovative fare and service options, and improve load factors. Historically, CAB regulation had inhibited airline fares from falling to reflect the cost savings of new equipment. Price competition, it was argued, would reduce the incentives for uneconomic service competition and would thus benefit consumers.[1]

Increased fare flexibility has indeed introduced innovation and experimentation in carrier fare policies. These changes are producing a fare structure that is markedly different from what the CAB had prescribed. Fare differences between markets are now more likely to be the result of cost differences. Also carriers are charging higher fares to passengers who travel at times of relatively strong demand. In some markets this is the product of an explicit peak-load pricing policy, whereas in others it is accomplished through a system of capacity-limited discount fares.

Reform of Price Regulation

After the Kennedy hearings in 1975, there was widespread discontent with existing Board pricing practices. Concern was rampant that consumers not be denied low-fare options. The Board responded with a series of decisions permitting lower prices for consumers. A chronology is given in table 3.1.

Fare Reform Policies Before Passage of the Act

The first reform steps reflected traditional Board practice of setting regulatory boundaries, with different policies applicable for different classes of carriers. For example, low-fare services were considered to fall logically into the domain of the charter carriers. Thus in 1975 the Board approved one-stop inclusive tour charters, subject to a fifteen- or thirty-day advance purchase, a four- to seven-day minimum stay, and a $15 per night ground package. In 1976 the Board adopted advance booking charters, which permitted the sale of air-only charter service subject to a thirty- or forty-five-day advance purchase requirement.

Table 3.1 Chronology of significant fare actions by CAB

Date	Title	Item ID	Description
9-13-75	One-stop inclusive tour charters	Rule SPR-85	Most liberal charter rule to date. Allowed the sale of charters with a ground package to a single destination, subject to a 15- or 30-day advance purchase, a 4- to 7-day minimum stay and a $15 per night ground package.
10-7-76	Advance booking charter	Rule SPR-110	Permitted the sale of air-only charters subject to a 30-day advance purchase requirement. There was no minimum price requirement, but round-trip travel along with a minimum group size of 40 were required.
2-25-77	Texas International Peanuts fare	Order 77-2-133	Permitted Texas International to offer fares at 50 percent discounts from the standard-class fares on certain flights in five selected markets.
3-15-77	American Supersaver fare	Order 77-3-80	Major promotional fare in New York to Los Angeles and San Francisco. Discounts up to 45 percent of the coach fare and a 30-day advance purchase and a 7-day minimum stay requirement. Capacity limited to 35 percent of the seats on a given flight.
8-23-77	Allegheny's Simple Saver fares	Order 77-8-109	Permitted price reductions on multi-stop flights, capacity controlled.
10-14-77 11-23-77	TWA Super-Jackpot fares	Order 77-10-68 Order 77-11-123	Board reversal of itself in which it decided not to protect charters from scheduled carriers but instead to rely on liberalized charter rules.
4-13-78	Suspend-free zone	Reg. PS-80 Eff. 9-5-78	Board vacated *DPFI* requirements that coach fares be established uniformly on a mileage formula basis, that first-class fares be prescribed at a fixed percentage of coach fares, and that discount fares be justified on the basis of the profit impact test. The Board also established a suspend-free zone ranging from 70 percent below to 10 percent above the coach fare formula.
6-11-80	Domestic passenger fare flexibility	Reg. PS-92	Expanded the suspend-free fare zone to full downward flexibility in all markets and substantially increased upward flexibility.

Source: Bibliography of important Civil Aeronautics Board Regulatory Actions, 1975–79, PS-92.

Table 3.2 Effect of Supersaver fare (April–December 1977 vs. April–December 1976)

	New York–Los Angeles			New York–San Francisco		
	1976	1977	Percent change	1976	1977	Percent change
Scheduled	1,012,289	1,322,720	+30.6	720,197	950,580	+32.0
Charter-scheduled	49,359	18,759	−62.0	28,794	35,400	+22.9
Supplemental	1,188	30,612	(25.8 times)	644	2,248	(3.5 times)

Source: CAB Early Warning System Data, Bureau of Accounts and Statistics, March 6, 1978.

Early in 1977 the Board, under Chairman John Robson, approved two innovative fare proposals by scheduled carriers. In February it allowed Texas International to introduce Peanuts fares in five selected markets. Peanuts fares offered reduced fares for a variety of flights which were operating with low load factors; these flights did not necessarily operate at night. More significantly, the following month the Board approved American's Supersaver fares. Recognizing the increased threat of competition from charters in two of its most lucrative transcontinental routes, American Airlines wished to offer fares that were fully competitive with charter fares (up to 45 percent below coach fares). These fares were offered between New York and both Los Angeles and San Francisco; they were subject to a thirty-day advance purchase requirement and limited to round trips of seven to forty-five days. In addition the number of discount seats available on a given flight was limited.

The approval of these fares was significant in at least two respects. First, the Board permitted the fares to go into effect despite substantial doubts about the carriers' claims that the fares would be profitable. Yet the Board was reluctant to deny the carriers the opportunity to carry out what they considered to "be a fully warranted pricing experiment." [2] Second, although the Board expressed concern about the effect of Supersavers on charter operators, it expressly refused to protect them, maintaining that it was unwilling to substitute its judgment for that of consumers.

The Board did, however, institute an early warning system of data collection to study the impact on charter operators. Although there was a substantial diversion of charter passengers to Supersaver seats in the two transcontinental markets, charter operations of the supplemental carriers (as opposed to those of the scheduled carriers) in fact increased in 1977 relative to 1976 (see table 3.2). [3] Later in the summer of 1977, after Alfred Kahn had spent a few months as chairman, the Board approved Supersaver fares in a number of other markets. These fares soon spread throughout the system.

The Kahn Board reviewed its fare policies during the early fall of 1977. On the one hand, it was feared that if overall fare levels continued to be controlled through the *DPFI* formulas, price reductions were likely to be selective and discriminatory; the benefits of price cuts were thus likely to be passed on only to certain discretionary travelers. Moreover there was concern that the dilution caused by the discounts might require increases in coach fares, even though the quality of service (measured by last minute availability of seats) was deteriorating. On the other hand, there was some indication that discount fares were in fact remunerative. By filling up empty seats, the deep discounts were raising load factors dramatically and thereby holding back increases in average costs. They thus benefited not only the airlines and discount passengers but regular passengers as well.[4] Another concern that arose during this period dealt with a type of discount that entailed lower prices for consumers willing to take less convenient one-stop service. Such discounts made sense for carriers, for it made their operations in less dense markets more economic. Yet in some cases it might be less expensive for a passenger to purchase a through ticket, and then to disembark at the intermediate point, than to buy a ticket direct to the intermediate point.

By late fall of 1977, after a good deal of hand-wringing over the issue of how fast and how broadly to deregulate, the Board had decided not to intervene with discount fare policies. It had adopted the view that letting airlines make their proposed changes in pricing could significantly improve the economic performance of the industry. The strategy it adopted was to make it known to the carriers that the Board would follow a liberal policy toward discount fares, approving any brought before it in a *pro forma* fashion. In Delta's Aerobus and matching Super-No-Frills fares (Order 77-11-124), for example, the Board declined to protect Delta's new high-density service from competitors' discount fares on their regular coach services. The Board also approved Allegheny's Simple Saver fares (Order 77-8-109), which offered discounts to passengers willing to take a multistop flight rather than the more convenient nonstop flight of their competitors.

As with Delta's Aerobus there were a number of cases where airlines introduced low unrestricted fares. The chronology behind the introduction of these fares parallels, to some extent, that for the discount fares. In late 1977 the Board suspended TWA's Super Jackpot fare to Las Vegas because it might affect the charter industry adversely, but a month later reversed itself under its new hands-off philosophy. At the beginning of the following year the Board approved Western Airlines No Strings fare (Order 78-3-106). This fare was introduced after the Board announced that the existence of low fares would influence the Board's choice of carriers in upcoming route awards.

Early in 1978 the Board made a ruling designed to encourage market-by-market pricing. It sought abandonment of the *DPFI* requirements that coach fares be established uniformly on a mileage formula basis, that first-class fares be prescribed at a fixed percentage of coach fares, and that discount fares be justified on the basis of the profit impact test.[5] The Board also codified the philosphy behind its case-by-case decisions on discount fares, by proposing a suspend-free zone ranging 70 percent below coach fare formula (Regulation PS-80). Fares within the zone were presumed to be lawful unless clear and convincing evidence to the contrary was presented. The rule granted upward fare flexibility to 10 percent above the coach fare formula, with more flexibility given to workably competitive markets than to markets where less than four carriers were authorized to serve. This limited the abuse of monopoly power during the period when there were still substantial barriers to entry.

The CAB decisions coincided with the most favorable part of the business cycle for the industry. Demand for air travel increased as personal income grew, while the substantial fare reductions stimulated travel by price-sensitive segments of the public. Moreover as the use of restricted discount fares expanded, profits increased. This turn of events provided an impetus for passage of the deregulation act for it effectively muted the doomsday argument that reduced regulation would be a financial disaster for the industry. Nevertheless, subsequent events combined with competition to put substantial pressure on fares, and many carriers have since experienced severe financial stress.

Pricing Reform after Passage of the Act
The pricing provisions in the act allowed carriers immediately to raise fares in nonmonopoly markets 5 percent or to lower them 50 percent in any market without CAB approval. The downward zone was less deep than the fare policies that the Board had adopted only a few months earlier. The act required the Board to adjust fare ceilings—the Standard Industry Fare Level (SIFL)—at least twice a year to reflect changes in actual industry costs. In most markets the SIFL was tied to the *DPFI* formula. The act called for complete deregulation of fares on January 1, 1983, one year after the Board's route authority ended.

Events in 1979 began to affect industry profits adversely. There was a fifty-eight-day strike at United Airlines, the nation's largest carrier. Also the grounding of the DC-10s after a major accident in the early summer of

1979 had a substantial and continuing effect on a number of carriers. However, of most significance was the more than doubling of the price of fuel. Beginning in the spring of 1979 the acceleration in oil prices began and it continued into the following year. After an initial few months of delayed response to the increased costs, the Board allowed the carriers to raise fares by adjusting the SIFL every two (rather than every six) months, but the higher fares along with the declining economy led to a traffic slump. As early as January 1980 the Board began to rethink the zone of upward pricing flexibility. Given the industry's declining profits and the ever increasing percentage of passengers traveling on discounts, increased flexibility might help the industry financially during this difficult period. Moreover in many markets there was reason to believe the Board's formula, even with the statutorily mandated fare flexibility, held fares below costs. The move toward a transition in pricing seemed all the more supportable because of the rapid conferral of new route authority that had taken place.[6]

The Cohen Board settled on a scheme of unlimited upward flexibility for markets up to 200 miles. It was thought that competition from surface modes would provide a check on prices in short-haul markets. Moreover these markets were largely served by commuter carriers whose fares were already unregulated. A 50 percent upward zone was proposed for markets from 201 to 400 miles and a 30 percent upward zone for all other markets in the lower 48 states. The difference in treatment among mileage bands was justified by the defects in the *DPFI* formula, which understated costs in the 201- to 400-mile zone. Thus, to permit a comparable degree of real upward flexibility, a larger zone had to be provided in the short- to medium-haul markets. The Board was aware that Congress preferred a 30 percent across-the-board increase, but it feared that such a policy would give an incentive for jet operators to leave the shorter-haul markets for longer-haul markets where the dollar flexibility in fares was so much higher. The Board anticipated that competition from commuters and, more significantly, surface transportation would discipline the price of jet operators in the short-haul markets. In addition the zones were set significantly above the SIFL, at least in part to discourage the use of the Board's fare formula as a coordinating device for industry pricing.

A number of members of Congress felt that small communities would be threatened by enormous price increases if prices in short-haul markets were completely deregulated at a time when longer-haul markets were capped at a 30 percent price increase. A compromise was reached in September 1980, which capped fare increases at $15 plus 30 percent across the board. The flat figure of $15 gave a much greater upward percentage of flexibility to the shorter-haul markets, as the Board felt was necessary, while satisfying congressional concern for the appearance of fairness by treating all markets equally. This would prove to be the Board's only pricing transition policy. Carriers' prices distributed themselves across the zones, and a great deal of unused upward flexibility was still available to carriers when prices were freed by the statute on January 1, 1983.

Pricing Strategies
Two basic pricing strategies have emerged under deregulation. The most prevalent strategy has been the offering of a wide variety of restricted discounts in addition to coach fares. Some carriers, however, most notably the new entrants, have introduced unrestricted low fares at or below the prevailing discount fares. Often these carriers charge higher prices for service in peak travel periods than in off-peak periods.

In some respects the discount fares that have been introduced under deregulation are similar to the discounts in the 1960s. They focus on discretionary passengers and are an attempt to offer reduced prices to the most price-elastic segment of the market. However, many of the earlier discounts (like the youth fares) were only available to specific types of individuals. Carriers are now more likely to use advance purchase and minimum stay requirements as the way to differentiate discretionary and time-sensitive passengers. The most significant feature of these discounts, however, is that the fares are capacity controlled on a flight-by-flight basis. Consequently discretionary passengers traveling on reduced fares can be routed on less-desired flights and do not prevent time-sensitive passengers paying full fare from traveling on their preferred flights. As we discuss later in this chapter, by limiting the number of discount passengers on a given flight, restricted discounts may achieve the same effect as peak-load pricing: passengers traveling during periods of high demand will, on average, pay higher fares.

An increasing share of air travelers are receiving a discount of some sort. The original Supersaver proposal had a thirty-day advance purchase as well as a seven-day minimum stay requirement. However, the restrictions on the use of discount fares have been eased since they were first introduced. For example, some restricted discount fares do not have a minimum stay requirement. Even where it is applied, the requirement is often no more than a stay over on a Saturday night. An Air Transport Association survey shows that the percentage of travelers paying the standard coach fare has fallen from over 60 percent of total coach revenue passenger miles (RPMs) in 1977 to just under 25 percent in 1982.[7] The ATA index considers any fare below the standard coach fare as a discount. Hence it includes some fares as discounts that are above the cost-adjusted *DPFI* fare formula.[8] Nevertheless, the ATA figures do indicate that an increasing array of fares is becoming available in airline markets.

Fares and Costs

In order to examine the relationship between fares and costs, we begin by examining how costs vary among markets. We show that, in general, the average cost of providing air service falls as the number of passengers per flight increases—both because of increasing load factors and increasing aircraft size. Hence in bigger markets, where larger aircraft can be used and load factors are higher, average costs are lower. We also show that cost per available seat mile of operating aircraft falls rapidly with distance.

An Overview of Airline Costs
Airline costs can be broken into three catagories: overhead, flight costs, and passenger costs. Overhead cost consists of those that in the short run are not affected by changes in service in a particular market. It includes the cost of the firm's capital, like aircraft, as well as general and administrative expenses and advertising.[9]

Flight costs and passenger costs vary with the number of flights and the number of passengers, respectively. Flight costs are the costs that could be avoided by not operating a flight including salaries of the flight crew, fuel, maintenance, landing fees, and services provided to the aircraft while it is on the ground, such as cleaning and fueling.

Passenger costs are those associated with services such as providing schedule information and taking reservations. They also consist of the costs of collecting tickets at the gate, food service on board, and passenger baggage.

Nearly 60 percent of the trunks' costs of operation in the year ending June 31, 1981, were flight specific costs (see table 3.3); about 17 percent of the costs were overhead or fixed costs. The remaining 22 percent were passenger costs; reservations and sales expenses accounted for one-half of them. The local service carriers had a very similar cost structure.[10] Since passenger-related costs are 22 percent of the total, costs do not rise substantially as the number of passengers on a less than full flight increases. Even this figure probably overstates the added expense of carrying an additional passenger. For example, the number of airline employees

Table 3.3   Cost elements by function for domestic operations of trunks, locals, and new entrants (12 months ended June 30, 1981)

	Domestic operations			
	$millions trunks	$millions locals	Percentage trunks	Percentage locals
Flight specific costs				
Aircraft operating costs:				
Flight deck crew	2,414	436	10.6	10.9
Fuel	6,706	1,117	29.6	28.0
Insurance and other	38	14	0.2	0.4
Maintenance-flight equipment	1,798	381	7.9	9.5
Aircraft servicing				
Landing fees	320	60	1.4	1.5
Other aircraft servicing	966	157	4.3	3.9
Cabin crew	1,184	161	5.2	4.0
Total flight specific	13,426	2,326	59.2	58.2
Traffic specific costs				
Food	686	83	3.0	2.1
Other passenger in-flight	196	37	0.9	0.9
Traffic servicing	1,757	429	7.8	10.8
Reservation and sales	2,372	384	10.5	9.6
Total traffic specific costs	5,011	933	22.2	23.4
Overhead				
General and administrative	707	153	3.1	3.8
Servicing administration	192	24	0.8	0.6
Advertising and publicity	396	45	1.7	1.1
Depreciation, amortization and rentals—flight equipment	1,151	155	5.1	3.9
Depreciation and maintenance—ground property and equipment	562	58	2.5	1.5
Other amortization	6	6		0.1
Interest	588	191	2.6	4.8
Imputed profit[a]	631	104	2.8	2.6
Total overhead	4,233	736	18.6	18.4
Total cost elements	22,670	3,945	100.0	100.0

a. 14.2 percent of average stockholder equity.

needed to collect tickets and handle baggage does not generally increase proportionately with the number of passengers on a flight. Traffic servicing expenses thus would not increase proportionately with the number of passengers; there may very well be economies of scale with respect to the number of passengers on a flight. In addition, since travel agent commissions are a specified percentage of a ticket's price, a reduced fare would yield a corresponding reduction in commissions.

Large airlines also may have lower average costs for activities like maintenance or traffic servicing because of economies of scale. Although a number of researchers have concluded that scale economies are not significant in the airline industry, the evidence adduced deals directly with system rather than city-pair market economies of scale. At the system level the studies are flawed; they do not generally control for differences in the markets served nor in the quality of service. In addition the observed costs which formed the basis for these studies were undoubtedly influenced by regulation: carriers that were authorized to serve the potentially most lucrative markets had the greatest incentives to develop high cost operations. A determination of the true extent of economies of scale in the airline industry will probably not be possible for a number of years.[11] In the subsequent discussion we assume that economies of scale are not significant in the sense that large trunk carriers are assumed to enjoy no significant unit cost advantage over, say, the smaller trunks. However, as we now discuss, we make no such assumptions about returns to scale at a market level.

Aircraft Size, Stage Lengths, and the Cost of Service
Table 3.4 provides operating cost estimates for a variety of aircraft over different stage lengths. For each aircraft type average cost falls as market distance increases.

The least-cost aircraft type depends on stage length. In shorter markets the smaller aircraft often have lower costs; as market distance increases, the size of the least-cost aircraft type also increases. For example, in a 1,250-mile market, the average cost per passenger of operating a B-727-200 is 18 percent higher than the cost of a DC-10-10 when both are operated at a 60 percent load factor. However, the DC-10-10 has more than twice the capacity of a B-727-200. Of course, though the larger aircraft are technologically most efficient over a wide range of markets, they are too big to operate at economical load factors in many markets.

The cost advantage of the B-727-200 over the smaller B-737-200 is not as great; at 1,000 miles the B-727-200 has only a 3 percent cost advantage over the smaller aircraft (with equal load factors). The larger aircraft has three

Table 3.4 Comparison of direct aircraft-operating costs for domestic trunks (12 Months Ending June 30, 1981, ¢ per RPM)

Aircraft type	DC-9-30	DC-737-200	B-727-100	B-727-200	DC-10-10	B-747
Seats	115	121	125	164	371	500
Mileage						
200	12.0	11.7	14.0	12.1	12.5	15.4
400	8.3	8.1	9.5	8.1	7.8	9.0
600	7.1	6.9	8.0	6.8	6.2	6.9
800	6.5	6.3	7.2	6.2	5.5	5.9
1,000	6.1	6.0	6.8	5.8	5.0	5.2
1,250	—	—	6.4	5.5	4.6	4.7
1,500	—	—	6.2	5.2	4.4	4.4
1,750	—	—	—	—	4.2	4.1
2,000	—	—	—	—	4.0	4.0
2,250	—	—	—	—	3.9	3.8
2,500	—	—	—	—	3.9	3.7

Sources: The cost comparisons are based on the *DPFI* Costing Methodology Version Six, developed by the Financial and Cost Division of the CAB's Office of Economic Analysis. The comparisons are based on trunk costs for the year ending June 30, 1981. Aircraft capital costs are based on used aircraft prices for aircraft at the midpoint of a 16-year life. The aircraft prices used are DC-9-30 = $5.1 million, B-737-200 = $6.3 million, B-727-100 = $2.5 million, B-727-200 = $6.5 million, DC-10-10 = $20.0 million, and B-747 = $24.5 million. (See *Avmark*, January 1, 1981.) Airlines return on equity was assumed to be the average of all manufacturing (see *Federal Trade Commission's Quarterly Financial Report*).
Note: Only two trunk airlines operated the B-737-200, and until fall of 1981, labor agreements required these carriers to operate them with three-man crews. In these cost comparisons we therefore used the pilot expense of the local service carriers for the B-737. Also the trunks maintenance costs for the B-737-200 were unusually high. We assumed that maintenance expense was an average of the trunks experience with a B-727-200 and the local service carriers B-737-200.

Seating densities were assumed equal to the greatest number of seats on an aircraft currently in operation, and load factors were assumed to equal 60 percent.

engines and a three-man crew, in contrast to the two-man crew and two engines of the smaller aircraft. The relative efficiency of the two aircraft is reflected in their relative purchase prices. In 1980 the average price paid by domestic airlines for a new B-727-200 was 24 percent higher than that for a new B-737-200 ($14.2 million vs. $11.5 million). As of January 1, 1981, the average price for used versions of the aircraft were essentially the same, about $6.4 million. When operating costs are calculated using capital costs based on new aircraft prices, the B-737-200 has lower costs than the B-727-200 in stage lengths up to 1,000 miles.

The DC-9-30, a two-engine aircraft which is only slightly smaller than a B-737-200, has higher operating costs, although it is more widely used. Of comparable size to these two-engine aircraft is the B-727-100, an earlier version of the predominant three-engine plane. Because both models of the B-727 have about the same operating costs on a stage of given length, the stretched aircraft, which is about 25 percent larger, has correspondingly lower costs per seat.[12] As we explore in more detail in subsequent chapters, one of the sources of some of the trunk airlines' financial problems under deregulation has been their relatively large stock of older fuel inefficient aircraft such as the B-727-100. Similarly the older four-engine DC-8s and B-707s in their fleets have operating ranges that are comparable to wide-bodied aircraft, but their average costs are substantially higher. These inefficient aircraft are being phased out of operation.[13]

Aircraft Size, Load Factors, and Market Characteristics
Airlines can minimize the average cost of serving a market, and hence the fare, by flying large aircraft at high load factors. However, such service would be relatively inconvenient for many passengers; it generally would not minimize total travel costs when the value of time is included. For example, someone who has to be in St. Louis on Tuesday morning may not be well served by a very inexpensive flight on Tuesday afternoon. To meet traveler demand for convenient service, airlines use smaller aircraft and operate them at lower load factors than simple cost (and fare) minimization implies. The aircraft size and load factor that minimizes passengers' total travel costs depend on the characteristics of the market, including distance and density, as well as the value that passengers place on their time.

An increase in the number of flights reduces the time between the passengers' desired departure times and their actual departure times. In most cases it also increases average costs. As more flights are added, passenger demand generally increases less than proportionately, so the number of passengers per flight declines.[14] By adding flights, carriers must operate the existing aircraft at lower load factors, or use smaller aircraft; both increase the average cost per passenger of serving the market.

The second aspect of convenience relates to a passenger's ability to secure a reservation on his preferred flight. The number of seats on a given flight is fixed, yet demand is random; therefore there is a chance that a passenger's preferred flight will be filled. For example, even though an airline expects on average to sell 70 percent of the 100 seats on an aircraft, on some flights more than 100 people will want a reservation. (Correspondingly, on other flights the number of people who want a reservation may be less than 40.) By reducing the percentage of seats that it expects to fill (either by increasing plane size or by raising fares to reduce travel), the carrier can reduce the probability that a particular passenger will be denied a reservation on his preferred flight. This, however, increases the average cost per passenger of serving the market.

An efficient air transportation system would minimize passenger total travel cost. As we have seen, this involves a trade-off between the fare and time-related costs. As we now show, load factor and aircraft size tend to increase with market distance and density. Moreover, at least relative to Board prescribed levels, fares generally decline as load factors and equipment size increase.

As market distance increases, surface travel becomes a poor substitute for air travel. Since air travel is almost always faster, the total cost of air transportation will be less for individuals who place a high value on their time. In short-haul markets, where the time savings of air travel are relatively small, airlines tend to specialize in serving travelers who place a high value on time. At longer market distances air travel demand becomes less sensitive to air service convenience.

Not only does the demand for convenient service decline as distance increases; the cost of providing a given level of convenience also increases. As we have noted already, the cost advantage of larger aircraft increases with distance. Thus it becomes relatively more costly to use smaller aircraft in order to provide more frequent flights in longer-haul markets. Moreover the total cost of each seat increases with market distance; so the cost of flying at low load factors increases as well. At longer market distances, equipment size and load factors will tend to increase, *ceteris paribus*.

Average aircraft size and load factor can be expected to increase with market density. There are diminishing returns to reductions in travel delay—beyond a certain point added flights do not substantially improve convenience. For example, in most markets, passengers would place little

Table 3.5   Average load factors and aircraft size (second quarter 1981)

Market distance (miles)	Market size (10–50)[a]		Market size (51–200)[a]		Market size (201–500)[a]		Market size (501 +)[a]	
	Load factor	Size (seats)	Load factor	Size (seats)	Load factor	Size (seats)	Load factor	Size (seats)
1–200	44	95	50	112	52	116	58	140
201–500	50	102	55	111	59	120	60	131
501–1,500	55	114	59	117	61	129	58	153
1501 +	61	132	61	151	65	177	62	258

Source: Service segment data.
a. O & D passengers per day.

additional value on having a flight every half hour rather than every hour. As market density increases, therefore, the airlines will increase the number of flights less than proportionately with the increase in passengers; instead, they will operate larger aircraft at higher load factors.

Table 3.5 shows that in the second quarter of 1981 average load factors and equipment sizes tended to increase with market density and distance as predicted.[15] For example, in the smallest short-haul markets, aircraft size (95 seats) and load factor (44 percent) are the lowest in the table. In the densest, long-haul markets the average coach load factor was 62 percent, and the average plane size was 258 seats. Generally, short-haul and less traveled markets have load factors below 55 percent, which is the load factor standard the Board used to compute costs and fares under the *DPFI*.[16] In longer and denser markets load factors are above 55 percent.

The load factor and equipment size observed at any given time is a function of a variety of factors, including the amount of connecting traffic traveling in the market, the fleet mix of the airlines, and transitory factors such as the business cycle. Nevertheless, these data indicate that differences in load factor and equipment size among markets are consistent with an efficient deployment of airline assets.

Air Fares and Market Characteristics

Table 3.6 shows the average fare as a percentage of the cost-adjusted *DPFI* fare formula for these same markets.[17] The relationship between the average fares and the *DPFI* tends to be consistent with the relative costs of service; the fare relative to the *DPFI* generally decreases with density and distance.

Of course, a market's average fare was not equal to the *DPFI* formula even under regulation. Discounts were available in many markets, and local service carriers could charge fares up to 30 percent above the formula.

Table 3.6   Fares as a percent of *DPFI* fare formula (second quarter 1981)

Market distance (miles)	Market size[a]			
	10–50	51–200	201–500	501+
1–200	116	109	103	79
201–500	117	111	103	76
501–1,500	110	94	88	88
1,501+	72	77	76	67

Source: *O & D Survey* for markets with nonstop flights.
a. O & D passengers per day.

Table 3.7   Comparison of load factor, equipment size, and fares as a percent of *DPFI* in tourist and nontourist markets (second quarter 1981)

Market distance (miles)	Market size (201–500)[a]			Market size (501+)[a]		
	Load factor	Equipment	Fare	Load factor	Equipment	Fare
501–1500						
Tourist	62	130	80	54	166	76
Nontourist	60	128	92	60	145	95
1501+						
Tourist	68	235	64	69	290	56
Nontourist	64	161	79	61	250	70

Source: Service segment data, *O & D Survey*.
a. O & D passengers per day.

Thus table 3.6 does not necessarily prove that fares in any given category are higher or lower than they would have been had regulation continued. Rather, it indicates that the relationship of fares among markets differs substantially from what the Board prescribed in the *DPFI*.[18] In chapter 9 we formally estimate the relationship between airline fares and factors such as distance, density, and market concentration.

To consider whether airlines are tailoring their operations to the demands of less time-sensitive passengers, we compared load factors, equipment size, and fares in a group of tourist markets and nontourist markets. Tourist travelers are generally not very time sensitive and consequently do not value reductions in travel delay highly. We defined tourist markets as those involving interstate service to Hawaii and Florida, as well as Reno and Las Vegas, Nevada. We also limited our evaluation to markets involving distances greater than 500 miles and with more the 200 passengers per day. In shorter tourist markets surface transportation is likely to be especially important, whereas in thinner markets it would be relatively difficult for carriers to realize any market economies.

As table 3.7 indicates, air fares are lower in tourist markets. In part, this reflects the lower cost service offered in these markets. In markets over 1,500 miles, load factors and equipment size are higher than in the nontourist markets. In the less dense markets between 501 and 1,500 miles, a similar relation is apparent, although the difference in load factors and equipment size is much smaller. In dense markets of 501 to 1,500 miles, load factors are actually lower in tourist markets, although aircraft size is somewhat larger. Nevertheless, the average fare as a percentage of *DPFI* is substantially lower in these dense, medium range markets.

Peak-Load and Other Pricing Practices

With increased fare flexibility the relationship between markets has changed from what the Board prescribed under the *DPFI* formula. Moreover a number of innovative pricing practices have been introduced under the deregulated regime. Most notably there has been an increase in the use of peak-load pricing. In addition carriers have reduced connecting fares in markets receiving nonstop service, have established special arrangements with travel agents, and have introduced frequent flyer programs.

Peak-Load Pricing

Demand for air travel varies by the season, by the day, and by the hour. (See figure 3.1 for an illustration of peaking during what is itself the peak month of August; the figure is derived from 1975 data.) Consequently, if airlines were to use their stock of aircraft intensively, and all passengers were charged the same fare regardless of when they traveled, load factors on different flights would vary considerably: they would be quite high at peak travel times and quite low on less popular flights. This is the type of service pattern that regulation encouraged.

Peak-load pricing entails different prices to consumers depending on when they use the service. This smooths out demand, because some travelers would be willing to change their desired departure time if they could travel at a reduced fare on a different flight. For example, a vacationing student and a salesman may both want to depart at 5 P.M. The student, however, might gladly delay his departure three hours for a 20 percent reduction in his fare, whereas the salesman would not. The institution of such a fare differential between the 5 P.M. and the 8 P.M. flight would increase the load factor on the later flight. At the same time it would decrease the number of travelers demanding service on the peak flight. This increases the probability that a full-fare passenger can secure a reservation. Since the student prefers the flight with the lower fare, he is better off. Any

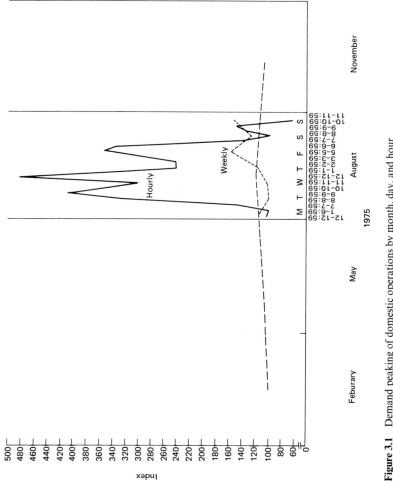

Figure 3.1   Demand peaking of domestic operations by month, day, and hour

full-fare passenger who might have been denied access on a peak-period flight and can now get it is also better off. Moreover with peak-load pricing carriers need a smaller fleet of aircraft to provide service to a given number of passengers.

A fare difference between peak and off-peak flights is cost-justified. An airline will buy an aircraft if the expected returns over its useful life exceed its cost. It is not necessary that each flight make the same contribution to the cost of the aircraft, only that, jointly, all the flights together pay for the investment. Aircraft capacity is fully used in the peak periods, and indeed the size of the aircraft fleet is tailored to serve peak-period demands. Consequently peak fares should cover a substantial share of investment costs. It is profitable to offer off-peak flights even though they make a much smaller contribution to overhead than more popular flights. Since empty seats at less popular travel times will produce downward pressure on fares, competition should produce a price structure in which fares are relatively high in peak periods and relatively low in off-peak periods.

As we have already noted, explicit peak and off-peak fares are available in many markets. Moreover two-tiered pricing schemes, with restricted discounts offered along with unrestricted fares, have many of the attributes of peak-load pricing. Although discounts are available on all, or almost all flights, the number of discount seats sold on each flight is limited. By rationing the availability of seats, full-fare passengers are assured a high probability of access to more popular flights, while relatively more discount travelers take off-peak flights.[19] Thus these two-tiered pricing systems can achieve the same efficiencies of utilization as explicit peak-load pricing systems.

In at least one respect capacity-controlled discount fares may be economically more efficient than explicit peak-load pricing. Since travel demands vary predictably by the season, day, and hour, the price that would fill all the available seats in a plane would be different for each flight. Although theoretically optimal, in practice, such a pricing system would be far too complex. Reservations would be cumbersome to make because travelers would want to know about the available fare options. Also passengers changing departure times would have to have their fare adjusted, which is costly for the airline as well as for the traveler. Yet by varying the proportion of full-fare and discount passengers on given flights, a system of restricted discount fares allows the average fare to vary on a flight-by-flight basis. Thus at least in theory a system of restricted discount fares should limit load factor disparity. In especially dense markets, however, carriers can adjust the number of flights to limit load factor disparity while employing explicit peak and off-peak fares.

Other Pricing Practices

Reduced connecting fares have been used to induce passengers to make an intermediate stop in markets where convenient nonstop services are offered by a rival carrier. In a hub-and-spoke system, which most airlines have implemented, carriers operate aircraft from a number of cities into a central hub where passengers make connections to reach their ultimate destinations. Such service is most common for passengers traveling to and from small- and medium-size communities, but in many markets where there is ample nonstop service, convenient connecting service is also available. Since connecting in such markets takes longer than nonstop service, passengers would prefer it only at a lower price. Carriers have increasingly offered reduced price connecting services in markets served by nonstop flights. For example, Piedmont, which provides service in the mid-Atlantic states, promotes Hop-Scotch fares to Chicago from Washington and New York. A number of carriers provide transcontinental service with intermediate stops at less than the prevailing nonstop fare. As with other discounts, carriers would be willing to accommodate a passenger traveling between two large cities at a reduced rate in order to help fill otherwise empty seats on their flights. In most cases the number of seats offered at these reduced fares is limited.

Historically the Board not only regulated the price of air travel, it also regulated the commission rates that airlines were permitted to pay their travel agents. In February 1980 the Board stopped regulating commission rates and prohibited their establishment by industrywide agreement. In September 1981 the Board allowed carriers to charge fares lower than the posted tariff price.[20] This maximum tariff rule made the relationship between the fares that the carriers post and fares that agents charge a contractual matter between the airlines and their agents. In December 1982, as we describe in more detail in chapter 10, the Board permitted airlines to decide whether or not they wanted to use alternate forms of ticket distribution in addition to distribution through travel agents.[21]

The changes in the Board's regulation of tariffs and distribution systems have allowed a number of innovations in the marketing and sale of airline travel. Carriers are now free to offer corporations volume discounts on air transportation. They are also able to establish special deals with individual travel agents. For example, some airlines have sold particular travel agents large blocks of seats that are resold at prices determined by the agent. In addition most airlines have developed commission rate structures that provide higher commissions to large volume travel agents. This is roughly equivalent to the volume discounts that are prevalent in many industries.

Such rate structures tend to encourage particular agents to deal primarily (but by no means exclusively) with a limited number of carriers.

In the spring of 1981 American Airlines instituted a frequent flyer program that gives bonuses to passengers who accumulate miles of travel on its system. Most of the larger airlines have developed similar types of programs. In one such program passengers that accrue 10,000 miles of travel on a carrier's system are able to travel first class with a coach ticket. Other incentives, including free travel, are awarded to passengers accruing more mileage.

Frequent travelers tend to be business people; hence someone other than the passenger is paying the fare. Yet the programs are designed to give the traveler, not the employer, the fare cut. The program is thus cleverly designed to help the airline by giving frequently flying businessmen an incentive to fly a particular airline rather than its competitor. All else equal, the airline that serves the most markets has a competitive advantage with a given frequent flyer program: the more markets a carrier serves, the greater the chance that a given passenger will be able to travel on that airline in a particular market. Consequently airlines with less extensive route networks tend to make it easier for passengers to qualify for the various bonuses.

Trends in Fares and Profitability

Airline pricing policies have changed substantially in the deregulated environment. As this discussion has shown, the relationships of fares among markets differ substantially from what the Board had dictated in the *DPFI*. Nevertheless, in the public's eye the most vivid testament to deregulation has come from the remarkably low fares that have been available from time to time in a number of markets. These fares, coupled with the industry's deteriorating profitability in the years following the passage of the act, suggest that prices may not be cost based. As we now discuss, however, both the "fare wars" and the industry's losses are consistent with the operation of an efficient industry.

"Fare Wars"
The effect of the changes in pricing policies on average industry fares is illustrated in figure 3.2 The figure presents indexes of average yields (fare per mile) for the trunk and local airlines, their average cost per available seat mile, and adjustments to the Board's fare formula. (All three indexes have a base value of 100 in the second quarter of 1977. The SIFL index does not reflect increases in the zones for flexibility.) Air fares rose substantially

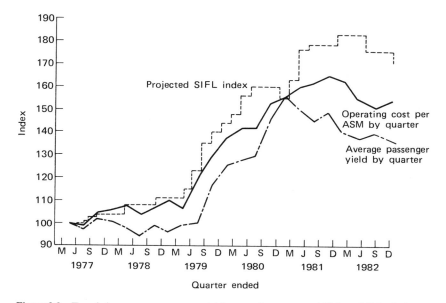

Figure 3.2   Trends in average passenger yield, operating cost per ASM, and SIFL index

less rapidly than costs and inflation through the second quarter of 1979. In the following twelve-month period the cost per average seat mile increased rapidly, and the Board adjusted its ceilings so average fares kept pace. Nevertheless, since load factors were falling, the increase in fares was not as great as the rise in the average cost per revenue passenger mile. Therefore, after the Board expanded its zone of flexibility in May 1980, carriers raised fares more rapidly than average costs rose. Part of this run-up may have been due to regulatory lag: without the delay in adjusting fare ceilings to reflect the fuel price increase over the summer of 1979, fares would have increased more rapidly in the preceding year than they had. Average industry fares trended downward after the first quarter of 1981 but firmed as the economy recovered in 1983.

The downward trend in fares during the recessionary period reflects remarkably low fares offered in many markets. One frequent cause for such low fares is introductory fares offered by an entering carrier which the incumbent carriers then match. Examples include markets like Salt Lake City to Denver, as well as larger ones such as the transcontinental markets. If the entering carrier is a formerly regulated carrier, prices often revert to their previous levels once a new equilibrium of market shares has been achieved.

Another source of lower fares since deregulation has been the growth of airlines that emphasis low-fare service. Currently there are a handful of carriers offering low-fare high frequency service in a number of short- to medium-haul markets. Their fares are often 40 to 70 percent below those of the incumbent carriers. These carriers as a group present a challenge to many of the formerly regulated airlines. Incumbent carriers that compete on the routes the new carriers enter tend to match the fares while simultaneously attempting to develop a cost structure that is closer to that of the new entrants. In markets where these new entrants serve, fares often do not return to their pre-entry levels.

A third reason for the recurrent low fares was the excess supply of equipment, and most notably wide-bodied equipment during the recession. Since regulation encouraged service competition, carriers faced incentives to purchase a larger stock of equipment than they needed. The freedom to exit and enter markets allowed carriers to more efficiently employ their narrow-bodied equipment, further exacerbating the excess supply of wide bodies. In addition the prolonged economic slump between 1980 and 1982, and the resulting downturn in demand for air travel, added to the excess capacity.

Three- and four-engine wide-bodied equipment was especially in excess supply. The Board's regulatory policy set fares in dense long-haul markets well above costs. Yet this equipment can only be efficiently deployed in these markets. Carriers have to ground the equipment if revenues are not sufficient to cover the direct operating costs. By using low fares in many dense long-haul markets, carriers have found they can stimulate enough traffic to keep the equipment operating, albeit with revenues that are insufficient to cover both direct and indirect costs.

Fourth, as we have already considered, tourist markets generally have lower fares than markets of similar distances and density. Because passengers in these markets are not particularly time sensitive, carriers tend to serve these markets with large equipment operated at high load factors. A carrier can attract business in a tourist market with few flights at less popular times if its fare is low enough. Consequently carriers find it relatively easy to enter vacation markets to increase equipment utilization.

The most widely cited low fare is a $99 transcontinental fare that has been available periodically. It is frequently proclaimed that low prices such as these are the result of fare wars and that they reflect destructive competition. As we have discussed, there are a number of rational explanations for the low fares. Falling fares in an industry where excess capacity exists is rational not irrational. If destructive competition in this latter sense were an important factor, we would observe carriers, without any cost advantage over their rivals, purchasing equipment even though fares did not cover costs. In fact we saw the opposite. Carriers have been canceling orders for new equipment and deferred deliveries. Moreover both Lockheed and McDonnell-Douglas ceased production of their three-engine wide-bodied aircraft. With the economic recovery in 1983 and 1984, airlines increased new equipment orders.

Profits
Despite the "fare wars" and fears of destructive competition, fares have increased considerably under deregulation. Nevertheless, they have not increased as rapidly as carriers' costs. Consequently as table 1.2 shows, carrier operating profit margins have declined since 1978.

The airlines' difficulties are epitomized by the bankruptcy of Braniff Airways in May 1982. Braniff, which had been the nation's tenth largest airline, was relatively profitable through most of the 1970s (see appendix C). However, Braniff expanded aggressively following the passage of the ADA. In the first year it added more than fifty routes, increasing the number served by over 60 percent. Braniff's expansion, which was far greater than any other carrier, proved overly ambitious as fuel prices rose and losses began to mount, and it was forced to curtail operations substantially. In late 1981, under new management, Braniff reconfigured its aircraft to all-coach seating, reduced the number of employees as well as their salaries, increased productivity, and consolidated operations around its hub at the Dallas–Ft. Worth Airport. These steps failed to stem the flow of red ink, and in mid-1981 Braniff was forced to cease operations. In March 1984 a smaller scale Braniff, under new management, resumed operations.

There can be little doubt that the rapid increase in fuel prices and the prolonged economic slump of 1980 through 1983 would have adversely affected industry profits regardless of the regulatory climate. Thus it is not clear that industry profitability would have been substantially different had the industry remained regulated. Airline demand has historically been quite sensitive to aggregate economic activity in addition to being reasonably price elastic. Regardless of the regulatory climate, therefore, the prolonged economic slump and the rapid cost increases would have depressed traffic and profitability. In fact the reductions in industry fares beginning in the first quarter of 1981 stimulated traffic and may have thereby ameliorated the effect of the industry slump. Moreover the PATCO strike and the resulting capacity restrictions, which began in

August 1981, undoubtedly had a negative impact on profits in 1981 and 1982.

A Long-Run View of Airline Pricing

Airline industry pricing policies have changed substantially in the deregulated environment. Fares have been somewhat volatile as carriers have been faced with excess capacity and as they have been rationalizing their route systems. Six years after the Board began liberalizing fares, the industry is still very much in disequilibrium. Nevertheless, the developments in the deregulated environment provide some indication of the nature of airline pricing in the long run.

As we have already noted, airline demand varies throughout the day and the week. The airlines have instituted a variety of pricing practices to smooth traffic patterns. Some carriers have employed peak-load pricing while others have used a system of capacity controlled discount fares, which in several respects accomplishes the same end. However, most carriers not only restrict the number of discount seats they offer on a given flight, they also require passengers to satisfy advance purchase and minimum stay requirements. These restrictions seem designed to distinguish passengers on the basis of their willingness to pay: a passenger who values his time highly is less likely to make travel arrangements in advance or to alter travel plans in order to qualify for a reduced fare. This suggests that carriers have an ability to price discriminate.

The minimum stay requirement is almost certainly not related to differences in the cost of providing service to passengers. The cost of serving a passenger who books well in advance and travels on flights for which space is available does not depend on the passenger's length of stay. It is the same regardless of whether he is spending two days or two weeks at his destination. The minimum-stay requirement appears to be mainly a device to discriminate among travelers of different time sensitivities.

On the other hand, an explicit "advance purchase" requirement may be cost related. A substantial share of passengers do not use reservations they make on particular flights. Since empty seats are costly, airlines strive to minimize the number of their no-shows. By requiring payment substantially before flight time, an advance purchase restriction may deter passengers from making reservations on flights they do not intend to take. If capacity-controlled discount seats are sold on a first-come first-serve basis, the "advance purchase" requirement becomes an implicit by-product of the capacity control, with the precise requirement varying across flights. In some cases discount seats are available the day before the flight, in others the discount seats might be sold out weeks before departure. A number of airlines currently offer such fares.

The ability of carriers to segregate passengers based on their willingness to pay suggests the airline industry is not perfectly competitive. Carriers have some discretion in setting prices in many markets, even in relatively large ones. This stems from the time sensitivity of passengers. If passengers have strong preferences about when they travel, they will not view flights at different times of the day as perfect substitutes (i.e., they will not always choose the cheaper flight). This gives each airline in the market the opportunity to position itself at an unserved time. Each can charge a premium for passengers who prefer to travel at that time and charge a lower price for passengers who are indifferent to flight time.[22]

As Panzar (1979, 1979a) points out, the product differentiation effect resulting from variation in flight departure times and the effects of flight frequency and load factor on service quality yield a monopolistically competitive model of airline markets. Such a model has two basic results. First, when the direct benefits to consumers of increased flight frequency are exhausted, excess profit of each active firm is driven down to zero. Simultaneously, potential entrants are afforded no profitable opportunity for entry, given the prices and flight schedules already supplied in the market. Thus the Panzar-type monopolistic competition model should turn into a perfectly competitive model (of the sort modeled by Dorman 1981) on high-density routes. These routes should have unrestricted low fares in long-run equilibrium. Second, a noncooperative free-entry equilibrium may well result in less dense markets in somewhat higher prices and greater frequency than would occur in a perfectly competitive world. In terms of the prices business and discretionary travelers pay in these less densely traveled markets, the monopolistic competition model predicts some discretion for firms to discriminate in price between these different classes of consumers. Nevertheless, it is not at all clear whether consumer welfare would be higher if time-sensitive passengers paid lower fares and were offered fewer flights or paid higher fares and had more flights.[23] In any case, since discretionary passengers are, by definition, largely indifferent to departure times, their fares should, if anything, be reduced by this pricing policy.

While we have stressed changes in demand over the day and the week, airline demand also varies seasonally as well as over the business cycle. We therefore should expect airline prices to fall during recessions and during low demand periods such as the winter. Board regulatory policy discouraged such pricing trends. However, the apparent ability of airlines to price discriminate has important implications for carriers' pricing during periods of cyclical and seasonal downturns. The demand of discretionary passengers is presumably more price elastic than that of time-sensitive passengers. At times of relatively low demand, therefore, carriers are more apt to reduce discount fares than they are to reduce unrestricted coach fares.

In the long run we would expect capacity-controlled discount fares or explicit peak-load prices to prevail and the particular type of fare system that exists in a particular market to depend on its characteristics. For example, in markets where a large proportion of passengers are discretionary, such as tourist markets, a system of unrestricted fares is apt to develop. In such markets a large proportion of passengers will be willing to alter travel plans to secure a low fare. Similarly, in dense markets where demand is relatively constant over time, the efficiency advantages of restricted discount fares may be relatively small.[24]

Throughout our discussion we have assumed that advance purchase and minimum-stay requirements are effective in differentiating passengers on their ability to pay. This is obviously not completely true. Some passengers otherwise willing to pay are able to qualify for discount fares, whereas other passengers preferring lower prices to convenience cannot. The efficiency and profitability of restricted discount fares depends on the ability of airlines to differentiate among passengers.[25] If in a particular market airlines cannot adequately differentiate among passengers on the basis of their willingness to pay, then the use of advanced purchase and minimum stay requirements will not be a profitable strategy.

Conclusion

In the period of regulation the CAB controlled the level and structure of air fares closely. With increased operating flexibility, carriers have adopted a variety of pricing strategies. These include restricted discounts and low unrestricted fares. Prices have apparently become more cost related; average fares vary among markets in a manner that better reflects differences in costs and the quality of service demanded. There is also a clear increase in the use of peak-load pricing, which has improved industry efficiency. Other pricing innovations, such as quantity discounts, corporate discounts, and frequent flyer discounts underscore the diversity in competitive strategies that are found in the deregulated marketplace.

Chapter 4

Routes and Industry Structure

Deregulation has caused the route system to be reshaped by the competitive pressures of open entry and exit. Carriers' route structures are no longer shaped by the incremental route awards of the CAB. Instead, carriers are engaged in overall planning to use their resources most efficiently. The strategy of local service carriers has been to expand into longer-haul routes, providing increased amounts of single-carrier service to small- and medium-sized communities. New entrants are, for the most part, concentrating on point-to-point traffic, with the majority of their operations focused at a single-hub airport. Trunks and locals alike have increasingly emphasized the development of hub-and-spoke operations at major airports. Commuters are increasing service to many of the smaller points formerly served by local service carriers and are expanding rapidly.

Reform of Route Regulation

The most restrictive era of route regulation occurred during the route moratorium of the early 1970s when the Board simply refused to entertain the hundreds of applications that came to it for new route authority. The Senate judiciary hearings preceding deregulation dramatized these shortcomings and reinforced the growing distaste felt by many for regulation in the presence of competition. A program of route policy reform began to be introduced; its results were relatively slow prior to the passage of the ADA but extremely rapid thereafter. Table 4.1 shows the Board's major route reform decisions.

Initial Route Reform Ideas
The first reform idea predated deregulation. The Board began systematically to remove the myriad of restrictions on carrier certificates that limited their operating flexibility. Many of these restrictions were imposed to protect carriers that no longer existed or for procedural reasons that were no longer relevant. The Board realigned carriers' certificates, beginning with the local service carriers in the early 1970s and proceeding to the trunks later in the decade.[1]

Table 4.1   Chronology of significant route reform actions by CAB

Date	Title	Type of action	Description
9-8-75	Reopened Service to Omaha and Des Moines Case	Order 75-9-19	First grant of new competitive authority in the post route moratorium period.
11-13-75	Remanded Reno–Portland/ Seattle Nonstop Investigation	Order 75-11-45	Board opted for competition *per se* even though it found incumbent's service was satisfactory. Diversionary impact on incumbents accorded limited weight.
5-17-77	Chicago–Midway Low-Fare Route Proceeding	Order 77-5-81	Commencement of first major low-fare route case. Board expressly requested parties to explore whether the authority conferred should be permissive (i.e., carriers would have the right not to inaugurate service or to cease operations) and whether more than one applicant should be granted authority in each city-pair market.
11-14-78	Piedmont "Boston Entry" Case	Order 78-4-69	Reversed precedent that full oral hearing procedures would be ordered upon incumbent carrier objections. Dispensed with traditional issues for litigation, such as profitability of planned service and amount of estimated diversion.
5-30-78	Oakland Service Case	Order 78-4-121	Board proposed to award authority to all fit applicants by nonhearing show cause procedures. Thus issue of comparative selection was eliminated; hearings limited to issues of fitness and whether each market could support some service. Order served as policy basis for subsequent multiple permissive or open entry route policy.
1-11-79	Dallas/Ft. Worth–New Orleans Subpart M Proceeding	Order 79-1-34	Proposed to grant multiple entry to all fit applicants and utilized standardized policy findings that served as precedent for all succeeding domestic route licensing action.

Source: *Bibliography of Important Civil Aeronautics Board Regulatory Actions 1975–1979*, CAB, December 1979.

The reform hearings prompted the Board to be more receptive to applications for new operating authority by existing and new carriers. By the end of 1975 the Board had reopened several service cases and began to grant new competitive authority. It began to find that even where the incumbent's service was satisfactory, added competition was warranted when the size and potential of the market were sufficiently large.

The Board also began to grant consideration to applications that were accompanied by low-fare service options. The Chicago-Midway case was the first route proceeding (Order 77-5-81) involving both new entrants and low fares. In this case the Board requested the parties to explore whether the authority that would be granted must be mandatory or whether instead it could be permissive (i.e., carriers would have the right not to inaugurate service or to cease operations). The Chicago-Midway case also raised as an issue whether the rights should be nonexclusive, so that more than one applicant might be granted authority in each city-pair market. In addition this case was one of the first designed to encourage service to satellite airports in order to relieve congestion at nearby major hub airports. By the end of 1977 three major low-fare route cases were in process; they were being given priority hearing schedules.

Another important policy change involved dispensing with two traditional issues for litigation: diversion and the demonstration of profitability. In the case involving entry into Boston, the incumbent carrier (Eastern) objected and alleged that Piedmont's services would divert up to $3 million in revenues from it and that the new service would be unprofitable. Eastern was put on notice that unless it was prepared to show that diversion by Piedmont's new Boston services would threaten its solvency or impair its ability to provide essential air transportation, diversion would not be considered to create an issue of material fact or the need for an oral hearing. Similarly profitability would no longer be required to be demonstrated; instead, it would be sufficient to show that the applicant had a plausible operating plan. In dispensing with these traditional issues for litigation, the Board wished to be able to move easily and quickly to permit additional entry in cases where a single applicant put forward a relatively conventional proposal for new and/or improved services in small- or medium-size markets.

Multiple Permissive Entry

Perhaps the most important new idea in route regulation reform was the exploration by the Board of the possibility of making multiple nonstop awards. This policy would permit authority to be received not just by one applicant (the traditional outcome) but by all applicants. The idea was not to overload a market with actual competitors, for the CAB recognized that the number of carriers that can operate profitably in a particular market is limited by such economic factors as local traffic demand and the availability of connecting traffic. Rather, the Board was intent on creating a pool of entrants able to enter if and when existing service failed to match consumers' needs or if prices in a market became too high. The Board relied on the idea that the forces of the marketplace are more likely to yield an economically rational carrier selection process than the Board could hope to achieve with its traditional regulatory mechanism. Thus, in deciding the Chicago-Midway and Transcontinental low-fare cases, the Board rejected arguments by new entrants such as World Airways and Midway Airlines that they should be awarded a monopoly corridor protecting them from competition to help them get established in the marketplace. The Board concluded that if the new carriers had an innovative product to market, no special protection was required. Thus in the Chicago-Midway case the Board granted all the authority that had been requested—service to all six cities at issue by the two new entrants (Midway and Midway Southwest); it also granted the new authority requested by Northwest, Delta, and North Central (now part of Republic). In addition the order imposed no restrictions on incumbent carriers that would prevent them either from matching fares at Chicago's nearby O'Hare airport or from instituting low-fare service at Midway.

The new policy set forth in the Midway case was expanded in the Oakland service case. This landmark route case anticipated open entry. Unlike the Midway case, which involved full hearing procedures, the Board proposed to award authority to all applicants by nonhearing, show-cause procedures. It could do this if it eliminated the issue of comparative selection. Hearings were to be limited to issues of fitness and to whether each market could support some service. The instituting order (Order 78-4-121) set forth exhaustive tentative legal, policy, and economic findings that justified open entry to applicants found by the Board to be fit to provide air service. In so doing, the Board abandoned forty years of protective entry control based on comparative selection among competing applicants.

The multiple permissive entry policies of the Board created a great deal of anxiety. Some feared that the intensified competition that would follow freer entry would be seriously distorted with victory going not to the most efficient firm, or the one with the most enterprising management, but to the one with the best existing route network. Since the trunks were perceived to have the best routes, they would be the clear winners. Others feared that massive new entry would occur, bringing in its wake destructive competition, excess capacity and falling load factors. Still others feared not that incumbent carriers would retrench in anticipation of entry by newly authorized carriers but that such entry would never materialize, thereby leaving the system less competitive than before.

The Board believed that once it was clear that entry was genuinely free of government restraint, the reaction of carriers was likely to be motivated by economic factors. Entry that did take place would be the result of calculation and selection by managements of the opportunities that would be most promising for their particular companies. The anxieties were believed to be inspired by the avid competition for routes that must and did occur as long as the selection process conferred some degree of exclusivity. Carriers filed applications, in part, to gain the value (now and in the future) of the certificate in an otherwise closed system and, in part, to prevent other carriers from getting authority. Sometimes carriers filed just to keep a high profile before the Board on the theory that they would gain more authority if they participated in a large number of cases. In contrast, if entry were really free, then certificates would have no inherent value, and regulatory-induced application filing and entry would cease. Thus the best answer to the fears of inefficient entry and operations was to wipe out the scarcity value of the certificate by making entry free and permissive. Eliminating the scarcity value would eliminate artificial inducements to enter or to hold onto an uneconomic operation merely in order to prevent anyone else from using the authority. The best answer to the differential handicaps to which carriers were subject because of the comparative efficiencies of their existing route systems was to give all carriers freedom to improve their systems by route realignment, new entry, and market exit.[2]

Other Board Policies toward Reform
During this period the Board also adopted a more permissive attitude toward market exit between city pairs where entry was liberalized. This attitude was illustrated in the increasing willingness to grant permissive and backup authority, both of which reflected a willingness to allow carriers not to exercise the licenses given them. More permissive entry carried with it as a logical counterpart the relaxation of the requirement to serve. In other words, as new competitors were permitted to enter markets, it was expected that incumbents in some cases would want to get out, and the Board was prepared to let them do so. The Board contemplated other

reform policies as well, such as using rule making to authorize unlimited entry into a group of very large markets.

A final and important thrust of Board policy just before the passage of the deregulation act was to relax the service and operational restrictions on the specialized carriers. The Board found it logical to remove the shackles on different kinds of carriers step by step and synchronously. In particular, the Board undertook to consider applications for scheduled service by supplemental carriers, for domestic markets by airlines traditionally restricted to international routes, and for interstate routes by intrastate carriers. In addition the Board acted to liberalize greatly the restrictions on charter carriers, with a decision to allow public charters.[3] The rule allowed the sale of one-way or round-trip flights, with or without a ground package and with no minimum price, minimum stay, or advance purchase requirements. Symmetrically, as we discussed in chapter 3, the Board permitted the scheduled carriers greatly increased pricing freedom to appeal to the same economy-minded passenger.

Route Reform under the Deregulation Act
Despite all of this activity very little, if any, authority was actually conferred under the new liberal ideas before the deregulation act was passed. This occurred in part because of the length of time it took to institute, hear, and decide cases, even under the most expedited procedures. In addition carriers (with Delta in the forefront) litigated the multiple permissive entry cases, faulting the procedural shortcuts and new criteria the Board was advocating. The Board was instituting new cases under new economic criteria at an ever-increasing pace, but the court system might well have held up actual entry under these new policies for a number of years had the Airline Deregulation Act not been passed.

The act essentially endorsed permissive entry policies by shifting the burden of proof in route cases from the entrant to the incumbent. This meant that entry would be permitted unless the Board made a finding in a particular case that monopoly was in the public interest. Suddenly it was up to those carriers who wanted to restrict entry to prove that such restrictions were in the public interest and beneficial. Moreover a joint House-Senate conference report explicitly mentioned the multiple permissive entry policies then favored by the Board and found these to be consistent with the intent of the new act. Consequently Delta withdrew its court case shortly after the act was passed.

Actual entry went from being effectively blocked before passage of the legislation to being rapidly implemented after passage. The Board was simply not willing to adopt a slow transition policy since this appeared to be unworkable, involving prolonged agony, inevitable discrimination among communities, and all sorts of perverse incentives.

Nevertheless, it seems clear that Congress did not anticipate that entry would occur as quickly as it actually did under the act. Indeed, the legislation contained a number of provisions designed to reduce the regulatory barriers to entry gradually. The Board's authority to regulate entry was not to end until December 31, 1981, over three years after the act was passed. In the interim several methods of encouraging entry were devised. First, a dormant authority program was established that allowed carriers to secure the route authority that other carriers were not using. In the week between the passage of the act and its official signing, a queue formed outside the CAB as carriers attempted to be the first to bid for various dormant routes.

A second provision of the act permitted automatic market entry into one route a year by existing carriers in each of 1979, 1980, and 1981 without CAB approval, although each carrier could protect itself from automatic entry by another carrier on a single route in the same year by filing with the CAB. This provision was controversial at the time of passage, but less so in its implementation, since it involved only thirty-two authorizations per year.

In fact route authority was conferred so rapidly that city-pair authorizations had increased from about 24,000 prior to deregulation to over 106,000 eighteen months after passage of the act. Most requested authority was conferred under a show-cause procedure based on standardized policy findings granting multiple permissive entry within two months of a carrier's request. Indeed, by January 1980, when each carrier could choose its second automatic entry routes, many of the carrier choices involved relatively thin routes to airports such as Orange County, West Palm Beach, and Boston, for which environmental impact studies were in process and entry (other than through the automatic entry provision) was being held in abeyance.

Route Networks since Deregulation

A major restructuring of the industry was expected to follow deregulation, and indeed it has. Carriers have seized the opportunity to redeploy their resources and have made major changes in their route networks. Almost all of the carriers have emphasized connecting service by developing hub-and-spoke operations. In addition carriers have entered routes to improve resource utilization. For example, carriers with predominantly east–west route structures, where traffic peaks in the summer, have entered north–south routes. The result of these route alignments has been improved efficiency, as well as reduced concentration in the industry.

The Incentives for Hubbing

Although passengers prefer frequent nonstop service, such service can be quite costly. Airlines thus face strong incentives to establish hub-and-spoke operations. Flights from various origins arrive at an intermediate point where passengers change planes to proceed to their ultimate destinations. By combining passengers with different origins and destinations, a carrier can increase the average number of passengers per flight and thereby reduce costs. Essentially the broader scope of operation lets the carrier take advantage of the economies of scale in aircraft. At the same time a hub-and-spoke operation provides more convenient service for travelers in less heavily traveled markets.

Since a hubbing airline serves more than just local traffic, on any given route it will have an advantage over a carrier that serves only local traffic. The hubbing carrier serves more passengers on its flights so it can use larger aircraft at higher load factors. Its greater traffic may also enable it to offer more frequent flights. There is some evidence that, over some range, a carrier can get a disproportionate increase in local demand for its service by increasing its share of flights on a route.

The incentives to establish hubs are strongest at cities where there is substantial local traffic and at points that allow relatively noncircuitous travel between a large number of city pairs. Also an efficient hubbing operation will minimize connecting times and therefore require that a carrier simultaneously accommodate many flights. Consequently at its hub airport a carrier must have access to a relatively large number of gates in convenient proximity to one another.

Because of these advantages of hub-and-spoke operation, both the trunks and local service carriers have increased their use of hubbing in the postderegulation period. However, the local service carriers inherited route structures that were in some ways better suited for exploiting the opportunities that deregulation produced. Before deregulation the local service carriers had been confined to serve largely short-haul and thinly traveled markets in particular regions of the country. In most city pairs there is not sufficient traffic to support nonstop service. Hence passengers in markets like Parkersburg, West Virginia, to St. Louis have to change planes at Pittsburgh enroute. In fact over 60 percent of the passengers that travel in the Chicago to Pittsburgh route are headed somewhere else. Many of the local service carriers' passengers had to take other flights, often with different airlines, to reach their ultimate destination. With deregulation the local service carriers branched out from their traditional service areas and enabled their passengers to remain on the same airlines when they traveled to farther destinations.

Passengers that make connections generally prefer making their trips on a single airline. By not changing airlines, they reduce the chance that they will miss a connection or lose their baggage. They also avoid long walks between airport terminal buildings.[4] To increase the amount of airline service they provide, carriers have tended to consolidate their operations at particular airports. They therefore offer service to a large number of cities from a given airport. In addition they strive to time the arrivals and departures to minimize the wait between flights, further increasing the convenience of their services. Since many local service operations were already concentrated in particular service areas, they were well positioned to establish hub-and-spoke systems.

The Growth in Hubbing
The expansion of USAir (then called Allegheny) after the passage of the act vividly illustrates the local service carriers' route strategy. Prior to deregulation Allegheny was largely limited to serving the mid-Atlantic region. Under deregulation it began to branch out from its traditional service area to a variety of places including a number of sunbelt destinations (see figure 4.1). For example, it established service to Phoenix, Houston, New Orleans, and several Florida cities out of its principal hub at Pittsburgh. Since passengers prefer single carrier service, USAir has become the leading airline in these new long-haul markets. The growth of USAir's hub at Pittsburgh is demonstrated by the change in the percentage of its connecting passengers that do not change airlines. In the second quarter of 1978, 73 percent of its connecting passengers made such online connections.[5] This had increased to 89 percent in 1981.

This situation was repeated for other local service carriers. They also began to take advantage of their own feed, rather than handing these passengers off to the trunks. Figure 4.2 shows that from the second quarter of 1978 to the second quarter of 1981, locals had more than doubled their RPMs in markets of 500 to 1,000 miles. Routes of over 1,000 miles, which the locals did not serve before deregulation, accounted for nearly 11 percent of their RPMs by 1981. (See appendix table D for an overview of changes in route networks of the locals.) As a result of these route realignments other

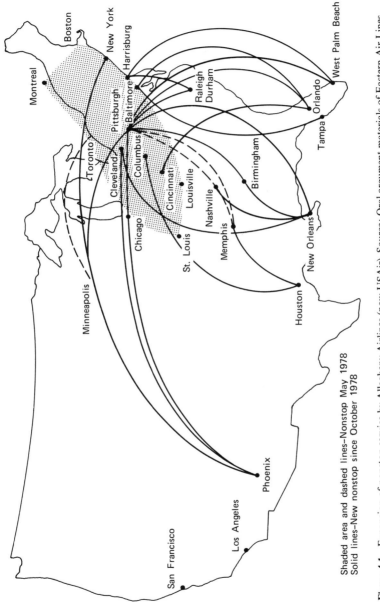
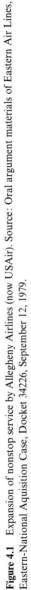

Shaded area and dashed lines–Nonstop May 1978
Solid lines–New nonstop since October 1978

Figure 4.1   Expansion of nonstop service by Allegheny Airlines (now USAir). Source: Oral argument materials of Eastern Air Lines, Eastern-National Aquisition Case, Docket 34226, September 12, 1979.

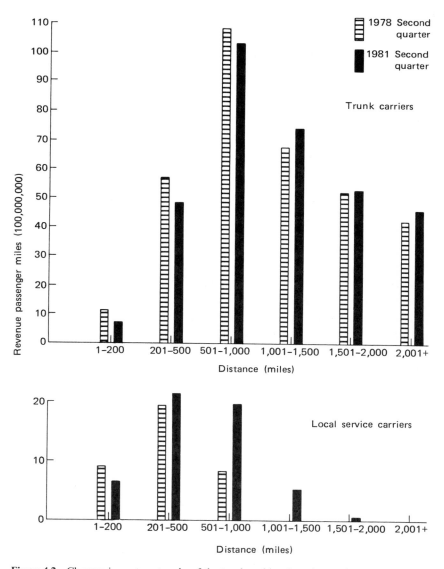

Figure 4.2   Changes in route networks of the trunk and local service carriers

local service carriers also experienced a substantial increase in the percentage of connecting passengers that they kept online. Frontier's online percentage at Denver increased from 48 to 80 percent between the second quarters of 1978 and 1981; for Ozark at St. Louis the percentage increased from 36 to 83 percent.

The trunks also moved to emphasize connecting service through hub-and-spoke operations. In fact Delta and Eastern had established hub-and-spoke systems at Atlanta while the industry was tightly regulated. Both of these carriers, like the local service carriers under deregulation, combined service in short thin routes with longer-haul service. With deregulation both carriers added service at Atlanta. American Airlines relocated its major offices to Dallas–Ft. Worth and built a hub there. United, after apparently deemphasizing hub-and-spoke operations and selling some of its B-737 aircraft, has expanded aggressively at Chicago and Denver.[6]

Aside from Delta and Eastern the trunks did not have many small jet aircraft necessary to serve efficiently thin feeder routes. Consequently despite their increased emphasis on hubbing the trunks, like the locals, have increased the stage lengths of their routes.

The increased emphasis on hubbing is illustrated in table 4.2, which lists the leading hub city for each airline. In 1978 none of the fourteen regulated airlines had 20 percent or more of their total domestic departures out of their leading city; by 1983 ten of them did. Indeed, six of these airlines increased operations by 50 percent or more at their leading hubs. Three—American, Western, and Piedmont—more than doubled their operations.

Because of the greater amount of local traffic trunk carriers have generally found it most profitable to establish their hub-and-spoke operations at large cities, where their large aircraft are best suited to operate. However, a few carriers have established such operations at smaller communities. Piedmont, for example, developed, as an alternative to Atlanta, service at Charlotte, North Carolina, as a connecting point in the southeast. In large part their success at Charlotte was responsible for the 125 percent increase in Piedmont traffic between 1978 and 1981. Piedmont also developed a hubs at Dayton, Ohio, and Baltimore, Maryland. As with Charlotte, it is continuing to focus on underserved communities.

Aside from increased reliance on hubs, carriers have also striven to improve the seasonality of their route systems. Under regulation carriers were often awarded route systems that had seasonality patterns substantially different from industry traffic. For example, United and TWA had largely east–west route systems; hence they had ample excess capacity in the winter. Both carriers entered markets to sunbelt points to improve

Table 4.2   The growth of hubbing (second quarter 1978 and 1983)

Airline	Leading Hub city in 1983	Percent of airline's domestic departures at hub		Percent change in departure's at hub
		1978 (2nd quarter)	1983 (2nd quarter)	
American	Dallas–Ft. Worth	11.2	28.6	113.7
U.S. Air	Pittsburgh	16.0	23.2	45.7
Continental[a]	Houston	12.8	22.9	45.8
Delta	Atlanta	18.3	21.4	11.4
Eastern	Atlanta	18.3	21.0	1.0
Frontier	Denver	18.0	33.8	23.8
Northwest[b]	Minneapolis–St. Paul	16.1	20.7	18.7
Ozark	St. Louis	15.5	35.6	53.7
Pan American[c]	New York	12.3	24.0	−1.8
Piedmont	Charlotte	3.7	19.6	583.0
Republic[d]	Minneapolis–St. Paul	3.4	7.7	91.1
Trans World	St. Louis	11.9	33.0	81.3
United	Chicago	13.8	18.9	1.5
Western	Salt Lake City	10.3	16.9	129.3

Source: Service Segment Data. Taken from CAB Report to Congress on Implementation of Deregulation Act.
a. Continental and Texas International departures were combined for 1978.
b. There was a strike at Northwest in the second quarter of 1978. Therefore in both years data for service during the first quarter are reported.
c. National and Pan American departures were combined for 1978.
d. North Central, Southern, and Hughes Airwest departures were combined for 1978.

equipment utilization. Similarly, Eastern, with many north–south routes, entered the summer peaking transcontinental routes. However, it encountered fierce rivalry in those routes and later largely withdrew. Eastern subsequently developed a hub at Kansas City to increase its participation in east–west traffic.

Changes in Industry Structure

Entry of New Competitors
One area that had been thought to be well understood before deregulation was the likely route expansion strategy that would be undertaken by new entrant carriers. The former intrastate carriers had become strong, not by scheduling connecting banks of aircraft but by scheduling point-to-point service with rapid turnarounds. A lack of feed had not prevented Pacific Southwest Airlines (PSA) from becoming a dominant carrier in the Los

Angeles to San Franciso route, or Southwest airlines from duplicating that record between Dallas and Houston. Both these carriers prospered by concentrating on serving a single market without trying simultaneously to serve a combination of other markets. Thus it was anticipated that new entrants would similarly achieve success by specializing in low-priced, high-frequency services in heavily traveled interstate markets. Although a number of new entrants have adopted strategies similar to Southwest's and PSA's, in fact these new carriers have employed a wider variety of operating plans. Deregulation has spawned a number of new airlines that are a small but rapidly growing segment of the industry. Some of these new entrants are newly formed airlines. Others are former supplemental airlines that have begun to offer scheduled service, former intrastate airlines that have expanded into interstate operations, or former commuter airlines that have begun jet operations.

These airlines operate in a variety of markets and offer a wide variety of services. At one extreme is Empire which operates jets in conjunction with its commuter fleet. Most of the rest have entered high-density routes serving major cities. The new entrants are for the most part relatively small, and they have less extensive connecting networks than do local service airlines. As did their intrastate predecessors, some tend to specialize in serving local point-to-point travelers, generally over short-haul routes at a major city.

These carriers generally have significantly lower labor costs than the established airlines. In many cases they price lower than the incumbents and consequently have grown rapidly. The formerly regulated airlines have responded to the competitive threat; therefore these new carriers have caused much greater changes in pricing and service than their small share of traffic would suggest. Chapter 5 examines their development and their impact on the industry.

Commuters
The commuter airlines have also grown rapidly since deregulation, continuing a period of rapid growth throughout the 1970s. Between 1978 and 1981 these carriers experienced a 43 percent increase in boardings and about a 75 percent increase in revenue passenger miles (see appendix F). They expanded service from a total of 381 points in May 1975 to 596 points in March 1981. The commuters have been replacing the formerly regulated carriers in their less profitable markets. These new markets are generally bigger and longer than the markets the commuters served before deregulation.

Several of these carriers, such as Air Wisconsin, Britt, Ransome, and

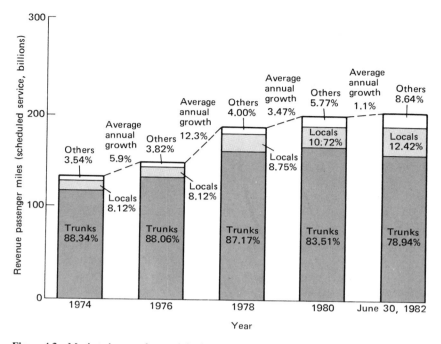

Figure 4.3 Market share and growth in domestic air transportation, 1974 to year ended June 30, 1982

Henson have established themselves as rather substantial regional carriers. Many of the commuters fly aircraft with 30 to 60 seats, much as the local service airlines did in the past.

Industry Market Shares

The change in the competitive balance that has resulted from route realignments and new entry is illustrated by the change in the shares of industry RPMs (see figure 4.3). The trunk airlines share of domestic RPMs has fallen from about 87 percent in 1978 to about 80 percent in 1981. The locals' share rose from about 9 percent to about 12 percent; in contrast to the trunks, each of the six local service carriers posted an increase in its share of industry traffic. The share of the new entrant airlines rose from 3.6 percent to 7.7 percent.[7] Since 1981 the new entrants have remained the most rapidly growing segment of the industry.

The influx of new competitors and the increased competition among the formerly regulated carriers have increased the number of airlines operating in many markets. Between the second quarters of 1978 and 1981 at least

Table 4.3 The average number of large aircraft operators providing nonstop service (May 1981 vs. May 1978)

Market distance (miles)	Market size (10–200)[a]		Market size (201–500)[a]		Market size (501+)[a]	
	1981	1978	1981	1978	1981	1978
0–500	1.27	1.31	2.17	2.02	3.90	3.45
501–1,500	1.30	1.11	1.89	1.66	2.84	2.23
1,501+	1.33	1.19	1.57	1.57	2.70	2.41

Source: *Official Airline Guide.*
a. O & D passengers per day.

one carrier entered in 122 of the 200 most heavily traveled markets; in a sample of smaller markets 24 percent experienced entry.

Table 4.3 shows that, on average, markets that were receiving nonstop service from jets had an increase in the number of carriers providing nonstop service since deregulation. (The table includes markets that had nonstop service in both May of 1978 and 1981.) However, in less dense short-haul markets the average number of carriers declined by 3 percent. In contrast, longer-haul, thin markets averaged more than a 10 percent increase in the number of carriers. Not surprisingly, the denser markets recorded that largest increases, with medium-haul dense markets showing a 27 percent gain in the number of carriers serving.

Table 4.3 clearly indicates that open entry has not lead to extreme proliferation of carriers on routes. There has been more competition in that the average number of carriers per route increased in the markets typically flown by trunks. But this increase was on the average less than half a carrier per route. Short-haul, less dense markets that were traditionally served by the locals have also experienced increased entry on their routes, but the average number of carriers per route continues to be lower than for the larger trunk routes. For example, approximately two carriers per route serve in the moderate-density, short-haul markets, whereas three to four carriers per route serve in the densest markets. Thus carriers serving the thinner markets continue to have less than half the number of competitors typical of the densest markets.

Changes in Service Patterns

The airlines' route restructuring has been accompanied by significant changes in the levels of service offered among communities and markets. The trends in departures by city size category are depicted in table 4.4[8] By June 1981 departures were about 19 percent greater overall than in 1976,

Table 4.4 Departures per week by hub type

	Large hubs		Medium hubs		Small hubs		Nonhubs		Total	
	Departures	Index	Departures	Index	Departures	Index	Departures	Index	Departures	Index
June 1, 1976	51,194	90	20,879	92	12,115	88	24,626	86	108,814	89
June 1, 1977	54,383	95	21,494	94	12,810	93	26,557	93	115,244	94
June 1, 1978	57,009	100	22,748	100	13,762	100	28,519	100	122,038	100
June 1, 1979	62,339	109	25,157	111	14,437	105	31,013	109	132,946	109
June 1, 1980	61,355	108	23,938	105	13,713	100	27,900	98	126,906	104
June 1, 1981	63,356	111	24,223	106	13,596	99	27,887	98	129,062	106
June 1, 1982	59,864	105	25,490	112	13,723	100	25,161	88	124,238	102

Source: *Official Airline Guide*, various issues.
Note: Index is a ratio, with June 1, 1978 = 100.

Table 4.5   Changes in weekly departures between major categories of airports

	Percent change (June 1978 to June 1981)
Between the 23 large hubs and	
Large hubs	9.3
Between the 36 medium hubs and	
Large hubs	10.5
Medium hubs	0.0
Between the 66 small hubs and	
Large hubs	18.3
Medium hubs	−7.1
Small hubs	−23.2
Between the 517 nonhubs and	
Large hubs	12.3
Medium hubs	10.5
Small hubs	−21.1
Nonhubs	−12.6

Source: *Official Airline Guide.* City categories are based on July 1982 hub classifications. Only nonstop flights between cities are counted. Nonhub departure statistics include eleven communities which lost service between June 1978 and the enactment of the deregulation act in October 1978.

with each city category gaining substantially. Since the major airlines have begun to concentrate their connecting networks at major airports, large and medium cities have gained in departures. Departures at large hubs increased by about 24 percent. The remaining categories experienced increases of between 12 and 16 percent.

Between 1978 and 1981 large and medium hubs registered an increase in the number of flights, while small hubs and nonhubs experienced slight declines. Although large hubs experienced the greatest increase, flights between large hubs and smaller communities increased more rapidly (see table 4.5). Since small communities have more flights to large hubs, they have better access to both major commercial centers and connecting flights. Thus the reduction in the total number of departures at any given community does not necessarily indicate a decline in service convenience. (In chapter 7 we examine the effect of these changes on service convenience.)

These changes in flights are consistent with the changes in airline route networks described earlier in this chapter. Since the major airlines have concentrated their connecting networks at several of the large-hub cities, flights between these airports and each of the other categories of cities have gone up. Both medium hubs and small hubs have declined in importance as connecting centers; so flights between medium hubs and between medium and small hubs have remained about the same or declined. In part, because of the restrictions placed on airports by the PATCO strike, the small and medium hubs have increased in importance since 1981.

In markets of all sizes the net changes mask substantial changes in the actual city pairs receiving service. For example, a growth in service between medium and large hubs from 377 to 415 markets encompasses 51 markets that lost service while 89 such markets gained service. The CAB's report to Congress (1984) finds that on average a trunk or local service carrier served only 40 percent of the city pairs it served in 1978. The report indicates that although the number of city pairs receiving nonstop air service increased by about 4 percent between 1978 and 1983, the gross changes that led to the added service to these 77 city pairs involved 865 separate movements, with 394 city pairs losing nonstop service while 471 city pairs gained such service.

These changes in route networks have also affected the patterns of connections made by passengers. We examined travel patterns in more than 5,000 markets in the second quarters of 1978 and 1981. Although the percentage of passenger trips requiring connections remained about the same, the proportion of connecting trips that were interline decreased by nearly 40 percent during that period.

In 1978, 72.7 percent of all trips had single-plane service; the fraction of trips with single-plane service rose only slightly to 73.3 percent in 1981.[9] (See table 4.6.) The patterns within market size/market distance categories changed little. Only about one in five passengers in markets with fifty or fewer passengers per day had single-plane service. In contrast, about two out of three have direct service in markets with 51 to 200 passengers per day. As market density increases, nonstop and single-plane service becomes more economical and the proportion of trips with direct service rises substantially. On the other hand, as the distance of the market increases, the fraction of the trips with direct service declines. For example, in 1981 markets with 201 to 500 passengers a day revealed the following pattern: 95 percent of passengers in the 201- to 500-mile block had direct service, while only about two-thirds of the passengers in the over 1,500-mile block had direct service.[10] The slight decline in single-plane service in long-haul routes may be partly due to passengers taking advantage of discount fares available on connecting flights in some of these markets.

As we have already noted, online connections reduce the time required between flights, along with the chance that a passenger will lose his baggage or miss a connecting flight. Table 4.7 shows that the percent of connections

Table 4.6 Fraction of trips with single-plane service (second quarter 1981 vs. second quarter 1978)

Market distance (miles)	Market size (O & D passengers per day)				All
	10–50	51–200	201–500	501 +	
1–200					
1978	91.9	98.4	98.3	98.9	97.8
1981	94.5	98.8	99.1	99.2	98.6
201–500					
1978	35.9	85.5	95.0	96.8	84.1
1981	36.5	85.0	95.2	97.1	85.8
501–1,500					
1978	14.6	61.1	83.8	91.4	67.0
1981	15.2	59.8	82.9	91.4	68.8
1500 +					
1978	6.2	46.2	67.5	84.9	57.6
1981	8.4	38.4	60.9	81.8	57.3
All					
1978	22.6	68.5	85.7	92.3	72.7
1981	22.7	64.9	83.1	91.8	73.3

Source: *O & D Survey*. Sample includes all O & D markets with more than ten passengers per day. Intrastate markets in Texas, California, and Florida are excluded because of the large amount of intrastate carrier service in those states prior to deregulation. Intrastate carriers did not file data to the Board in 1978.

Table 4.7 Percentage of trips with online service (second quarter 1981 vs. second quarter 1978)

Market distance (miles)	Market size (O & D passengers per day)				All
	10–50	51–200	201–500	501 +	
1–200					
1978	96.5	98.8	98.7	99.2	98.7
1981	97.3	99.0	99.3	99.3	99.0
201–500					
1978	71.0	94.0	97.6	97.9	92.6
1981	77.7	95.7	97.8	98.7	94.9
501–1,500					
1978	57.7	89.1	95.1	96.3	86.5
1981	76.6	93.7	96.7	96.7	92.4
1,500 +					
1978	60.3	84.2	87.1	94.8	84.3
1981	76.6	90.7	91.3	94.3	90.2
All					
1978	63.6	90.5	94.8	96.8	88.8
1981	77.8	94.0	96.2	97.0	93.1

Source: *O & D Survey*. Sample Includes all O & D markets with more than ten passengers per day. Intrastate markets in Texas, California, and Florida are excluded because of the large amount of intrastate carrier service in those states prior to deregulation. Intrastate carriers did not file data to the Board in 1978.

that are made online has increased substantially between 1978 and 1981. The rise in online connections was greatest in thin long-haul markets (those with less than 200 passengers per day but more than 500 miles). However, increases were experienced in nearly every category. The increases in the proportion of the service provided online continued since 1981. In 1978, 40 percent of those passengers that had to change airplanes made interline connections; by 1983, this had declined to less than 15 percent (see U.S. CAB 1984).

A Long-Run View of Airline Routes

The outcome of the service pattern transition in routes was somewhat different than that anticipated. Congress was concerned that free entry would permit the bigger airlines, with ample feeder and main route operations, to funnel intermediate traffic on competitive routes into their own aircraft and thus make it impossible for smaller, more specialized carriers to compete on those routes. Although it was recognized that such an operation would raise efficiency, it was feared that such integration would result in increased concentration in the industry. Yet these industry observers failed to recognize the advantages of the locals' fleet mix in providing service to both the feeder routes and the more heavily traveled ones. In retrospect it seems surprising that the importance of feed traffic and the ensuing success of some of the locals was not foreseen. It is significant, however, that by 1982 many of the trunks had enhanced their own hub-and-spoke operations to such an extent that the growth of the locals was slowing somewhat.

We have described carriers' strong incentives to establish hubs. It should be mentioned as well that there are several factors that limit the size of a carrier's operations at an airport. First, if there is adequate demand in a market, it is less costly to provide nonstop service rather than connecting service. In addition the size of a carrier's hubbing operation will be limited by the availability of more convenient flights over alternative connecting points: increasing the number of flights a carrier includes in a connecting bank generally reduces the convenience of making connections. A carrier operating a hub brings in flights from numerous destinations, allows time for connecting passengers and baggage to be exchanged, and then sends the flights off to their ultimate destinations. Obviously the greater the number of flights involved, the longer will be the average connecting time for passengers. Thus, as connecting banks are made larger alternative routings become more desirable to a subset of passengers. For example, a passenger traveling between a point in the midwest and the west will often be able to choose among connections at St. Louis, Denver, and Minneapolis, as well as other cities. If the transit time increases at one of these hubs, alternative routings become more desirable.

This suggests an equilibrium industry structure in which carriers establish hubs at most major cities and smaller hubs at a number of medium-sized communities. However, the number of airlines that hub at a particular city will be limited by several factors. First, the S-curve (as discussed in chapter 9 passenger demand increases disproportionately with flight shares) provides incentives for carriers to offer a large share of departures on any given route. In addition there are economies of ground station operations. A carrier that operates a hub needs to control a relatively large number of gates and to have the necessary support equipment to handle flights at these gates simultaneously. As we will discuss in chapter 10, airport capacity constraints may limit the number of carriers that can establish hubs at most major cities.

A substantial fraction of flights are provided to major cities where carriers have the greatest incentives to establish hub operations. Since the number of carriers that establish hubbing operations at any particular airport will be limited, the number of carriers serving a given route will also be limited. Thus most airline markets will tend to be concentrated, even markets large enough to support a large number of frequent flights by efficient-sized aircraft.

Although entry is relatively easy, carriers will operate integrated route networks, and thus the viability of service in any single city pair will be related to the other routes the carrier serves. For example, a carrier that has established a hub at an airport may introduce service from the airport to a particular point. Alternatively, entry may come from a carrier that provides tag-end service to a community. For example, a carrier who does not hub at Atlanta may extend a St. Louis–Atlanta flight to Savannah, Georgia.

Entry can also occur by carriers who serve neither end point. However, such entry will generally be part of a decision to enter simultaneously a number of interrelated markets. Moreover the new entrant will probably not concentrate operations at an established hub unless the carrier plans to differentiate its service substantially from that of the incumbent carriers.

Passengers travel for a number of different reasons and have different preferences. Some place a high value on convenience, whereas others are primarily concerned with air fares and still others with onboard amenities. However, regulation encouraged carriers to offer a relatively homogeneous type of service. Since more than one airline will offer air service in many markets, there is some room for carriers to differentiate their product to appeal to diverse interests. A number of new entrants have established significantly different service than that provided by the incumbents. This trend may continue. Thus some carriers will offer higher levels of service at higher prices than others. The ability of airlines to differentiate their product is limited to some extent by economies of aircraft size, which provide incentives for carriers to offer multiclass service. These incentives are strongest in long-haul markets where the economies of scale tend to be greatest.

Conclusion

The air service network has changed rapidly as the established airlines have realigned their routes and new airlines have entered interstate markets. Departure statistics indicate carriers are focusing on hub-and-spoke operations and concentrating their operations at large hubs. Although the proportion of trips involving connections has changed only slightly, a much greater share of connections is now made online. In nonhub markets there is a tendency for more direct service to major airports. We believe many of these new patterns are permanent features of the route system rather than merely transitory. Sunbursts of routes rather than linear systems will characterize the typical airline route map of the future, and travelers using connecting services will be able to chose among a variety of routings.

Chapter 5

Emerging Competition from Low Cost Airlines

The airlines that have begun providing interstate air service since deregulation are already becoming a major competitive force. Their origins and operating strategies are diverse, but for the most part they all have lower operating costs. Their lower costs are partly explained by the simplicity of their operations, partly by their lower input costs, especially wages, and partly by their no-frills service policies. In most cases they set fares lower than the prevailing fares prior to their entry, and as a consequence their share of industry traffic has grown to more than 8.0 percent. Because of their rapid growth their influence on industry behavior goes well beyond what their market share would suggest.

In this chapter we consider the source and the extent of the new entrants' cost advantages, as well as their performance in the deregulated marketplace. We then give an overview of the cost differences among airlines. Though operational differences account for some of the variation, lower labor costs are also an important source of the advantage. We therefore consider labor relations under regulation and conclude that regulatory policies probably contributed to the industry's relatively high labor costs.

Cost Comparisons

System Costs
In order to place the new entrants' costs in perspective, we compare the operating costs per available seat mile (ASM) of jet carriers that operated for most of the full year ending June 30, 1982.[1] Since the cost per ASM declines with stage length, we control for differences in stage length among the carriers. The costs reported in figure 5.1 include international operations. Since most of the airlines also carry cargo (a few in fact operate freighters) and operate charters, we estimated the cost per ASM of scheduled service by subtracting cargo and nonscheduled revenues from total expenses and then dividing by ASMs. Essentially we assume that cargo and nonscheduled operations broke even. It should be noted that operating expenses do not include returns on capital, that is, profits and interest on long-term debt.

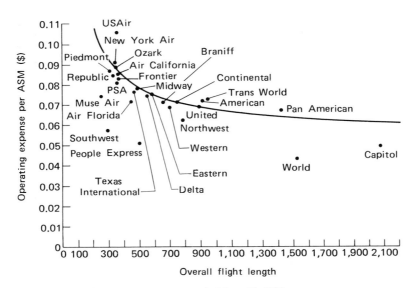

Figure 5.1 Airline system costs, year ended June 30, 1982

Obviously stage length is not the only factor that produces differences in costs per ASM among efficient carriers. For example, carriers that serve low-density routes may use smaller aircraft and therefore have higher costs per ASM than other carriers. Also ground costs will vary among carriers depending on the region they serve and their average enplanements per airport. Figure 5.1 shows the estimated relationship between the cost and the stage length for the formerly regulated carriers. The depicted relationship is: cost/ASM $= 5.74 + (1023.4) \times (1/\text{stage length})$.

After controlling for differences in stage lengths, seven of the ten new entrants have a cost advantage over the incumbents. Muse, Southwest, People Express, Capitol, and World have average costs per ASM that are far below the fitted cost curves of the incumbents. Pacific Southwest Airlines (PSA) and Air Florida have small cost advantages, while Midway and Air California do not appear to have any. New York Air's costs are actually higher than those of the incumbents.

Figure 5.1 only approximates the true cost differences among carriers. For example, to the extent that the new entrants provide less service than the formerly regulated carriers, the figure overstates their cost advantage. Also some of the new entrants' work forces have much less seniority. Part of their cost advantage therefore will automatically narrow as their work force ages. Of course carriers like PSA and Air California have existed for many years and have senior work forces.

On the other hand, there are a number of factors that inflate some of the new entrants' costs. New York Air, for example, concentrates its operations at congested airports. The costs of operating at these airports are high, and the congestion requires relatively circuitous flight paths. If incumbents operated a similar proportion of their flights from La Guardia in New York City, their costs would undoubtedly be higher. In addition the new entrants tend to run less capital-intensive operations than the established airlines; thus operating costs are a greater share of their total costs. For example, over half of Midway Airlines' ASMs were provided on DC-9-10s, which are more expensive to operate than newer models. The capital savings of using the less efficient aircraft are not fully reflected in operating costs, because though depreciation is included in operating costs, returns to capital are not. Similarly, because the new entrants typically lease rather than buy ground facilities, and contract out their maintenance rather than establish maintenance facilities, their cost structure tends to include higher operating costs and lower capital costs. To gauge the source and the extent of their cost advantage better, we compare the estimated costs of Southwest, a well-established intrastate carrier, with those of two formerly regulated carriers.

Cost differences in Serving a Particular Route

As we mentioned in chapter 2, Southwest has been one of the nation's most rapidly growing and profitable airlines. It specializes in serving short-haul point-to-point markets with B-737-200s, offering few on-board amenities. It does not interline with other carriers. Southwest employs high-density seating and offers a system of peak and off-peak fares that has enabled it to operate at relatively high load factors. In addition Southwest has achieved very high productivity for both its work force and its aircraft. For example, Southwest uses its B-737-200s significantly more hours per day than other airlines.

In order to sort out Southwest's apparently significant cost advantage, we compare estimates of the costs of serving a 200-mile route segment with its B-737 operations against the costs of Piedmont (a local service carrier) and United (a trunk). We assume that the cost of each carriers' aircraft is the same. We use the *Avmark* estimated value of an aircraft at mid-life, which was $6.25 million as of January 1, 1981. The aircraft is assumed to have a useful life of sixteen years and residual value of 2 percent. A carriers' costs of capital are assumed equal to a weighted average of the rate of return for all manufacturing and the trunks' average interest costs on long-

Table 5.1   Comparison of airline costs for serving 200-mile markets

Cost category	Southwest	Piedmont Actual	Piedmont Adjusted	United Actual	United Adjusted
Flight crew	$130	251	251	460	307
Aircraft, fuel, loading fees, and aircraft servicing	$1,215	1,469	1,374	1,683	1,359
Cabin crew	$70	86	72	149	124
Passenger-specific costs	$349	927	1,122	989	1,171
Overhead (excluding aircraft)	$136	134	144	332	338
Fully allocated costs	$1,900	2,867	2,963	3,613	3,298
Seats per aircraft	118	110	118	103	118
Load factor	0.67	0.56	0.67	0.60	0.67
Fully allocated costs per passenger	$24	47	37	58	42

Source: *DPFI* Costing Methodology, Version Six. Data are for twelve months ending June 30, 1981.
Note: Adjusted costs assume crew complements, landing fees, load factors, and seats are the same for United and Piedmont as are observed for Southwest.

term debt. United's fleet of B-737s is relatively old, and its reported maintenance costs are quite high. We therefore assume that United's maintenance expenses on its B-737-200s are equal to its maintenance expenses on the larger B-727-200. (It is noteworthy that United's average block hour maintenance expense for the larger aircraft is lower than the average of the local service carriers' B-737-200 maintenance expense.)

As table 5.1 indicates, United's average costs per passenger are more than double Southwest's; they are higher in every one of the five cost categories included in the comparison. Piedmont's costs per passenger are nearly twice Southwest's. The bulk of Southwest's cost advantage is in passenger-specific costs, which include reservation and sales as well as baggage handling and preflight and inflight services. Part of the cost difference is related to Southwest's simplified reservation and ticketing system and its decision not to interline. It limits the number of fares in its system, so it can use preprinted tickets; it also uses cash register receipts as boarding passes. In addition Southwest provides no food service. (However, the incumbent carriers' food cost on a 200-mile segment is only about a dollar per passenger.)

Undoubtedly part of the cost difference relates to the higher productivity of Southwest's employees. Differences in labor compensation can be seen most clearly by comparing cost differences for the flight crew (pilots) and the cabin crew (flight attendants). In the case of the flight crew, Southwest's pilots fly more hours per month than either Piedmont's or United's. In 1981, for example, while Southwest's pilots flew 73 hours per month, United's flew 43 hours, and Piedmont's flew 49 hours. (See table 8.5.) In addition United's labor agreement (which was revised in late 1981) required that it operate its B-737s with a three-man crew, while most other carriers, including Piedmont and Southwest, used two-man crews.[2] Relative to the cost differences for flight crews, the cost differences between the carriers' cabin crew expenses is not as great; still United's costs are considerably higher than those of Southwest. A major source of the difference is the greater productivity of Southwest's attendants; they fly more hours per month, and fewer flight attendants are employed per flight.

The differences between the carriers' flight-specific costs are not as great and are chiefly due to differences in aircraft utilization and aircraft servicing expenses. Southwest operated its aircraft on an average 9.5 hours per day, while Piedmont and United operated their aircraft on an average of 7.3 and 5.2 hours, respectively. In part, Southwest's higher utilization stems from its concentration on point-to-point service.[3] United's higher overhead expenses stem, at least in part, from the concentration of its operations in higher cost areas.

Table 5.1 also contains cost figures which control for some of the operating differences between Southwest and the formerly regulated carriers. Specifically we assume that Piedmont and United use the same crew complements (both flight and cabin) as Southwest. In addition we assume that they use the same seating configuration and that they achieve the same aircraft utilization rates and load factors. Finally, we assume Piedmont and United offer no food service and that they pay the same landing fees. No other adjustments were made. Thus even the adjusted cost figures assume that Piedmont and United continue to use their more complex and more costly reservation system. These adjustments reduce the average passenger costs of United and Piedmont by 21 percent and 28 percent, respectively. Nevertheless, the average cost of each carrier is still over 50 percent higher than Southwest's.

Regulation and Labor Costs

Regulation's lack of price competition encouraged service competition and reduced carriers' incentives to control costs. In the 1960s when fares did not fall as rapidly as costs, labor costs rose at the same time service competition was increasing. In this section we explore why labor had a strong bargaining position. We then briefly discuss the history of labor negotiations with pilots and the relationship between changes in industry productivity and wage rates.

Regulatory Misincentives
In competitive industries a firm that is able to reduce its costs can increase its profits on current production while using its cost advantage to expand relative to other firms. (Similarly inefficient firms would shrink and eventually be driven out of business.) CAB regulation inhibited such expansion because carriers were not free to enter new markets or to reduce their prices to draw business away from their competitors. This limited the incentives for carriers to reduce costs.

For a variety of reasons regulation also insulated carriers from the risks caused by high costs. Since efficient carriers could not expand or cut fares, inefficient carriers were often protected. In many cases the Board explicitly awarded new routes to unprofitable (i.e., inefficient) airlines attempting to strengthen their finances. In addition industry fares were based on average costs, so a portion of any individual airlines' costs would be "passed through" into fares. (This was most significant for larger carriers.) Furthermore CAB restrictions on entry ensured existing carriers of protection from the entry of more efficient new airlines. Finally, the Board's protective policies essentially eliminated the risk of financial ruin for inefficient airlines. CAB route rights were highly valuable, making a troubled airline an attractive merger prospect for a healthy airline. In sum, CAB regulation substantially reduced the long-run payoff from achievement of a lean, efficient airline.

Workers' negotiating leverage was also augmented by several other characteristics of the airline industry. First, as a service industry, airlines cannot store output, so sales lost during a strike are lost forever.[4] Since regularity of service is an important competitive element, the effects of a strike may persist even after the settlement. (Following deregulation some carriers have used promotional discounts to regain traffic following strikes. This alternative was not open to the airlines under regulation.) Finally, many of the employee groups are highly skilled and highly specialized, thus limiting the availability of substitutes. This was especially important during periods of rapid growth that followed the introduction of new aircraft and no doubt helped the unions in their dealings with the airlines. Regulation also created a small number of stable, easily identifiable firms to organize.

Labor Relations: The Pilots

The economic characteristics of the airline industry, the regulation of the industry, and the institutional arrangements between management and labor apparently placed the airline unions in a strong bargaining position with the airlines. More information is available on pilots' negotiating history than the history of any of the other employee groups. In this section we describe how regulation and the economics of the industry affected pilots' labor relations.[5]

The airlines have experienced several phases of technological advances in the past three decades as larger and faster aircraft have been brought into use. Those advances have been labor saving: passenger miles of service per employee hour are greater with new aircraft. Pilots have succeeded in capturing a considerable share of the cost savings created by these technological advances, and as a result pilot costs have not fallen as much as technological change would have allowed. These gains were achieved not only through higher pay but also through changes in work rules that increased the required number of employees.

The basic form of today's pilot compensation formula goes back to the very beginnings of the industry. In the early years of the industry the Post Office Department's mail service program established the original structure of the pilot pay formula. Pilot salaries were calculated from a base pay rate, which increased with experience as measured by accumulated flight hours and a mileage rate. Pay differentials existed for night flights and flights over dangerous terrain. When commercial carrier contracting replaced the Post Office's service in 1927, the same formula and rates were adopted.

On October 1, 1933, the five largest carriers proposed to change the pay formula structure to a simple hourly rate.[6] However, the newly formed union of airline pilots, the Airline Pilots Association (ALPA), opposed that proposal. ALPA insisted that the mileage component be retained and requested a maximum limitation on the monthly flight hours or mileage flown by pilots. Responding to that conflict, a National Labor Relations Board investigation released a recommended pilot pay formula in May 1934, as National Labor Board Decision #83. Decision #83, which was to apply only for one year, included three components in the basic pay formula: base pay, hourly pay, and mileage pay. Also the Decision recommended an 85-hour limitation on actual monthly flight hours.[7] (FAA safety guidelines limit pilots to 100 flight hours per month.)

The first changes in the Decision #83 rates were made in 1941, when the Boeing 307 Stratoliner was introduced. Faster and larger than other commercial aircraft of that time, the Stratoliner increased productivity substantially. As a result a new debate arose between pilots and management over the basic question of how the benefits of new technologies should be split between labor and management. This initial conflict was settled by an arbitration board award in 1941 that increased the hourly rates of pilots flying the Stratoliner. This established a precedent: as faster aircraft have been introduced, pilots' hourly pay rates have been increased.[8] In succeeding negotiations the industry and the unions developed an elaborate mechanism for determining pilots compensation. For example:

1. When calculating pilot pay, aircraft speeds are determined by negotiated "pegged speeds." Pegged speeds often differ substantially from actual speeds. A concern over rising inequities in flight crew salaries, when jets were being introduced, prompted this change. (Using the prevailing pay formula with its actual speed rate factor, pilots who flew jet aircraft would receive large salary increases. On the other hand, pilots of piston aircraft would not receive any of the benefits coming with new jet technology.) Therefore negotiated pegged speeds were set lower than actual speeds for jet aircraft and higher than actual for piston planes.

2. Instead of using actual map distances, flight mileage is calculated by multiplying flight times by pegged aircraft speeds. Originally adopted to compensate pilots for delay times, such as time spent circling congested airports, hourly mileage rates also provide automatic pay increases when aircraft speeds increase.

3. As heavier aircraft are introduced, pilot pay increases automatically. Since newer planes are generally larger and heavier this also generates pilot pay increases as new aircraft are introduced. After lengthy negotiating disputes this rate component was added to the basic pilot formula in the late 1940s.

With these aspects of the pilot compensation formula automatically increasing pilot pay when more productive aircraft were introduced, the cost savings from the improved technologies were obviously limited.

In addition the pilots were able to negotiate changes in work rules so that they spent fewer hours flying aircraft. Pilot layoffs in the mid-1940s, following the introduction of four-engine propeller aircraft, spurred a fear of "technological unemployment." Airline employees perceived that larger and faster aircraft would reduce labor requirements. With more productive aircraft fewer flights are needed to serve a given number of passengers. Thus, if employment levels are related closely to the number of aircraft flights, the level of employment would be expected to fall when larger and faster aircraft are introduced. If, however, the new aircraft lead to substantial increases in demand for air service, demand for airline employees will not necessarily decline. As a result during negotiations throughout the

1950s ALPA acted to maintain employment levels and counter the technological unemployment anticipated when carriers began jet services. By the end of the decade all major pilot contracts included full sets of duty time and trip time ratios. These provided a guarantee of flight time for duty time and time away from base.[9] Time guarantees and other working condition provisions were also included in the contracts. As the jets were introduced, ALPA also succeeded in lowering the monthly limit on pay and credit flight hours, further reducing the number of hours per month pilots actually flew aircraft.

These new provisions reduced pilots' average monthly flight hours dramatically. By 1961 actual flying hours had fallen by at least eight hours from the levels prevailing during the 1950s. In 1960–61 pilots were flying an average of 60 to 65 hours per month.[10] Since that time pilots' work rules at the major carriers have become progressively more restrictive. Specific ratios guarantee more flight pay and credit hours while on duty; in addition minimum pay and credit requirements have increased. Most important, the limit on monthly pay and credit hours was reduced from 85 to 75 hours at most carriers, though most contracts allow temporary increases above that level. By 1975 average pilot utilization (actual flying hours) had dropped to only 50 hours per month.[11] Pilots' average flight hours at major carriers subsequently have fallen below 50 hours per month.

It appears that other airline employee groups have also been successful in increasing pay and employment. Flight attendants work about the same number of flight hours per month as pilots.[12] Although weekly hours of mechanics and other ground personnel are apparently comparable with other industries, these employee groups have adopted restrictive and specialized job descriptions which tend to increase employment. In addition, despite the strong daily and weekly peaks in air travel demand, many airline contracts restrict the use of part-time employees.

Labor Productivity and Unit Labor cost
To the extent that restrictive work rules have been adopted, airline productivity growth has been held below the levels that could have been achieved. The result has been to increase the employment necessary to provide any given level of airline service. (Whether a change in work rules affects total industry employment depends on how the work rules change total industry output as well as the number of employees required per unit of output.) Thus worker productivity in the airlines has not improved by as much as the technological change would have allowed. Nevertheless, technological change has lead to enormous increases in worker productivity, when

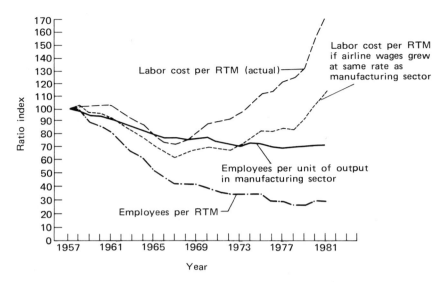

Figure 5.2   Trends in trunk airline employee productivity and pay

output is measured by revenue ton miles. The trends in worker productivity and pay for the trunk and local airlines are charted in figures 5.2 and 5.3.[13] The trunk airline productivity curve falls rapidly between 1958 and 1967, reflecting the introduction of jet aircraft over that period. It leveled off in the early 1970s but began to improve later in the decade with the integration of wide-bodied aircraft into their systems and improving load factors.[14] (In absolute terms productivity per employee is higher for the trunks than for the locals, reflecting the differences in the route networks they serve.) The local service airlines' labor productivity growth follows a somewhat different pattern. Productivity did not begin to increase sharply for these airlines until 1960–61. Productivity continued to improve throughout the 1970s, although at a slower pace than during the 1960s. Their relatively better performance during the 1970s reflects the Board's decision to allow the local service carriers to expand into longer and denser routes, as well as their conversion to jet aircraft.

As figures 5.2 and 5.3 indicate, employees per unit of output for U.S. industry declined from its base of 100 in 1957 to about seventy in 1981. Clearly productivity growth in the airlines greatly exceeded productivity in the economy as a whole. Not surprisingly, the difference in the rate of productivity growth is greatest in the 1960s when the conversion to jet aircraft occurred. Productivity growth in both the trunk and local airlines

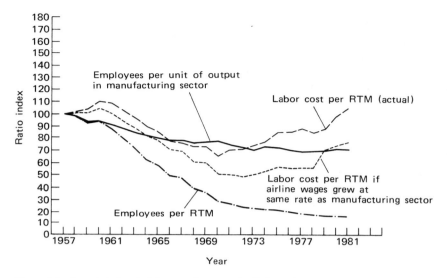

Figure 5.3   Trends in local airline employee productivity and pay

has continued to exceed the growth in the overall industry productivity by a substantial margin since 1970.

The figures also present an index of airline labor costs per RTM and an index showing how airline labor costs would have changed had airline workers received the same percentage pay increases as workers in the nonfarm manufacturing sector. Comparison of these two pay curves shows that trunk airline wages have risen much more rapidly than manufacturing wages since 1967. In competitive labor markets wages should tend to equilibrate among industries if workers with similar skills can migrate readily. While the airline industry requires highly skilled workers, it is questionable whether the differences in skills fully account for the apparent wage differential that has developed. Indeed, as we shall see later in this chapter, it appears that airline workers are paid more than workers doing similar work in other industries. If airline wages had just remained competitive with the manufacturing sector of the economy, pay per unit of output for the trunk airlines would be about 30 percent lower today.

The pay pattern is similar for the local service airlines. The gap between the growth in their pay and pay in the manufacturing sector is slightly less than that of the trunks: the local employees' pay would be about 28 percent lower per RPM if their pay increases just kept pace with the rise in manufacturing wages. However, these airlines have experienced faster productivity growth than the trunks. As a result their labor costs per RTM have risen only about 6 percent since 1957, whereas the trunk airlines' labor costs per RTM have risen more than 70 percent.

We have compared the wages paid by the major airlines with wages for similar jobs in other industries. Wages in the airline industry appear to be substantially higher, even for jobs where no industry-specific skills are required. For example, in 1980 keypunch operators who worked for the airlines earned 31 percent more than the average wage for all keypunch operators.[14] Typists at airlines were paid 41 percent more; for computer operators the differential was 38 percent. Job categories where skills may differ somewhat from those in other industries show similar earnings differentials. Air freight agents earn about 58 percent more than shippers, and aircraft cleaners (interior) earn about 82 percent more than the average for janitors.

It is difficult to assess differentials for jobs such as aircraft mechanics and inspectors, flight attendants, and pilots because many of the skills are specific to the airline industry. Nevertheless, aircraft mechanics earn about 28 percent more than the average for motor vehicle mechanics, while aircraft inspectors earn about 48 percent more than the average for blue-collar supervisors.[15] Flight attendants earn about the same salary as school teachers[16] or nurses.[17] Pilots for the major airlines earn substantially more than either military pilots or corporate pilots.[18]

In sum, although the airlines have experienced enormous productivity growth relative to other industries, they have also had very large relative increases in wage rates. This rise in relative wage rates is not fully explained by differences in skills in the airlines relative to other industries but at least in part seems to reflect the airline workers' success in capturing a share of the industry's productivity gains.

The New Jet Airlines

The new entrants have evolved from diverse origins, and their route networks, service policies, and prices differ accordingly. Several carrier were certificated in 1979, but only Midway Airlines actually inaugurated service that year. Former charter carriers, such as World and Capitol, were certificated early in 1979 as part of the *Transcontinental Low-Fare Route Proceeding* (Order 79-1-75). The former intrastate airlines were all certificated for interstate service by mid-1979, and they have mainly expanded into states neighboring their original home state. PSA and Air California have expanded up the West Coast, inland to Nevada and Arizona as well as into Mexico. Similarly Southwest has expanded beyond its Texas markets to serve states in the south and southwest. Air Florida expanded more aggressively than the other former intrastate airlines, but in 1982 it retrenched its domestic operations. Nevertheless, it continued to serve many domestic and international markets before declaring bankruptcy in the summer of 1984.

A number of newly formed airlines got certificates in 1980 and 1981, and by September 1981, ten such airlines had begun service. People Express established a hub at a secondary airport, Newark. New York Air concentrated its operations at two airports in the New York area. Muse Air initially concentrated services in the Houston–Dallas market in competition with Southwest and has begun to expand into other markets in the southwest. The remaining new entrants are Jet America, which served Chicago and Dallas from Long Beach, California; Pacific Express, which served several markets along the West Coast; Northeastern, which served vacation markets from Long Island, New York; Best, which is based in Buffalo, New York, and served several cities in the East; Emerald, which served several cities in Texas; Hawaii Express and Pacific East, which served mainland to Hawaii markets. Pacific Express and Hawaii Express subsequently ceased operations. Since 1981 five additional carriers began service, and a number of others have announced their intention to enter the industry.

These airlines typically serve short-haul markets, or markets dominated by discretionary travelers. The competitive advantage of the new entrants is greatest in short-haul markets because a smaller share of costs in these markets is associated with fuel and the cost of aircraft, the areas in which the new entrants do not have an advantage. In discretionary markets the new entrants' lower costs and lower fares are more apt to stimulate demand. Since passengers are not time sensitive in these markets, a carrier does not have to offer a full range of flights in order to establish market identity.[19] It is also possible to offer flights at less popular times and still serve the markets profitably.

Moreover these newly certificated airlines have generally entered relatively dense markets already served by several formerly regulated airlines. However, they generally offer different types of service at less than pre-entry fares. For example, in 1982 over half of the new entrants had based their operations at an airport other than the predominant one in a major city they serve. Several of them offered different on-board amenities than the regulated carriers.

The equipment these airlines employ also varies. Although some of the carriers operate new aircraft, most operate used equipment. Two-engine

Table 5.2   Service offered by new entrant airlines

Airline	Snacks and drinks	Food	Inter-line tickets and baggage	Ticket offices	Auto-matic ticketing	On-board ticketing	Ticket by mail
Air California	Yes[a]	No	Yes	No	Yes	No	Yes
Air Florida	Yes	Yes	Yes	Yes	No	No	Yes
Capitol	Yes	Yes	Yes	Yes	No	No	Yes
Jet America	Yes	Yes	Yes	No	No	No	Yes
Midway	Yes	No	Yes	No	No	No	Yes
New York Air	Yes	No	No	No	Yes	Yes	Yes
Pacific Express	Yes	No	Yes	No	No	No	Yes
PSA	Yes[a]	No	Yes	Yes	Yes	Yes	No
People Express	Yes[b]	No	No	No	No	No	No
Southwest	Yes[a]	No	No	No	Yes	No	No
World	Yes	Yes	Yes	Yes	No	No	Yes

Source: Telephone survey of airline marketing personnel. This survey was conducted in spring 1982.
a. Service on some flights.
b. No free services.

narrow-bodied jet equipment is the most prevalent, though several of the long-haul carriers like Capitol, World and Hawaii Express use wide-bodied equipment. Northeastern uses some of the old DC-8-50's that the larger carriers have been retiring because they are too fuel inefficient.

World, Capitol, Air Florida, and Jet America provide amenities similar to those of the formerly regulated carriers, but, as table 5.2 indicates, many of the others do not. Three of these airlines provide no interline service, and most do not provide meal service. All of the airlines provide snacks, beverages, and baggage handling. However, People Express charges for these services.

Ticketing services also vary widely among these airlines, although they all offered telephone reservations and sold tickets through travel agencies. Only four of the eleven operated ticket offices; four offered automatic ticketing; and New York Air and PSA offered on-board ticketing. All but three will mail prepurchased tickets. People Express, which handles ticketing and seat selection at its gates, is the only airline without airport ticket counters.

The new entrant airlines have followed very different strategies with respect to fares and the number of flights they offer. Table 5.3 provides an overview, as of spring 1982, of the strategies of several of the new entrants.

Table 5.3   New entrant marketing strategies

Airline	Number of markets in survey	Range of new entrants' fares as a percent of *DPFI* formula		Range of new Entrants' share of markets		Range of total passenger growth in markets, (1981 vs. 1978, second quarter)	
		Min	Max	Min	Max	Min	Max
Air California	8	0.63	0.86	10	100	−31	250
Air Florida	10	0.51	0.83	7	33	−17	132
Capital	1	0.43		10		45	
Midway	8	0.78	0.88	10	22	−12	1
PSA	7	0.61	0.82	16	42	−15	63
Southwest	8	0.43	0.60	22	100	57	120
World	3	0.44	0.46	5	7	−20	45

Source: Traffic and fare data are from CAB *O & D Survey*. Departure data are from the *Official Airline Guide*.

At one extreme Southwest has generally entered markets with very low fares and a large amount of capacity relative to the size of the market. For example, in May 1981 Southwest's shares of flights in its interstate markets ranged between 20 percent and 100 percent of the total, while its fares ranged from 43 to 60 of the *DPFI* fares. As a result of Southwest's aggressive fare and service offerings, most of the markets it has entered have grown enormously. Between the second quarter of 1978 and the second quarter of 1981, traffic grew between 57 percent and 120 percent in Southwest's interstate markets.

Midway typifies the other extreme. Midway's share of departures (including O'Hare and Midway together) ranged from about 10 to just over 20 percent in the eight markets it served in May of 1981, while its fares ranged from 78 to 88 percent of the *DPFI* fare. Because of this philosophy Midway apparently has not had a very large impact on traffic. Indeed, between the second quarter of 1978 and the second quarter of 1981, traffic increased in only two of the eight markets entered by Midway, and in the remaining six markets traffic fell by 1 to 12 percent. During this period Midway established its market niche by slightly undercutting its competitors and settling for relatively small shares of its markets.

This strategy of a new entrant offering only a small share of capacity, so that the incumbent carrier would not find it profitable to match their lower fares, was also followed by Air Florida and Capitol, which were more successful initially than Midway in attracting passengers by offering proportionally lower prices.[20] The initial success of these carriers apparently demonstrated that passengers were quite sensitive to price differentials of sufficient magnitude. Consequently the incumbent carriers became more aggressive in meeting the new entrants' fares. Sometimes there was direct matching as in the Buffalo–Newark market. In other instances, matching has been much more tailored, such as to the specific time slots of new entrants flights.

People Express, like Midway, started after ADA. But it has used a scheduling strategy similar to that of Southwest. Using Newark Airport as its hub, it started operations in April 1981 and within a year and a half had grown to over $210 million in assets, over a thousand employees, and a fleet of seventeen B-737 aircraft serving twelve cities. It has continued to grow at a rapid pace; by the end of 1983 it had a fleet of thirty-nine aircraft and was offering low-fare service between Newark and London, England. People Express strives to have the lowest costs of any airline in the country. It initially purchased a matched fleet of aircraft and pioneered a unique integration of employees, each of whom has responsibility in several job areas. Moreover each employee is required to have an equity position in the company; People Express will even provide loans to new employees to purchase the equity position.

The Buffalo–Newark market offers a typical illustration of the problems encountered by a new airline offering slimmed down service (see table 5.4). When People Express entered this market in August 1981, USAir had been running load factors of 87 to 90 percent. USAir responded to People's entry not only by lowering its $97 fare to match the $35 level, but also by expanding its capacity from 325 flights per month to 412 flights per month between July and September. Analysis of the load factors of the two carriers shows that in every month between August 1981 and June 1982, People Express load factors averaged more than 20 points lower than those of USAir. Still, by June 1982 the total number of departures was 745 (compared to 258 a year earlier), and the load factor for USAir was 84.6 compared to 69.2 for People Express. The data thus suggest that many consumers chose to travel on the carrier with the greater name-recognition and amenities when the fare is the same. People Express' experience in the Buffalo–Newark market shows also that, even if passengers have incentives to prefer the incumbent, a low enough price can stimulate enough traffic so that simple price matching will not be a successful deterrent to entry. In fact USAir greatly expanded its capacity in the market, yet People Express was able to achieve satisfactory load factors.

As a response to the matching activities of the incumbent carriers, the new entrants have responded by adopting a strategy of picking some

Table 5.4 Buffalo–Newark market

	May 1981	June 1981	July 1981	August 1981	September 1981	October 1981	November 1981	December 1981	January 1982	February 1982	March 1982	April 1982	May 1982	June 1982
Load factor														
Industry	89.78	87.63	90.36	80.55	70.12	37.24	53.02	52.84	45.26	38.42	53.11	85.29	90.42	77.86
USAir	89.78	87.63	90.36	87.18	77.42	76.98	69.08	69.74	57.49	48.62	62.86	93.07	93.64	84.63
People				74.40	62.26	21.88	39.16	39.02	34.25	27.08	41.48	76.54	86.28	69.23
Passengers														
Industry	20,941	20,269	25,699	61,168	57,224	57,664	47,801	46,595	31,420	27,765	42,903	59,894	68,324	64,381
USAir	20,941	20,269	25,699	31,847	32,759	33,230	28,857	27,669	18,851	18,497	27,633	34,604	39,817	39,221
People				29,321	24,465	24,434	18,944	18,926	12,569	9,268	15,270	25,290	28,507	25,160
Departures														
Industry	253	258	325	697	745	818	822	817	645	663	735	621	686	745
USAir	253	258	325	363	412	422	412	406	335	373	423	341	406	437
People				334	333	396	410	411	311	290	312	280	280	308

markets for service that are substitutes for but not identical to the markets served by incumbents. Thus People Express chose to enter the Melbourne, Florida, market not the Orlando market. It also chose to enter Burlington, Vermont, thereby attracting passengers to cross over the border to take advantage of the lower U.S. fare rather than to initiate travel in Canada.

As a group the new entrants have had substantial impact on the airline industry. As we discuss in chapter 9, average fares are substantially lower in markets they serve. At the same time the low costs and consumer acceptance of new entrant services have encouraged the formerly regulated carriers to become more efficient. The carriers they compete with respond competitively to their fares and thus have incentives to develop cost structures that are closer to those of the new entrants. Thus the increased competition is giving all carriers an incentive to use their work forces more productively. Methods to increase the productivity of work forces are beginning to include new concepts of risk sharing between labor and management, as well as efforts to arrive at more productive work rule and salary packages. This emphasis on minimizing costs will continue even though the new entrants will undoubtedly give up some of their cost advantages as their work forces mature, their equipment becomes more varied, and their growth rates slow.

Although all of the new entrant airlines have enjoyed substantial growth, not all of them have been profitable (table 5.5). In 1983 six of the ten new entrants that we have considered were profitable. Two of the four former interstates lost money in 1981 and 1983. Air Florida appears to have been hurt by expanded service of other carriers into Florida markets. PSA has attempted to revitalize its operations by switching to a flat rate system of low fares, which greatly increased traffic in the second half of 1982. Southwest, however, remains one of the most profitable airlines in the industry.

The former charters, World and Capitol, seem to have suffered from fare wars due to the glut of long-haul wide-boded aircraft, and neither made money in 1981 or 1982; Capitol had a small profit in 1983.

Of the newly formed airlines, People Express seems to be doing particularly well. For much of 1982 Muse was troubled by its inability to obtain the airport access rights necessary for expansion. New York Air made several changes in its route and service policies in 1982. It now appears to be positioning itself as a high-service airline, one that offers more comfortable seating and amenities than its competitors on the routes it serves. This policy seems to have been successful financially. Midway Airlines, after an initial period of loss, temporarily turned the corner

Table 5.5 Selected traffic and financial data of the new entrant airlines (domestic operations)

	RPM growth rates (%)[a]		Average on-flight passenger trip length (Miles)[a]		Passenger load factor (%)[a]		Profit margin (%)	
	1981	1983	1981	1983	1981	1983	1981	1983[b]
Former interstate								
AirCalifornia	23.4	5.8	380.7	385.2	58.2	58.2	(1.3)	7.2
Air Florida	65.4	(17.3)	614.7	645.7	59.6	56.9	4.0	(6.1)[c]
PSA[d]	6.9	16.6	352.1	379.7	53.0	55.2	(4.3)	(2.3)
Southwest	14.1	28.8	300.6	360.8	63.6	61.6	17.9	15.3
Former charters								
Capitol	346.1	(38.7)	1,910.3	1,612.0	82.2	75.2	e	1.5[c]
World	33.5	(12.9)	1,985.9	2,313.4	79.0	64.9	e	(22.8)[c]
Newly established carriers								
Midway[f]	177.3	0.3	498.8	488.3	59.1	48.4	11.9	(11.9)
New York Air[g]	h	8.2	295.0	312.1	62.7	57.3	(14.8)	6.7
People Express[i]	h	111.8	423.9[j]	519.9	58.3[j]	73.5	h	6.8[c]
Muse[k]	h	139.8	241.0[j]	452.2	34.5[j]	50.9	h	6.3

a. Scheduled service.
b. December 1983 financial data are based on preliminary reports.
c. Comparison data are for twelve months ended September; carrier failed to file December 1983 financial reports.
d. Due to strike, operations were suspended from September 25 to October 17, 1980.
e. Carrier did not file entirely financial reports prior to 1983.
f. Midway began operations and traffic reporting in November 1979 and quarterly financial reporting in December 1979.
g. New York Air began operations and all reporting in December 1980.
h. Full twelve-month data not available in 1980 and/or 1981 for comparison.
i. People Express began operations in April 1981 and financial and traffic reporting in May 1981.
j. Calculations based on available data. See also footnotes i and k.
k. Muse began operations and all reporting in July 1981.

financially. In 1983 it reconfigured its aircraft and began to offer high levels of amenities to appeal to business travelers. The mixed performance of these airlines suggests that, though they are a strong competitive force in the industry, the success of any single airline is not ensured.

Conclusion

It is appropriate to relate these outcomes to economic theory. In theory all players in the market have access to the same technological arrangements and therefore to the same cost structures. We have seen here that costly labor contracts and associated restrictive work rules bind the older certificated carriers, whereas the new entrants are largely free from such constraints. The entrants are also free from costly equipment errors made by past managements. Thus new entrants have a cost advantage under which they can earn profits at prices that are not compensatory to incumbent carriers. The older incumbents, on the other hand, have the advantages of name-recognition, amenities, and service convenience, particularly at their hub airports. The actual situation in the airline industry in the period after passage of the ADA is thus characterized by disequilibrium. It is fortunate for the competitive process that in this disequilibrium some advantages are enjoyed by the entrants and some by incumbents.

Chapter 6

Small Community Service

In the debate over deregulation there was considerable concern about small community air service. The act was designed to make it easier for airlines both to enter into new markets and to exit from old markets. It was feared that this added flexibility would result in an exodus of service from small communities. Carriers would redeploy their aircraft away from relatively low-density markets into the higher-density routes that had previously been closed to them. Thus Congress included in the act a program to assure small communities that they would not lose all air service. This program was something of an anomaly since it increased in some ways the regulation of small community air service in order to allow a massive reduction of regulation for the rest of the system.

In this chapter we describe the changing character of air service to small communities. As anticipated, the local service carriers have continued the withdrawal from service to small communities that began over a decade ago. The withdrawal has been all the more rapid because of the jump in fuel prices in 1979 and 1980. Nevertheless, an evaluation of systemwide patterns of service changes shows that travelers from many small communities now have better access to the nation's air transportation system. This service improvement, as commuter carriers have replaced local service airlines, has been accompanied by improved efficiency, as is shown by the sharp reductions in the level of subsidy required.

Subsidy Program under Regulation

In no area of airline deregulation were the fears of reform so pronounced as in the service to small communities. The opponents of reform argued that small community air service would collapse if entry were opened. The line of reasoning went like this. Airlines currently used revenues earned on profitable (near monopoly) routes to subsidize service on short, less dense routes. If competition were permitted on the profitable routes, there would be no revenues to subsidize services to small communities, and carriers would abandon them. Since there are small communities in every state, Congressmen could not accept the risk associated with reform.

One enormous contribution of the Kennedy hearings in 1975 was that these fears were addressed head-on in a systematic and scholarly fashion. Evidence was accumulated, partly through academic studies and partly through government reports, that indicated that trunk carriers had long lost interest in serving small communities and that even the local service carriers had been abandoning them.[1] Other economic studies showed that, at current prices, longer-haul markets could indeed be expected to produce large profits, but the existing carriers had competed away this profit by means of scheduling competition—planes in the long-haul markets were flying about 40 percent full in markets that had three competing carriers, 50 percent full in markets that had two competing carriers and 60 percent full in monopoly markets.[2]

Fears concerning small community service continued to be on the minds of congressmen, however, and were fed by industry representatives who stated that under deregulation airlines would pull out of a substantial number of "losing" city pairs. The Kennedy staff responded by conducting a detailed analysis of 327 "losing" city pairs served by United Air Lines, where "losing" refers to failure to cover full costs.[3] A similar analysis was later carried out by the Department of Transportation for a list of 160 "losing" domestic segments provided by Eastern Airlines.[4] In both cases it was found that all but two dozen or so of the losing segments were served on a discretionary, not a mandatory, basis and that in the majority of these, more service was being provided than was required by the CAB. Of the remaining city-pair markets, pullout by a trunk carrier would, as it had in the past, lead in most cases to unsubsidized replacement by commuter or local service carriers. Only in a few instances would direct subsidy be needed. Thus the Kennedy forces would recommend direct subsidy rather than cross-subsidy as the best approach in any reform package. But the direct subsidy should be based on somewhat different criteria than had been established in the past, for there was substantial dissatisfaction with the system of subsidy that was being paid to the local service carriers.

The Local Service Airlines
When the local service airlines were created, they used small aircraft (the DC-3 was the most common aircraft used), and their route certificates prohibited them from competing in markets already served by the trunk airlines. In the early 1950s several of the local service airlines began acquiring larger aircraft (40-seat Convair-240s and Martin-202s). In a significant decision—which reversed earlier policy—the Board decided to subsidize the costs of using the larger aircraft.[5] The Board paid higher

subsidy for large aircraft service, and by 1963 nearly 80 percent of the locals' revenue passenger miles were provided in large propeller aircraft.[6] Hand in hand with the introduction of these larger aircraft came several major route proceedings in which the Board attempted to "strengthen" the local airlines' route networks.[7] In these proceedings the Board rescinded some of the restrictions on the locals' routes, transferred routes from the trunk airlines to the locals, and added additional new stations to the locals' certificates. (In 1962 the number of points authorized for service from the local service airlines reached its peak of 499.)[8] While both larger and small markets were added to the local carriers' certificates, the carriers clearly found it profitable to shift their newly acquired large aircraft into these larger markets. Thus by 1962 the fraction of passenger miles provided in markets competitive with trunk airlines (or possibly other locals) rose to 34 percent from 19 percent in 1955.[9] Subsidy rose sharply over this period, from $22 million in 1955 to to $66.8 million in 1962.

Early in the 1960s the local service airlines lobbied for the expansion of their route networks to allow them to serve even larger and presumably more profitable markets. In 1966 the Board decided that this indeed was the way to reduce subsidy costs. The Board undertook an ambitious program of lifting restrictions from the local carriers' certificates and granting them larger and longer-haul routes. (These added routes were not eligible for subsidy.) At the same time the local service airlines dropped many smaller communities. Under the Board's use-it-or-lose-it policy eleven points were dropped between 1964 and 1966. Between 1967 and 1970 local service airlines were replaced by commuters at thirty-one points.

The local service airlines converted rapidly to jet aircraft operations. Between 1966 and 1970 they acquired 135 jet aircraft, giving them a total fleet of 157 jets by 1970. The number of propeller aircraft, meanwhile, declined by 115 to 258 aircraft.[10] Thus this period saw a rapid transition of the local service airlines. While the Board was successful in reducing subsidy (see figure 6.1), in the process it transformed the locals to regional jet airlines that served many of the densest markets in their service areas. They became far removed from the small community specialists that were originally envisioned when their service began to be subsidized. By 1976 the percent of the aircraft in the local service fleet that were turbo prop or piston powered had shrunk from a 99 percent level achieved in 1965 to just 35 percent.

The policy change in the 1960s reduced subsidy from about $67 million in 1962 to about $40 million in 1970; however, it also contributed to the decline in the quality of service to communities eligible for subsidy. Eads

(1972) found that departures declined in 56 percent of the 97 points served by local service airlines in both 1959 and 1969. Moreover departures declined in 81 percent of the cities with fewer than 50,000 inhabitants.[11] Since the Board did not control scheduling of subsidized service, the carriers' focus on their major markets may have caused the convenience of scheduled service at small subsidized points to decline even more than the decline in departures suggests. However, the expansion of the locals no doubt improved the convenience of airline connections available to small community travelers.

The Commuter Carriers

The small communities that lost certificated service did not always lose all air service. Instead, much of this service was assumed by the commuter carrier industry. This industry was exempted from CAB price and entry regulation just after World War II. Thus commuters were able to enter and exit freely from any market they chose and to charge whatever fares they wished. However, the industry had a size limit imposed on the aircraft it could fly. Initially, there was a single weight limit of 4,500 pounds for the aircraft. Then in 1972 the CAB increased the aircraft size limitation to the dual limit of 30 revenue seats and 12,500 pounds of cargo capacity. The line was drawn to exclude the F-27/Convair CV-240 to Convair CV-580 class of propeller aircraft, since these were at the time employed by local service carriers in small community subsidized service.

As in other matters the CAB had attempted to regulate perfectly by setting up a regulatory boundary—with certificated carriers on one side of the boundary and exempted air service on the other side. Two unfortunate but related side effects occurred. One of these was technological. The rules encouraged the development of aircraft which just met the specified limit, such as the 30-seat Shorts 330. The second was that as the local service carriers expanded their aircraft size, there was no incentive to build a replacement for the Convair 580 which had roughly 55 seats; the commuters would be unable to operate such an aircraft without assuming the burden of full rate and route regulation. Thus an aircraft suitable for service to many communities that were larger than the smallest but not so large as to warrant jet services was stifled. This would have untoward consequences for the small community air service program after deregulation, as we will shortly see. Even with this regulatory limit, however, the commuter industry grew at a rapid pace. By 1976 commuters were serving 7.3 million passengers without subsidy. This traffic was carried by 174 passenger carriers serving 781 airports and 1,412 city pairs in 47 states.

Some 150 points served by commuters enplaned fewer than fifteen passengers per day. Thus the commuters had freely chosen to supply the hoped-for service to many small communities and were doing so without federal support.

Commuters were often able to stimulate traffic when their services were introduced. Usually this was done by offering more frequent flights at more convenient times rather than by offering lower fares. This strategy proved attractive to the business passengers who constitute the majority of short-haul passengers. The results were particularly positive in the case of the Allegheny Commuter program, which represented a well-designed transfer of routes to commuters with access to many of the reservation and other facilities of the local service carrier. In addition Allegheny (now USAir) timed its flights to make connections from its commuters convenient to passengers.

Because of the expense and poor service characteristics of the subsidy program, in 1972 the CAB proposed a two-year experiment in which subsidy would be paid under a low-bid contracting system. Under this system service levels and aircraft types were to be specified according to the isolation of the community and expected levels of traffic.[12] Such a system promised the benefits of greater control over the minimum quality of service, enhanced incentives for cost efficiency as well as for commercial development of the market, and a substantial reduction in subsidy costs. Although the Board's proposal was not then adopted, a similar type of program was ultimately incorporated in Section 419 of the Airline Deregulation Act. But this did not occur without a struggle since the local service airlines naturally wished to protect their subsidy.

Utilizing a booklet entitled "Five Myths about about Subsidized Airline Service to Small Cities," the local service airlines attempted in 1977 to prevent a more economic system from being legislated.[13] In this booklet the local service carriers attempted to show that they were interested in small community service, had no universal exit policy toward them, and were indeed in some instances still purchasing small aircraft. They cited a number of cases where small communities were pleased with the existing system, and a number of cases where replacement service by commuters did not offer an improvement to the communities. They contended that subsidy would not be less if commuter replacement were widespread, and defended the class-rate system as providing incentives for efficiency.

Their booklet elicited a point-by-point rebuttal from the CAB staff in March 1978.[14] The staff admitted freely that there were likely to be gainers and losers under a changed system. In economists' terms the move from a local service carrier to a commuter carrier orientation would not offer a Pareto improvement, with each community better off. Rather, the overall benefits of the change would greatly outweigh the losses.

Congress decided in favor of the agency's position. Reliance for small community air service would be transferred during a period of transition from the local service to the commuter carriers and would be based on community need rather than carrier system need. To satisfy the fears of service withdrawal, Congress would guarantee at least some service to all communities that currently had service.

Subsidy Program under Deregulation

The essential air service program provided, for the first time, assurance to all communities listed on air carrier certificates on the date of enactment of the act a guarantee that they would continue to receive air service for ten years. In some ways the mandate was quite rigid. The Board was given no discretion based on cost/benefit relationships to eliminate a point from the program if it was close to another larger airport or if it was isolated but enplaned very few passengers per day. Similarly it could add no new point, unless the point was eligible because it had received some service during the decade before the ADA was passed. In other ways the Board was granted substantial discretion. The Board could judge between proposals that met criteria it would devise about what level and kind of services would be subsidized. The Board could also negotiate levels of direct payment of the requisite subsidy to those carriers that it selected as best able to provide the service. Thus the new mandate chose direct subsidization of service rather than of carriers, and it permitted the Board to make subsidy payments to carriers without requiring their certification.

On other fronts, such as the size limit applicable to the commuter carriers, Congress acted to rectify the anomaly that had arisen with the 30-seat rule for aircraft, by augmenting the size limit to 55 revenue seats. The Board increased this to 60 seats shortly thereafter. Congress also decided that with the new reliance on commuters in the essential air service program, these airlines must go through a formal fitness procedure. Finally, the ADA required the Board to extend joint fares to commuter carriers. [15]

Guidelines for Small Community Replacement Services: Section 419 Subsidy

The Board issued a set of guidelines in September 1979 that attempted to balance the needs and desires of the communities and the act's general philosophy of relying on competitive forces to determine service level and quality at these communities. Regional hearings were held before the guidelines were issued in order to obtain comments from state, community, and other interested parties. The guidelines guaranteed support for levels of traffic of up to a maximum of 80 seats daily in each direction. Larger volumes were deemed able to support themselves. The Board guaranteed access to a city (or sometimes to two cities) that had close commercial, political, and geographic ties to the community and that provided it with access to the national air transportation system. Flights were required to be well timed and to allow for the possibility of same day round-trip service. In general, aircraft had to have two engines and to be operated by two pilots.

The replacement process was designed to proceed fairly smoothly. A certificated carrier had to notify the Board ninety days before suspending service at a community. The Board covered the incumbent's losses for subsequent periods of thirty days until a replacement carrier was found. At those communities where no carrier was willing to provide subsidy-free air service, the CAB invited service proposals including subsidy requests from interested carriers. On the basis of the service proposals, the carrier's service record, and the community's preferences, the Board selected a carrier to serve the community generally for a two-year period. The ADA also ordered substantial changes in the local service subsidy program effective on January 1, 1983, at which time any carrier could replace or bump an existing 419 carrier by showing that it could improve service and reduce subsidy.

Local Service Carriers: Section 406 Subsidy
The act stipulated that the Board would be required to continue subsidizing local service carriers at those communities that were entitled to receive a subsidy until January 1, 1985. Moreover the subsidy was to be sufficient to support service of the same extent and quality as the service provided in 1977. However, appropriations for Section 406 Subsidy were reduced by about one-half for fiscal year 1983 and eliminated for fiscal year 1984. These changes phased out the local service subsidy program sooner than was anticipated in the ADA, and induced a more rapid decline in the number of small communities receiving service from local service carriers.

When the deregulation act was passed, there were 198 small communities receiving federally subsidized air service in the forty-eight contiguous states. Although local service subsidy payments were not immediately changed by the ADA, the legislated timetable for termination of the program and the increased opportunities to enter markets reduced the

Table 6.1 Subsidy outlays ($ thousands)

Fiscal year	Section 406 subsidy	Section 419 subsidy
1970	36,546	
1971	55,152	
1972	62,977	
1973	72,223	
1974	73,362	
1975	63,581	
1976	71,343	
1977[a]	79,787	
1978	73,999	
1979	72,665	380
1980	80,867	9,438
1981	94,433	13,837
1982	45,582	18,667

Source: CAB Budget Estimates, Salaries, and Expense Payments to Air Carriers, fiscal years 1972–1981.
a. Fiscal year change from twelve months ending June 30 to twelve months ending September 30, 1976, not included.

carriers' incentives to continue serving subsidized points. As small community service has shifted from the locals to the smaller commuter airlines, subsidy cost has been reduced by more than half. These changes have led to a substantial decrease in the amount of government subsidy (see table 6.1). The average annual cost for seventy-eight communities covered by the new Section 419 Subsidy in mid-1981 was $267,000 per city per year, whereas under the old Section 406 program the average annual cost at these communities had been $718,000.[16]

Transition Policy for Medium-Sized Cities

Another area that should be mentioned pertains to Congress' concern about specific gainers and losers from regulatory changes. This concern was assuaged in the case of the smallest communities through the requirement that no eligible community lose service. However, there was one type of loser not fully anticipated at the time the ADA was designed. This resulted, for the most part, from the lack of a satisfactory number of commuter carriers in some parts of the country and from the lack of appropriate sized equipment resulting from the former regulatory policy on size of commuter equipment.

The situation in California was especially difficult. At the time of deregulation, there were only forty-two commuter aircraft in the entire state of California, primarily as a result of the California Public Utility Commission (PUC) policies. Whereas commuter service was deregulated in terms of price and entry in most parts of the United States, the PUC controlled entry within California and maintained restrictive entry policies. When the ADA was passed in 1978, the effects of previous state regulation and the desire of certificated carriers to take advantage of new opportunities elsewhere resulted in significant cutbacks in service to such cities as Bakersfield, where first Hughes Airwest and then United filed notices of intent to terminate all air service to the community in 1979. The difficulty facing this city, and others like it, was that their traffic levels were well above the level which would enable them to qualify under the maximum guarantee of seats under the essential air service program. Yet a decision to terminate service would mean that a significant portion of the city's traffic could not be served by the small commuter aircraft available for replacement purposes. Thus the Board adopted a transition policy for some middle-sized communities. In the case of Bakersfield, California, traffic had averaged 475 to 520 passengers per day, so the Board required United to continue to provide 600 daily seats during the transition until commuter carriers both in California and nearby states could enter and obtain more appropriate sized aircraft. For Bakersfield and five other communities, the transition period lasted on the order of six months after the terminations would otherwise have taken place.

Effects of Fuel Costs on Service

Changes in the subsidy program have clearly had an effect on service in small community markets, but changes in fuel prices have also had an influence. Before we evaluate changes in service, it is important to outline the direction of change caused by fuel cost increases.

Most markets emanating from small communities are short hauls. In these markets rising fuel costs have made jet operators less competitive relative to the commuter airlines and ground transportation. In many short-haul markets rising fuel costs have simply made jet service increasingly uneconomical.

The doubling of fuel costs between 1979 and 1980 widened the gap between the costs of jet service and turboprop service for short hauls. As Table 6.2 shows, turboprop operations are much less fuel intensive than jet operations. For turboprops about 3 gallons of fuel are required per available seat for a 100-mile flight. A jet requires more than four gallons per

Table 6.2 Flight speed and fuel costs for 100-mile segment

	Props		Jets
	DeHavilland Twin Otter	DeHavilland DHC-7	B-737-200
Seating capacity	19	50	110
Flight time	42 min	38 min	32 min
Fuel used	57 gal	148 gal	451 gal
Fuel per seat	3.0 gal	3.0 gal	4.1 gal

Source: CAB, Aircraft Operating Cost and Performance Report.

available seat. In practice, the difference in relative fuel used per passenger is substantially greater. Jets are simply too large to operate at high load factors in small markets. For example, if ten passengers were carried over the segment, the fuel used per passenger would be about six gallons in the 19-seat turboprop and about 45 gallons in the 110-seat jet. When fuel costs went up, therefore, the cost per seat or per passenger of turboprop service did not rise as rapidly as the costs of jet service. Hence the relative price of the faster service rose. Indeed, as the table shows, the effective speed advantage of jets is not substantial in short-haul markets. The replacement of jet operators by commuters is a natural consequence of the economic forces created by fuel price increases.

Changes in Service

One measure of the change in the quality of air service is the enormous shift that has taken place in the types of flights offered.[17] As table 6.3 shows, there has been a dramatic increase nationwide in the number of nonstop and one-stop flights offered and also a dramatic reduction in the number of multistop flights. It is impossible to say the degree to which these trends can be attributed to the fuel price increase as opposed to the policy changes toward small community service, but the trend clearly shows a move away from the hedgehopping flights that were characteristic of service under the class-rate subsidy system in favor of more nonstop and one-stop service.

Since much of our analysis concerns the turning over of communities from the trunk and local service airlines to commuters, it is instructive to divide nonhubs[18] into three broad categories: (1) communities that have lost service from a trunk or local service airline, (2) communities that have retained some trunk or local service, and (3) communities that were not served by a trunk or local service airline in either 1978 or 1981. Table 6.4 contrasts service changes in these three categories. In addition the table

Table 6.3   Nationwide reduction in multistop flights, June 1978 to June 1979

Stops per flight	Weekly change in number of flights
0	+60,363
1	+8,361
2	−5,576
3	−6,331
4	−4,745
5	−2,236
6	−910
7	−363
8	−126
9+	−41

Table 6.4   Weekly departures at nonhub airports

	Departures		Percent change
	1978	1981	
Points losing trunk or local service (74 communities)	3,643	4,606	26
Eligible for local service subsidy (46 communities)	1,717	2,185	27
Unsubsidized (28 communities)	1,926	2,421	26
Points retaining trunk or local service (156 communities)	11,146	11,172	0
Eligible for local service subsidy (118 communities)	7,143	6,786	−5
Unsubsidized (38 communities)	4,003	4,386	10
Points not served by trunk or local airlines in 1978 or 1981 (306 communities)	12,418	10,883	−12
Total for all nonhubs	27,207	26,661	−2

Source: *Official Airline Guide* for June of each year. Note that total departures in this table are lower than the total departures reported in table 2.5. This table omits communities that lost service between June 1978 and passage of the deregulation act in October 1978.

Table 6.5   Percent change in weekly departures at nonhubs by aircraft size (1981 vs. 1978)

	Aircraft size			
	0–30	31–60	61+	Total
Points losing trunk or local service (74 communities)	76	−53	−93	26
Points retaining trunk or local service (156 communities)	56	−18	−26	0
Points not served by trunks or local service in 1978 or 1981 (306 communities)	−13	2	−99	−12
Nonhub total:	13	−20	−34	−2

Source: *Official Airline Guide* for June of each year.

breaks out changes in departures according to whether the community received a local service subsidy in 1978.

The nonhubs that have experienced the biggest increase in service are those that have been dropped by the major carriers. In the seventy-four communities where trunk and local airlines dropped service, total departures went up 26 percent. The markets served voluntarily by the formerly regulated carriers had more moderate increases, while those still under local service subsidy have experienced a 5 percent reduction. Departures fell by 12 percent at the points which were served only by commuter airlines in June 1978.

The increased role of the commuter airlines in serving small communities means that many had reductions in jet service. Table 6.5 examines the changes in the kinds of aircraft used by breaking departures down by aircraft size categories. Aircraft with more than 60 seats are jets; smaller aircraft are propeller driven. In total, the nonhub airports have experienced a 34 percent decline in jet departures, a 20 percent decline in large prop aircraft departures, and a 13 percent increase in small prop aircraft departures.

Communities that have lost trunk or local service experienced a 90 percent reduction in jet service and have lost 53 percent of their large propeller service. Their increased service came entirely from the expanded use of smaller aircraft. Points that retained the trunks and locals have experienced similar but less dramatic changes in the kinds of aircraft providing the service.

Table 6.6 shows that departures to large and medium hubs are up sharply for the seventy-four communities that have lost all trunk and local service. The points retaining trunk or local service have more flights to large or medium hubs but fewer flights to small hubs and nonhubs. These

Table 6.6   Percent change in weekly departures at nonhubs by hub size (1981 vs. 1978)

	Large or medium hub	Small hub or nonhub	Total
Points losing trunk or local service (74 communities)	37	16	26
Points retaining trunk or local service (156 communities)	22	−16	0
Points not served by trunk or local service in 1978 or 1981 (306 communities)	−5	−19	−12
Nonhub total:	11	−13	−2

Source: *Official Airline Guide* for June of each year.

communities have apparently benefited from the carriers' increased reliance on hub-and-spoke operations. Thus the quality of service to these communities has apparently improved despite the lack of change in the number of departures. At the points that have never had trunk or local service, departures have declined to large- and medium-hub airports, but the reduction is much smaller than the cutbacks to small hubs and nonhubs.

Conclusion

Small community service has been affected by the Board's subsidy policies, changes in route regulation, fuel price increases, and the economic recession. Overall, service to small communities declined slightly between 1978 and 1981, but the subgroups of communities were affected very differently. One particularly noteworthy finding is that though the CAB subsidy evidently was successful in retaining local service carriers in markets serving eligible subsidy communities, service convenience at these communities has declined relative to communities that lost certificated service. Nevertheless, small cities that retained larger carrier service are receiving an increased number of departures to large and medium hubs. Communities dropped by these carriers experienced sharp increases in flights, albeit with smaller aircraft than before. Since 1981 service to small communities has improved further as the economy has recovered.

Part **III**

Analyses of Changes in Convenience, Productivity, and the State of
Competition

Chapter 7

Convenience of Air Service

There was concern that deregulation would lead to a severe disruption of the integrity of the service network, that it might simply no longer be possible to get from here to there. Less dramatically, a typical trip might take a lot longer, requiring a number of reroutings through intermediate points. Without the guiding hand of the regulator, service to and from all but the largest cities might decline, and decline precipitously.

As with many of the fears about change, the truth was more complex. Practically every community has experienced changes in air service as the airlines have realigned their route networks. As we discussed in chapter 4, medium and large hubs experienced increases in departures, small hubs remained about the same, and nonhubs experienced declines. The pattern of departure change in small communities has been affected by carriers' increased reliance on hub-and-spoke operations. A larger share of flights from small communities are now bound for large and medium hubs.

In this chapter we investigate whether the change in typical routings has led to an improvement in the ability of citizens from small communities to reach their desired destinations conveniently. In other words, we seek to learn whether the more direct access has compensated for the implied reduction in service convenience as a result of the reduced number of departures. The logic of our analysis is easily stated.

Smaller communities generally do not have sufficient traffic to support frequent service to many destinations. On the other hand, large and medium hubs because of their larger populations have service to more places. In theory increased service between a small community and a nearby large city provides small community passengers greater access to the banks of flights available at the larger city. This in turn should reduce travel time from these communities to their destinations.

By using a simulation technique, we find that, though there is a great deal of variation among cities in the changes in convenience, the development of hub-and-spoke operations has indeed led to a small net improvement in travel time and hence convenience of service on the average. Service convenience between larger cities has remained about the same. Service convenience from smaller cities has improved somewhat. Service from the smallest cities has improved at locations where commuters have replaced trunk and local service carriers and has declined at locations where trunk and local service carriers remain.

Measuring Service Convenience

A traveler wants flights at or near the time he wants to travel and prefers nonstop or direct flights over circuitous flights. Convenience thus depends on the timing and directness of flights, as well as on the number of flights. Assessing changes in convenience therefore requires measuring the combined influences of changes in departures, flight timing, and connecting patterns. To do this, we constructed an index of service convenience that reflects the correspondence between flights and desired travel times as well as the actual time required in making a trip. To determine the probability of a passenger being denied a reservation on his preferred flight requires information on, among other things, airlines' allocations of restricted seats and the variability of demand in a given market among hours of the day and days of the week. This information is unavailable; so we limit our analysis to the timing and speed of flights. To the extent that smaller aircraft are now being employed in smaller communities, access to flights can be expected to have declined.

The index was obtained by simulating trips in about 200 markets since 1978. Hypothetical travelers are assumed to have desired arrival times spread every fifteen minutes throughout the peak travel hours of the day. They choose from a menu of available direct and connecting flights by trading off between schedule convenience and flight speed. In general, the speed of a flight depends on the kind of aircraft, the number of stops made, and the circuity of the trip.

The flights available in a market were identified using the *Official Airline Guide* (*OAG*) listings, which are available on computer tapes. These tapes list all the direct flights between city pairs that appear in the printed *OAG* volumes. Connections are constructed from the direct flight listings by matching direct flights from the origin city to a connecting city, with flights to the destination city from the connecting city. As many as fifteen connecting cities were considered for a single city-pair market. In constructing connections time limits were set so that only reasonable connections would be included for consideration. The minimum layover is twenty minutes. A maximum layover of two hours was set for flights where both the origin and destination is a large hub or a medium hub. A maximum of three hours was allowed whenever the origin or destination was a small hub or a nonhub.

For each traveler we calculated the weighted sum of the difference between the actual arrival time of the chosen flight and the traveler's preferred arrival time ("schedule delay") plus the total elapsed time of the flight ("flight duration"). Schedule delay is a term introduced by Douglas and Miller (1974). Their definition included the difference between desired arrival or departure time and the actual time of arrival or departure plus an expected delay due to the possibility of not getting on the flight of first choice. Our definition does not include this adjustment for availability of seats. The index thus reflects the time costs associated with air travel. Higher values of the index indicate that travelers must take flights that are less convenient, or that take a longer time to arrive at the destination. We assume an equal weight for each traveler, so the index for the market is the average of this sum over all the hypothetical travelers. Likewise, aggregate indexes are averages over markets weighted by the number of travelers in each market.

The duration of a flight depends on aircraft speed, whether the route is direct or circuitous and the time required to make connections. Schedule delay depends on the frequency of flights and their timing relative to the timing preferred by a traveler. If one particular flight is the fastest and arrives exactly when the traveler wants, it clearly dominates alternative flights and will be chosen by the traveler. But sometimes a trade-off is involved in choosing among flights: for example, a traveler who wants to arrive in Chicago at 5 P.M. may have a choice between a two-hour connecting flight that arrives right at 5 P.M. and a one-hour nonstop flight that arrives at 7 P.M. Many travelers would take the fastest flight no matter what time of day it arrives. Others place more weight on the arrival time and in some cases would take a connecting flight that arrives near the desired arrival time even when a direct flight is available at some other time of day. In the simulations we have assumed that a traveler places slightly more weight on travel time than on schedule delay. Several assumptions were tried in the analysis, and our year-to-year comparisons were not sensitive to the value of the trade-off assumed. The trade-off used in the simulation is 1 hour of schedule delay to 3/4 hour of travel time; that is, a traveler would willingly incur up to an extra hour of schedule inconvenience if it allows him to save 45 minutes of flight time.

A total of 210 markets were selected for the analysis. Of these, 120 are markets among communities which are classified by the FAA as hubs.[1] To ensure that a substantial number of markets of all sizes were included in the analysis, we constructed a random sample of twenty markets from each of the six possible combinations of airports, (i.e., large hub–large hub, large hub–medium hub, large hub–small hub, . . . , small hub–small hub).

We used a more systematic selection procedure for the markets involving nonhubs because we found that when nonhub markets were drawn at random, the result was often a market with little or no traffic. (One such randomly selected market was between Sheridan, Wyoming, and Tupelo, Mississippi.) We first selected ninety nonhub cities. Thirty were randomly selected from each of three categories of community: those that have lost trunk or local service, those that have retained trunk or local service, and those that never had trunk or local service. One market was then created for each nonhub city using New York, Chicago, or Los Angeles as the destination, depending on the region in which the community is located. These large cities were considered to form the most appropriate markets because they are among the top destinations of all communities within their part of the country, and they represent markets in which service is highly valued by small city residents. At the same time it allowed us to avoid focusing too narrowly on only the traffic between the nonhub and its principal neighboring hub airports, which can lead to biased results when the hub airport changes in response to changing airline service patterns.

Only flights with a single connection (but possibly several intermediate stops) were included in the analysis. For most of the markets included, this was not a serious limitation, and the added complexity of selecting multiple-connection itineraries was considered prohibitive. In some of the nonhub markets selected, one-connection service was not available in 1978; we therefore replaced these communities with communities that had one-connection service.

To establish daily travel patterns, we examined the distribution of arrival times in three dense markets—New York–Boston, New York–Chicago, and New York–Los Angeles—in 1978 and found a peak travel period in each of these markets between 3 P.M. and 10 P.M. Morning peak periods are also evident in the shorter-haul markets, but the New York–Los Angeles market had no nonstop arrivals between 8 A.M. and 11 A.M. in either direction. Since a morning peak was not found consistently while an afternoon peak was, the simulation focuses on the afternoon peak period. Traffic remained at a relatively uniform plateau throughout afternoon peak hours, so a uniform distribution of travel demand was assumed.

Table 7.1   Description of markets used in simulations (data for June 1980)

Market category	Market density (average travelers per day)	Average trip length	Average speed in transit (mph)	Average schedule delay (min)
Large hub–large hub	386	995	351	40
Large hub–medium hub	180	1,223	328	47
Large hub–small hub	33	1,047	259	63
Medium hub–medium hub	21	927	231	55
Medium hub–small hub	12	935	250	90
Small hub–small hub	3	904	204	68

Source: Simulations based on *Official Airline Guide* and *O & D Survey*.

Table 7.2   Indexes of service convenience in hub markets

	Baseline markets	Hub market categories						Average
		Large– large	Large– medium	Large– small	Medium– medium	Medium– small	Small– small	
June 1978	100.0	100.0	100.0	100.0	100.0	100.0	100.0	100.0
June 1980	100.3	101.2	100.9	92.8	100.5	102.6	95.7	100.7
June 1981	100.6	99.0	99.5	93.7	96.2	101.1	102.8	98.8

Source: Simulations based on *Official Airline Guide* and *O & D Survey*.

Changes in Service Convenience

Table 7.1 describes the size categories of markets included in the simulations and presents summary statistics for the simulation in June 1980. Not surprisingly, as market density increases, travel speed increases and schedule delay decreases. For example, average speed (total elasped time divided by distance) is 351 miles per hour between large-hub cities but only 204 miles per hour between small-hub cities. The passengers traveling between two small hubs choose flights that are, on average, 68 minutes before or after the preferred arrival; the comparable schedule delay is only 40 minutes for the passengers traveling between large hubs. This pattern seems efficient because more densely traveled markets can support more frequent, direct service.

Table 7.2 presents indexes of convenience for the six hub-market categories from 1978 to present, using June 1978 as the base period. The indexes show the relative time cost of travel; therefore smaller values indicate improvement. In addition to the market categories already described, the index was calculated for three heavily traveled markets (New York–Boston, New York–Chicago, and New York–Los Angeles) to obtain a baseline.

Table 7.3 Service convenience at nonhubs

| | Market categories | | | |
	Dropped by trunk or local	Retained by trunk or local	Never had trunk or local	Average
June 1978	100.0	100.0	100.0	100.0
June 1980	93.9	107.2	101.0	102.0
June 1981	93.2	105.9	104.5	101.9

Source: Simulations based on *Official Airline Guide* and *O & D Survey*.

The baseline markets and the large hub markets exhibit little variation in time costs since 1978. The convenience and speed of service in these very dense markets has remained essentially unchanged. This is not surprising. Most of these markets already had a lot of nonstop service; so flight times have not declined substantially. Thus in the large hub to large hub markets, in which flight time accounts for more than 80 percent of total trip time, it would take relatively large reductions in schedule delay to affect overall convenience substantially. Thus a 9 percent increase in the number of flights in the large–large category produced only a 1 percent improvement in convenience. Similarly the large- to medium-hub markets, which are also relatively heavily traveled, did not show appreciable change.

The improvement in convenience has been greater in the large- to small-hub markets as well as the medium- to medium-hub markets. The 6 percent drop in travel time costs for the large-small category is the greatest improvement in convenience for any category in these simulations and is largely the result of the 18 percent increase in departures in these markets. The improved convenience in service between medium hubs takes place even though departures were virtually unchanged. Since these markets have less direct service than the markets between major hubs, they have greater potential for improvement in convenience via changes in scheduling and connecting networks. At the same time service convenience has declined by about one to two percentage points between small hubs and medium hubs and between small hubs and small hubs.

The results of the simulations for the nonhub markets are presented in table 7.3. Between 1978 and 1981 the convenience of service has improved by about 6 percent for the cities that have been dropped by trunk or local airlines and has deteriorated by about the same percentage for those cities that have retained trunk or local service and for those cities that have never had it. Overall, the nonhub communities have experienced a 2 percent decline in convenience.

Opponents of deregulation argued that the pullout of these carriers would constitute a major loss to small communities. It is noteworthy that convenience has improved for those communities that have lost trunk and local service. The simulations show that trip time has increased slightly—no doubt because the commuter airlines use smaller aircraft—but this has been more than offset by large reductions in schedule delay. On the average the number of flights has increased about 26 percent for these communities and convenience has increased about 7 percent (see also table 6.3).

The communities that never had trunk or local service have had about a 12 percent reduction in flights, and convenience has declined by about 4.5 percent. In the simulations enroute travel times remained virtually unchanged between 1978 and 1981 for these communities, but schedule delay went up by about 17 percent.

The communities that have retained trunk or local service have had very mixed experiences in terms of changes in departures. Communities on subsidy have lost departures, while the other communities have gained departures. Our index shows that service convenience has declined on average (see table 7.3). (Although we showed in chapter 6 that total flights to these communities have remained about the same, our sample for the simulation contains a disproportionate share of communities that are receiving subsidized service.) In the simulations we found that enroute travel times have remained about the same, but schedule delay has increased by about 20 percent. We observed a similiar pattern in markets that never had trunk or local service airlines. Thus in these smaller markets it appears that convenience has tended to fall except where commuters have replaced trunk or local service airlines.

Conclusion

We have shown that the convenience of air service has not changed appreciably under deregulation. The simulations show that convenience has increased slightly in the hub market categories and declined slightly in the nonhub market categories. It is noteworthy that convenience has improved in those small communities where trunks and locals have suspended operations. These changes in convenience are consistent with the changes we have observed in the carriers' route networks, and they confirm the view that in the period since deregulation carriers have realigned their routes to match travel flows better.

Chapter 8

Productivity Growth

Comparisons of the costs and fares of CAB regulated airlines with intra-state airlines in California and Texas were prominent elements in the case for regulatory reform. The clear implication of these comparisons was that costs and fares would be lower for the interstate airlines if CAB regulation were relaxed. Thus one key test of deregulation is whether it has in fact led to increased productivity and lower costs.

Several of the developments in the industry have obviously contributed to increased productivity: load factors have risen, aircraft utilization has improved, and competitive pressures are forcing airlines to improve worker productivity. In addition average industry costs are falling because low cost airlines are growing relative to high cost airlines. This chapter considers deregulation's impact on these aspects of the industry's efficiency and concludes by presenting some estimates of the overall extent to which deregulation has increased productivity.

Load Factors

As was predicted by the proponents of deregulation, load factors increased dramatically when the Board began granting carriers greater pricing flexibility early in 1977. In fact, in 1978 the industry had the biggest year-to-year increase in load factors since the outbreak of the Korean War. Load factors increased further in 1979 largely due to a fifty-eight-day strike at United Airlines and the grounding of the DC-10's; they then fell in 1980 and 1981 as the economy softened, before increasing in 1982 and 1983. Nevertheless, the trunks' load factors in both recession years remained higher than they had been in any year since 1966. Indeed, load factors in the 1980–82 period were substantially higher than in either of the two preceding recessions. (Figure 8.1 shows trunk airline load factors since 1950 along with an indication of the approximate timing of the six recessions that occurred during that period.) In the recent recessionary period average load factors ranged between 57 and 59 percent. In the preceding recession years of 1974–75, load factors averaged only 54 to 56 percent. Yet during part of that period fuel allocations decreased airline operations which

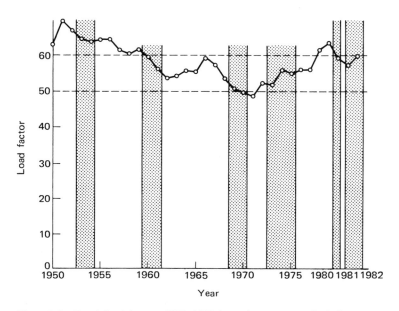

Figure 8.1   Trunk load factors, 1950–1982 (recession years are shaded)

undoubtedly affected load factors. Also the government allocations interrupted gasoline supplies for consumers, making intercity automobile travel frought with uncertainty and thereby increasing air travel demand. Moreover in the 1969–70 recession load factors hovered around 50 percent.

Exogenous factors, particularly the sharp increases in fuel prices in 1974–75 and again in 1979, have undoubtedly increased the equilibrium load factors. Arguably these changes would eventually have led to regulatory policy changes that would have increased load factors had traditional CAB regulation continued. However, the CAB may have attempted to control capacity directly through collusive agreements or route moratoriums, rather than alter the economic incentives facing the airlines by changing its fare policies. Thus we conclude that the improvements in load factors observed since the mid-1970s can be in large part attributed to the fundamental changes in pricing philosophy associated with deregulation.

It is also important to note that the distribution of load factors across markets of differing size and distance also reflects improved efficiency. Under regulation fares in long-haul markets were deliberately set too high; moreover fares did not reflect cost differences inherent in serving markets of different densities. Consequently load factors tended to be depressed in denser, long-haul markets. It was in those markets that the gap between the regulated fare and the competitive equilibrium fare was the largest. In addition analyses of regulated markets showed that increases in the number of airlines authorized to serve a market increased the extent to which such a fare gap induced added service competition (and hence lower load factors).

The positive effect of the number of carriers on market load factors under regulation is readily explained. Where only a single carrier was allowed to serve, it would pay to add flights only up to the point where the added market demand was enough to cover the cost of the added flight. However, when more than one carrier operates in a market, each views its own demand curve as being more elastic than the demand curve for the market as a whole. In that case a carrier can assume that if it were to increase the number of flights in the market, it wold attract business from the other carriers in the market as well as increasing the quantity demanded in the market as a whole. Thus each carrier acting independently will tend to expand capacity beyond the amount a monopolist would provide. These models predict that at any regulated price, capacity would be expanded to the point where profits would be driven toward zero as more and more carriers are added to the market.[1]

Douglas and Miller (1974) examined these relationships between load factors and market distance, density, and competitiveness using data for 1969. They found that load factors fell with market distance. This is contrary to the positive relationship that would be consistent with welfare-maximizing equilibrium but consistent with the theory that regulation induced carriers to offer excess capacity. This was taken as strong evidence that CAB fare regulation was inducing market distortions.

To see how these relationships have been altered by deregulation, our analysis compares Douglas and Miller's estimated relationships with our own estimates for later years using a similar sample of markets. We estimated the relationship for the year ending June 1981, because this is the first full year for which the airlines had essentially complete pricing freedom. To provide an intermediate observation, we also estimated the relationship for 1976. This observation follows the completion of the *DPFI* reforms of the structure of fares and precedes the liberalization of fares that began in early 1977. (The parameter estimates are contined in table 8.1.)

Before turning to a detailed discussion of our findings, it must be noted that these regression results reflect changes other than deregulation across the sample years. Douglas and Miller's 1969 data cover a recession year

Table 8.1   Equations explaining market average load factors, 1969, 1976, and year ending June 1981

C	Ln (distance)	Ln (passengers per day)	Ln (market con- centration)	$\bar{R}^2$
1981—324 observations[a]				
0.130	0.026	0.045	0.061	0.33
(3.9)	(5.1)	(8.1)	(4.4)	
1976—324 observations[a]				
0.123	0.029	0.047	0.126	0.29
(3.2)	(5.9)	(2.8)	(8.2)	
1969—351 observations[b]				
0.257	−0.019	0.073	−0.146	0.14
	(1.8)	(7.0)	(5.5)	

Note: Dependent variable = average load factor; t-statistics in parentheses.
a. In the 1976 and 1981 equations we used the Herfindahl index of market concentration.
b. The 1969 equation is taken from Douglas and Miller (1974), p. 53. They used the number of carriers serving as their measure of market concentration.

when load factors averaged only about 50 percent. A recovery year, 1976 showed load factors of about 56 percent, and 1980–81 was a recessionary period, with average load factors about 58 percent.

Comparison of the statistical results shows that the relationships have indeed changed over time, much as predicted. In both 1976 and 1981 load factors rise with distance, rather than fall as they did in 1969. Thus the perverse result noted by Douglas and Miller has reversed itself. It is noteworthy that the distance coefficients in 1976 and 1981 are quite similar. Because the *DPFI* held fares above costs in long-haul markets, we would have expected load factors in 1981 to have risen in long-haul markets relative to short hauls. This would have been reflected as an increase in the distance coefficient. However, there was a recession in 1981, which had a disproportionate impact on discretionary demand. Discretionary traffic is relatively more important in long-haul markets. This may explain why the coefficient did not increase in 1981 as one would expect. It may also be a contributing factor to the negative distance coefficient in 1969, which was also a recession year. Nevertheless, the changes made to the structure of fares in the *DPFI* brought the fare-distance taper much more closely into line with the competitive market outcome than the taper that had existed prior to the *DPFI*.

Other exogenous changes that might have altered the distance-load factor relationship have had mixed effects: the introduction of wide-bodied aircraft reduced the costs of serving long-haul markets relative to short-haul markets and should have caused load factors to fall in these markets, *ceteris paribus.* On the other hand, increases in fuel prices should have caused load factors to rise in all markets, and particularly in long-haul markets, thus reinforcing the pattern observed.

The passenger variable is also quite similar in both 1976 and 1981, although it is substantially smaller than in 1969. The introduction of wide-bodied aircraft in the early 1970s increased economies of scale in dense markets, just as it reduced the costs in long-haul markets. Given our theories of airline behavior under regulation, we would therefore have expected load factors to have fallen in dense markets relative to thin ones. The decline in the passenger coefficient between 1969 and 1976 is consistent with this. However, the *DPFI*-based fares in 1976 did not reflect cost differences caused by size differences across markets. Deregulation of fares would thus be predicted to cause load factors to rise (and fares to fall) in large markets relative to small markets. We expected this to be reflected as an increase in the passenger coefficient.

Since the *DPFI* there has not been a significant change in the effect of density and distance on market load factors. However, there has been a substantial change in market structure's effect on load factor. Load factors have risen in less concentrated markets. In 1969 and 1976 our estimates indicate that doubling the market concentration variable (e.g., going from two equal-sized firms in the market to a monopoly) would increase load factor in the market by eight to ten points.[2] In 1981 the estimated differential is about four points. This represents a substantial reduction in the difference between load factors in unconcentrated markets and more concentrated markets.

In summary, we find that load factors have been high by historical standards since the CAB began to liberalize fare regulation in 1977. Moreover the available evidence on the changes across markets provides confirmation of the theories that gaps between CAB regulated fares and competitive fare levels would be reflected in carrier load factors.

Other Operational Changes

In addition to increasing load factors, carriers have added seats to their aircraft, reconfigured their route networks to increase utilization, retired inefficient aircraft, and taken steps to increase employee productivity. These changes have also contributed to the increased productivity of the formerly regulated carriers.

Aircraft Utilization

One of the goals of the carriers' route realignments has been to increase the number of hours per day aircraft are operated. Table 8.2 shows changes in aircraft utilization rates calculated for a baseline fleet of fuel-efficient aircraft. We focus our analysis on fuel-efficient aircraft because this helps control for the effects of phasing out B-707s and DC-8s and also controls for cyclical variations in the use of relatively inefficient aircraft.[3] In the period following the Board's liberalization of its fare policies, carriers offered increased service in the markets they had authority to serve. Consequently between 1976 and 1978 average aircraft utilization rates increased sharply. Aircraft utilization rates declined in 1980 and apparently in the first six months of 1981. The utilization rates nevertheless have remained substantially higher during the recent recession than in the 1974–75 recession for the trunk airlines. Overall, it appears that postderegulation utilization rates are from one-half to one hour greater per day. The local service airlines seem to have experienced a somewhat similar increase in utilization.

It is to be expected that utilization rates would increase during the expansionary period and fall as traffic contracted. Airlines will fully utilize their efficient aircraft during peak periods even when demand is relatively soft. During periods of relatively weak traffic, most of the cutbacks in flights will occur in the off-peak periods, thereby reducing utilization rates. Based on the industry's experience during 1978 and 1979, the ability to offer reduced fares during off-peak periods can be expected to allow carriers to achieve significant increases in utilization when the economy resumes its expansion. The airlines' ability to enter new routes has probably also increased utilization. As mentioned earlier, carriers have taken steps to reduce seasonal variations of their route networks by diversifying the kinds of markets served.

It must be noted that the airlines' increased emphasis on developing connecting banks has probably tended to limit the observed improvement in utilization rates. If twenty aircraft arrive within an hour of one another and are to exchange passengers, and then proceed to their ultimate destinations, the first plane that arrives cannot depart until the other nineteen have arrived. In contrast, Southwest, which concentrates on serving point-to-point (as opposed to connecting) passengers, strives both to deplane incoming passengers and board outgoing passengers within ten minutes. A connecting-bank operation is antithetical to such rapid turnaround of equipment.[4] Thus the improvements in utilization due to the other factors mentioned have probably been greater than our statistics imply.

Table 8.2 Airlines' aircraft and use, 1971–1981

	Trunks				Share of ASMs wide-bodied aircraft	Locals			
	Load factors (percent)	Average seating density (seats per aircraft)	Aircraft utilization rates (block hours per day)	Average on-flight trip length (miles)		Load factors (percent)	Average seating density (seats per aircraft)	Aircraft utilization rates (block hours per day)	Average on-flight trip length (miles)
1971	48.3	158.9	8.6	786	12.0	45.3	96.9	8.6	286
1972	52.4	177.9	8.6	792	17.7	49.2	97.9	8.8	292
1973	51.9	182.7	9.2	797	25.0	48.7	98.1	9.1	303
1974	55.7	186.8	8.0	795	29.0	52.7	98.0	9.0	307
1975	54.8	192.2	8.7	810	30.8	51.7	98.1	8.8	314
1976	55.8	192.6	8.9	819	33.5	52.9	98.9	8.7	320
1977	55.9	195.4	9.5	820	34.3	53.9	99.2	9.0	324
1978	61.2	202.9	9.7	837	34.5	58.6	99.7	9.2	339
1979	63.2	206.4	10.3	854	32.8	58.7	102.3	9.2	386
1980	58.3	207.5	9.6	884	35.9	54.8	105.7	9.2	420
Year ending 6/30/81	57.5	209.1	9.2	899	37.0	55.0	105.9	9.0	437

Source: *Form 41.* Based on use of efficient aircraft, defined as B-737, B-727-200, DC-9-30, and wide-bodied aircraft. The averages were based on available seat mile shares.

Stage Lengths

Both the trunks and the local service carriers have increased the proportion of their flights in long-haul segments. Table 8.2 shows that the trunks increased their stage lengths by about 10 percent following deregulation. On an annual basis the trunks' average stage lengths have increased by 2.5 percent per year since the passage of the ADA, as compared to 1 percent per year before. The table shows that local service airline average stage lengths have increased by about one-third since deregulation, which is nearly 10 percent per year.

Fleet Mix

The trunks have substantially reduced the amount of service provided in their fuel-inefficient aircraft. Service in the B-707 and the B-727-100 has declined from 25 to 15 percent between 1978 and 1981 (see table 8.3). In fact the number of available seat miles (ASMs) provided in these inefficient aircraft declined by more than 35 percent even though total ASMs increased by 8 percent to 284 billion.[5] High fuel prices are the primary reason for these retirements, but undoubtedly the more competitive environment was a factor in the airlines' decision as well.

Seating Density

Another step airlines have taken to improve productivity has been to increase the number of seats per aircraft. For the trunks, seating density rose sharply in the early 1970s (see table 8.2). Between 1971 and 1973 average seats per aircraft rose 15 percent, with most of the growth occurring between 1971 and 1972. Then between 1973 and 1977 growth slowed considerably: average seats per aircraft increased only 7 percent over the four-year period. Seating density increased somewhat more rapidly immediately following fare liberalization but has slowed in recent years.[6] Seating density has grown by 7 percent between 1977 and the year ending June 1981, with most of the growth coming between 1977 and 1978.

Employee Productivity

Chapter 5 discussed at length the substantial differences that currently exist between the pay and worker productivity of the large, established airlines and the newer, smaller airlines.

Deregulation has spawned much new entry into markets both by established airlines and their lower cost competitors. In addition traffic growth has slowed, and this has put added pressures on carriers to scale back their operations and control their costs. We would expect that com-

Table 8.3 Domestic trunk and local aircraft fleets (percent distribution of available seat miles)

	1978[a]			1981[b]		
	Trunks	Locals	Total	Trunks	Locals	Total
Wide-bodied passenger aircraft						
Four-engine (B-747)	8.9	—	8.0	9.0	—	7.9
Three-engine (DC-10 and L-1011)	25.1	—	22.8	26.8	—	23.4
Two-engine (A-300)	0.2	—	0.2	1.8	—	1.6
Total wide-bodied turbofans	34.2	—	31.0	37.6	—	32.8
Regular-bodied passenger aircraft						
Four-engine—nonstretched (B-707-100B/300B/C, B-720, DC-8-50/62);	10.5	—	9.5	4.3	—	3.8
stretched (DC-8-61/63)	4.2	—	3.8	3.2	—	2.8
Total four-engine	14.7	—	13.3	7.5	—	6.6
Three-engine—first generation (B-727-100);	14.3	1.2	13.0	10.8	6.4	10.2
second generation (B-727-200)	28.1	1.9	25.7	37.9	5.4	33.7
Total three-engine	42.4	3.1	38.7	48.7	11.8	43.9
Two-engine—first generation (DC-9-10 and BAC-1-11);	0.6	23.0	2.7	—	15.4	2.0
second generation (B-737-200, DC-9-30/50/80 and F-28)	7.0	65.3	12.5	6.2	70.1	14.4
Total two-engine	7.6	88.3	15.2	6.2	85.5	16.3
Total regular-bodied turbofans	64.7	91.4	67.2	62.4	97.3	66.8
Turbojets (B-707-100/300, B-720, DC-8-10/20/30)	1.1	—	1.0	—	—	—
Turboprops	—	8.6	0.8	—	2.7	0.3
Total regular-bodied	65.8	100.0	100.0	62.4	100.0	67.2
Total passenger aircraft	100.0	100.0	100.0	100.0	100.0	100.0

Note: Table based on computerized program used to run the CAB's *Aircraft Operating Cost and Performance Report*. Aircraft of very limited utilization are excluded; table accounts for over 98 percent of total aircraft hours.
a. Twelve months ending June 30, 1978.
b. Twelve months ending June 30, 1981.

petitive pressures will eventually force an equalization of pay and productivity across airlines. However, our examination of work rules, flight crew utilization, and total employment indicates that through 1981 the larger airlines have had limited success in reducing their labor costs. Since 1981 there has been a substantial increase in labor productivity (see U.S. CAB 1984).

United Airlines and Western were able to reduce the crew complement of B-737 aircraft from three down to two pilots. At a number of carriers there has been a liberalization of work rules to allow carriers to increase the flying hours of their flight personnel. Increases came largely from reductions in the minimum guarantees of pilot compensation for the time they are on duty but are not actually flying. During the 1982–83 recession there have been some salary reductions as well as relaxation of work rules at a number of airlines.

However, these changes in labor agreements have come slowly. Flight crew contracts were not changed until well into 1981. Consequently their productivity changes are not entirely reflected in our productivity estimates. For example, data on block hours per cockpit crew member in table 8.4 show that between 1977 and 1981 there were no significant increases in the average productivity of the cockpit crew.[7] Similarly there has not been an increase in the seat block hours of cabin attendants.

The trends in total employment and output indicate that the trunk airlines have not experienced rapid labor productivity growth between 1977 and 1981, whereas the local service airlines have (table 8.5). In that period the trunk airlines' available ton miles (a measure of output capacity) per employee have increased only 3 percent. Of course, since load factors increased considerably during this period, productivity in terms of revenue miles would show a larger increase. Total employment of the trunks has actually declined about 1 percent since 1977. (Employment increased through 1979 and has declined since.) Between 1977 and 1981 the local service airlines' available ton miles per employee increased about 27 percent while employment was increasing nearly 42 percent (see table 8.5).

Between 1981 and 1983 both the trunk and local service airlines experienced a substantial increase in employee productivity. The trunks' productivity, which had increased at an annual rate of less than 1 percent between 1977 and 1981, accelerated to a rate of more than 6 percent per year. The rate of change for local service carriers also increased in that later period, although the improvement was not as large as that of the trunks.

Neither the trunks nor the locals have experienced labor productivity

Table 8.4 Annual block hours per cockpit crew member, 1977–1980

	1977	1978	1979	1980	1981
Trunks					
Northwest	641	712	685	710	695
Delta	594	609	605	605	579
Braniff	549	527	504	582	521
United	559	584	492	555	517
Trans World	576	595	581	550	497
Eastern	516	519	518	509	512
Continental	489	468	487	496	446
Western	522	580	535	486	534
American	533	549	565	478	494
Pan Am[a]	681	674	643	696	588
Total	556	569	547	547	527
Locals					
Texas International	616	602	620	620	676
USAir	590	578	590	595	558
Frontier	601	551	593	589	594
Piedmont	666	556	490	539	591
Ozark	649	619	474	512	607
Republic[a]	568	556	590	539	547
Total	599	578	542	565	601

Source: *Form 41*. The average number of block hours per cockpit crew members were derived by first multiplying for each carrier the block hours for each aircraft type times the number of crew members required. This was summed over all aircraft types and the total number of crew block hours divided by the number of crew members (full-time equivalents).
a. Pan Am includes National; Republic is an aggregate of North Central, Southern, and Hughes Airwest.

gains that approach the levels attained in the 1960s when jet aircraft were coming into the fleets. Between 1960 and 1970 the trunk airlines' labor productivity increased 142 percent, whereas the locals experienced an increase of roughly 200 percent. In the first half of the 1970s labor productivity growth slowed substantially. Between 1970 and 1975 labor productivity increased only 14 percent for the trunks and 11 percent for the locals. During this period the route moratorium slowed the growth of the airlines' networks, which undoubtedly slowed productivity growth.

Comparison of the productivity changes since deregulation (see table 8.6) indicates that relative to the early 1970s, the trunks have experienced much slower labor productivity growth as their share of industry traffic shrinks. The locals have experienced accelerated productivity growth as their share of the industry has expanded.

Table 8.5 Industry employment and worker productivity (full- and part-time)

	Trunks				Local service carriers			
	Available ton miles (millions)	Number of employees	Available ton miles per employee (thousands)	Percent change in output per employee	Available ton miles (millions)	Number of employees	Available ton miles per employee (thousands)	Percent change in output per employee
1957	6,543	132,878	49.2		171	8,251	20.7	
1958	6,721	133,502	50.3	2.2	185	8,928	20.7	0.0
1959	7,633	139,337	54.8	8.9	238	10,603	22.4	8.2
1960	8,622	146,739	58.8	7.3	282	12,012	23.5	4.9
1961	9,645	145,739	66.2	12.6	329	13,146	25.0	6.4
1962	11,040	146,829	75.2	13.6	389	14,071	27.6	10.4
1963	12,711	150,800	84.3	12.1	441	14,978	29.4	6.5
1964	14,915	159,995	93.2	10.6	504	15,810	31.9	8.5
1965	17,990	173,642	103.6	11.2	585	17,114	34.2	7.2
1966	21,058	195,306	107.8	4.1	761	19,382	39.3	14.9
1967	27,800	228,808	121.5	12.7	1,024	21,865	46.8	19.1
1968	33,877	253,603	133.6	10.0	1,470	24,404	60.2	28.6
1969	38,386	269,884	142.2	6.4	1,859	26,266	70.8	17.6
1970	39,827	267,159	149.1	4.9	2,147	26,248	81.8	15.5
1971	42,524	258,455	164.5	10.3	2,195	25,708	85.4	4.4
1972	43,581	257,403	169.3	2.9	2,264	26,563	85.2	(0.2)
1973	46,126	270,521	170.5	0.7	2,534	28,386	89.3	4.8
1974	43,568	263,369	165.4	(3.0)	2,578	29,312	88.0	(1.5)
1975	43,798	256,989	170.4	3.0	2,620	28,948	90.5	2.8
1976	45,822	258,764	177.1	3.9	2,929	30,688	95.4	5.4
1977	48,431	265,777	182.2	2.9	3,269	31,402	104.1	9.1
1978	49,559	273,837	181.0	(0.6)	3,685	35,078	105.1	1.0
1979	53,226	294,930	180.5	(0.2)	4,269	40,794	104.6	(0.5)
1980	53,423	289,829	184.3	2.1	4,906	41,472	118.3	13.1
1981	50,504	273,704	184.5	0.0	5,331	44,437	120.0	1.4
1982[a]	49,993	250,963	199.2	8.0	5,451	40,334	135.1	12.6
1983	50,652	243,209	208.3	4.5	6,271	42,294	148.3	9.8

Source: *Form 41*. Includes international and nonscheduled services.

a. Texas International (local) merged with Continental (trunk) in November 1982. Texas International data for 1982 are included with the trunks.

Table 8.6   Estimates of annual rates of productivity change, 1971–1981 (excludes capital)

	Trunks			Locals		
	Total change	Change due to load factor	Change due to other factors	Total change	Change due to load factors	Change due to other factors
1971–72	13.0	9.1	3.9	7.1	7.9	−.7
1972–73	.3	.7	−.4	6.0	1.8	4.2
1973–74	9.9	17.5	−7.6	10.3	14.4	−4.1
1974–75	−5.7	−15.3	9.6	−11.1	−16.8	5.8
1975–76	11.0	9.0	2.0	14.8	7.7	7.1
1976–77	2.3	.2	2.1	4.7	−.6	5.3
1977–78	11.1	7.6	3.5	10.0	7.8	2.2
1978–79	6.1	4.8	1.3	8.5	2.5	6.0
1979–80	−5.3	−8.8	3.5	1.4	−4.5	5.9
1980–81	−.6	−2.7	2.1	6.4	−.1	6.5
1971–81	4.6	2.6	2.0	6.1	2.3	3.8
1971–75	4.7	3.2	1.5	3.5	2.2	1.4
1975–81	4.5	2.1	2.4	2.9	2.4	5.5
1975–78	8.1	5.6	2.5	9.9	5.0	4.9
1978–81	.5	−1.8	2.3	5.7	−.5	6.1

Source: Appendix I, Cost and Yield Indexes. The changes reported are from the first quarter of the first year to the first quarter of the second year.

Estimates of Productivity Gains

This section assesses the changes in productivity that have occurred under deregulation and the extent to which they are due to the changes in airline operations described in the preceding sections. To measure productivity, we compare changes in average costs with changes in average input prices from 1971 through the second quarter of 1981. If airline output, service quality, and productivity are all constant, average airline costs would increase at the same rate as input prices, because the amount of inputs required to produce the given amount of output remains the same. When productivity is increasing, or the quality of service is declining, fewer inputs are required to produce each unit of output, so average costs increase less than the increase in input prices.[8]

We calculate the changes in productivity (*PR*) as follows:

$$PR_t = \frac{CR_t/CR_{t-1}}{P_t/P_{t-1}},$$

where CR_t is the average cost per revenue ton mile in period t and P_t is an index of airline input prices in period t. We also developed an index of productivity based on changes in the cost per available ton mile:

$$PA_t = \frac{AR_t/AR_{t-1}}{P_t/P_{t-1}},$$

where AR_t is the cost per available ton mile in the period. The difference between the total productivity measure and the ATM productivity measure is approximately equal to the productivity change due to increased load factor. It would be equal if there are no additional costs associated with increasing the number of passengers on a flight.

The input price index used as the basis against which to compare changes in average costs is a weighted average of prices airlines paid for variable inputs where the weights are each input's share of costs in 1978. Neither the input price index nor the measures of costs used in the price index include depreciation or a return to capital. Since capital costs represent approximately 15 percent of the carriers' expenses, their omission should not seriously bias the results.[9]

It must be emphasized that this relationship between average costs and input prices is an inexact measure of productivity changes, because there have been changes in convenience and quality of air service. Indeed, the product itself changes as travelers shift from large to small markets or from short to long markets. (Historically the cost savings observed in the airline industry have reflected changes in the length of passenger trips, as well as the pure productivity improvements brought about by the new aircraft technologies.) The magnitude of the bias due to ignoring changes in service quality is not certain. Overall, it would appear that service convenience has remained essentially unchanged for the average traveler (see chapter 7). There has probably been a slight decline in on-flight comfort because of higher seating densities and higher load factors.

Our calculation of productivity change since 1971 are presented in table 8.6.[10] In comparing the productivity changes across years in this period, it must be kept in mind that these changes are very sensitive to changes in the overall growth of the economy and industry. In the period covered by the table, the economy experienced three recessions: 1973 to 1975, 1980, and 1981 to 1982. As noted earlier, industry load factors tend to decline in recessions. We would also expect other operational changes to occur as well, which would tend to decrease the utilization of capital and labor and thus reduce productivity growth. To provide a clear picture of how productivity has been changing, we therefore calculate the changes in productivity for a number of alternative time periods and show the year-to-year changes in productivity.

The table reports the productivity gains for the entire period, 1971 to

1981, as well as for several subperiods. We divide the decade into pre-1975 and post-1975 periods since this creates subperiods for which the end points are recession years or early recovery years. The trunks experienced productivity growth of 4.7 percent per year prior to 1975 and 4.5 percent after 1975. Although the growth in productivity was about the same in these periods, the reason for it differed. Prior to 1975 load factor accounted for 3.2 percent per year of growth, and other factors accounted for only 1.5 percent. After 1975 load factor accounted for 2.1 percent, and other factors accounted for 2.4 percent.

It might at first seem surprising that load factor increases did not account for a more substantial share of productivity growth after 1975, because the deregulation of fares led to sharply increasing load factors. However, examination of figure 8.1 shows that those increases in load factors were partly reversed in the recession years of 1980 and 1981. Table 8.6 breaks down the post-1975 period further, and we see that indeed load factor caused productivity growth of 5.6 percent per year between 1975 and 1978 but caused a decline in productivity growth of -1.8 percent per year after 1978.

The significant difference between the pre-1975 and post-1975 periods is in the productivity gains due to other factors, which increased from 1.5 to 2.4 percent per year. These productivity gains appear to be relatively stable in the post-1975 period.

The locals experienced sharply improved productivity growth in the post-1975 period: 7.9 versus 3.5 percent per year. Like the trunks they experienced a big jump in productivity due to load factor increases in the 1975 to 1978 period, and a decline after 1978. They also experienced an increase in productivity due to other factors, but it was much larger than for the trunks, averaging 5.5 percent per year after 1975.

Productivity estimates using a measure of total factor productivity have recently been reported by Caves, Christensen, and Tretheway (1982). They find that total factor productivity has increased by 4.9 percent per year since 1975 for the trunks through 1980 and 6.3 percent per year for the locals. Their estimates would have been a bit lower had they included 1981. It appears our estimates would have been a bit lower had we included a capital cost component, since Caves et al. generally get somewhat lower estimates of total factor productivity than we get for variable inputs.[11]

Conclusion

Both the trunks and the locals have made operational changes that have increased productivity since deregulation. As noted at the beginning of this chapter, load factors rose to the highest levels in the late 1970s, following the liberalization of discount air fares. Although load factors declined from those peaks, they remain substantially higher than in the preceding recessions of the 1970s. Changes in other operational factors appear to have contributed to an increased rate of productivity growth that has continued right through the recessions of the 1980s. Increased utilization of aircraft, increased seating density, increased stage lengths, and accelerated retirement of inefficient aircraft appear to have resulted from deregulation and have contributed to a higher growth rate in productivity.

Some of the other operational characteristics examined did not contribute to productivity growth. The proportion of wide-bodied aircraft in the trunk airlines' fleets stabilized at around the middle of the decade. The introduction of these aircraft undoubtedly accelerated productivity growth in the first half of the 1970s but contributed very little to productivity growth after 1975. It also appears that the airlines have generally been unsuccessful in negotiating labor contracts that improve workers' productivity. We find, for example, no increase in cockpit crew utilization through 1981. Consequently between 1977 and 1981 the productivity of the trunk airline's work forces improved only 3 percent. Although the locals were also not successful in renegotiating contracts, they experienced about a 27 percent increase in worker productivity. Since 1981 there is some evidence that the combination of renegotiated labor contracts and the economic expansion has led to substantial increases in labor productivity.

The significance of the various operational changes in terms of their effect on productivity clearly varied over time. Prior to 1978–79 the airlines operated in a growing economy and were given new freedoms to offer discount fares but were essentially constrained from altering their route networks. After 1978, the airlines did have the freedom to alter their routes, though in 1979 when fuel prices shot up, the economy began its decline. In this period the major gains in productivity appear to stem from increased stage lengths and the retirement of inefficient aircraft. (Seating densities increased for both the trunks and the locals, but the trunk airlines' growth rate slowed to the levels of around the mid-1970s.) Load factors and aircraft utilization actually declined in this period but not by enough to offset fully the gains in productivity from other sources.

Although the fleet mix was changing and stage lengths were increasing while the industry was regulated, the changes since 1978 were undoubtedly accelerated by deregulation. The freedom to exit and enter routes provided carriers with unprecedented flexibility to design their route systems. Moreover the increased competition from local service carriers and new entrants increased the rate at which trunk carriers grounded their inefficient aircraft and increased the stage lengths of their flights using three-engine aircraft.

Thus our findings showed that rapid productivity growth occurred immediately following the liberalization of discounts. This growth slowed for the trunks in the recession-ridden years 1979 to 1982, largely because of falling load factors and aircraft utilization. The locals, in contrast, sustained high rates of productivity growth despite the recession. It should also be noted that another reason why the average productivity growth for the industry has been growing is that the more efficient airlines are growing the most rapidly and accounting for an increasing share of industry traffic.

Chapter 9

Analyses of Airline Competitive Behavior

Airline markets are highly concentrated compared with markets in other industries. Although regulation clearly contributed to the market structure, proponents of an end to entry restrictions recognized that in most markets, economies of aircraft size would limit the extent of deconcentration. Nevertheless, they argued that the ability of airlines to enter and exit easily would prevent fares from exceeding the cost of service. Our test of this view shows that markets are not perfectly contestable, so that carriers in concentrated markets are able to charge somewhat higher fares than carriers in less concentrated markets.

We also present evidence showing how the nature of market rivalry has changed. The restrictions imposed by regulation led the airlines to rely mainly on flight frequency as the means for competing. The effect of market concentration on market load factors has declined under deregulation. In fact, under regulation the leading carrier in the market tended to have the highest load factor. This tendency encouraged carriers to engage in schedule rivalry. We show that a carrier with a small share of flights in a market now can offer lower fares to counter the advantage of its larger rivals. We also find that a carrier's load factor on a route tends to be positively related to the number of connecting flights the carrier is providing.

A Test of the Contestability Hypothesis

The theory of contestability provides the basis for the hypothesis underlying deregulation—that airlines cannot exercise market power even when there is little head-to-head competition among incumbent airlines in particular markets. The theory specifies conditions under which the threat of entry into markets is sufficiently powerful that firms will price competitively regardless of whether the market is structurally competitive or noncompetitive. Essentially, firms must be able to engage in "hit-and-run" entry into markets without incurring losses due to sunk costs. This requires that (1) all factors of production are mobile among markets, (2) consumers are willing and able to switch quickly among suppliers, and (3) existing firms are unable to change their prices quickly in response to the entry of a new firm. Of course all these extreme conditions are unlikely to exist in any industry. Nevertheless, the theory does provide an alternative view of the competitive process, which may have important implications in industries such as the airlines where factors of production are highly mobile among markets.

In some ways the airline industry approximates the conditions for contestability, but it does not conform to the conditions in every respect. The strongest argument that airline markets may be contestable is the high degree of mobility of aircraft. Moreover at most airports the requisite ticket counter and gate space are readily available for lease by airlines.

Despite the apparent factor mobility, other sunk costs might exist. Passengers exhibit a preference for incumbent carriers' flights because the incumbents' schedules and service reliability are better known than the entrants' until the latter have been in the market for awhile. Start-up costs and advertising therefore represent a sunk cost associated with entering the market. Also the condition that incumbents' prices must be relatively "sticky" is not in general met. In many cases incumbent airlines respond immediately to meet a new competitor's lower fares. In some cases airlines have actually pledged that they would meet the fares of their competitors. Thus the assumption that fares are rigid is clearly not applicable in the airline industry.

Nevertheless, we can focus on the behavioral issue of whether fare-setting practices are consistent with the contestability hypothesis. If airline markets behave as though they were contestable, then we would find that fares are independent of the competitive structure of a market and depend only on variables that determine the costs of serving the market. (A finding that fares depend on the structure of markets after controlling for differences in costs, shows that markets are not perfectly contestable. It does not, of course, rule out the possibility that potential competition exerts some influence on pricing.)

When testing for contestability, it is important whether the competitive structure of a market is itself jointly determined with the fares and traffic in a market (i.e., is endogenous) or is determined only by other factors (i.e., is exogenous). In the long run technology and demand are the key determinants of market structure. Technology determines how many flights an airline must have to have competitive costs, whereas demand determines how many firms of efficient size can coexist in the market. Hence structures would be jointly determined with the volume of travel. However, structure may not be uniquely determined by technology and traffic volume. If average costs are flat over a wide range of outputs, there may be a wide range of viable scales of operation and hence a wide range of possible industry structures. The observed structure may thus reflect a history of random shocks that determine the relative sizes of the existing firms. In this case industry structure can only be bounded by economic analysis, and the observed structure is a function of unobserved exogenous variables.

Apart from this problem of indeterminacy of industry structure, there are two additional reasons why the structure of a particular market may be exogenous. First, not much time has passed since CAB regulation was relaxed, so the structure in particular markets (as well as of the industry) imposed by the CAB has probably not yet been fully eroded. Although CAB decisions were endogenous in the sense that the agency probably took many economic factors into account in allocating routes—in particular the number of airlines it allowed in a market depended to some degree on traffic volume—the rapid changes in the industry show that the old network was not a competitive equilibrium and therefore did not completely reflect economic variables.

Second, although the industry is still changing quite rapidly, regulation undoubtedly remains important exogenous factor influencing the structure of both the industry and particular routes. Regulation conferred route structures that contained certain routes that did not dovetail well after deregulation and did not contain routes that did so dovetail. Routes that fit in with the networks of several airlines are likely to be less concentrated than those that fit in with few. Thus markets of a given size may have more or fewer airlines depending on how each market fits in with the air service network.

The proper method for testing the contestability hypothesis, and the statistical results vary depending on whether market structure is assumed to be exogenous or endogenous. We therefore provide estimates using both assumptions. When structure is assumed to be exogenous, we find that fares tend to be higher in more concentrated markets. When structure is assumed to be endogenous, we find fares do not depend on concentration, but there are certain statistical problems that undermine the reliability of this estimate.

We tested to determine which treatment of structure is most appropriate, and found that structure was uncorrelated with the error term in the fare equation, and therefore should be considered exogenous. Graham, Kaplan, and Sibley (1983) tested whether market structures are endogenous or exogenous for a small sample of densely traveled markets during the same period. They also did not reject the hypothesis that structure was exogenously determined. It will be important to retest this hypothesis as the industry continues to evolve, and the influence of CAB regulation on the route system continues to erode.

Market-Cost Model

As we noted in chapter 3, the cost per mile of serving a market declines as the distance and the number of passengers carried (density) increase, and cost increases as the quality of service provided increases. There are several additional factors that explain cost differences among markets that should also be included in a model explaining the costs of serving a market. One is the scarcity of landing rights at certain airports. The Federal Aviation Administration limits operations at four airports: Chicago's O'Hare, Washington National, as well as New York City's Kennedy and La Guardia airports. Carriers therefore can offer fewer flights at these airports than they would in the absence of the FAA's restrictions. Consequently slots have a scarcity value at these airports which will be reflected in the average fares charged in the market serving these airports.

Second, as we discussed previously, the new entrants generally have lower costs than the formerly certificated carriers. Because of this cost advantage, these new entrants tend to set lower fares than the incumbents. The formerly regulated carriers frequently meet these lower fares, even when these fares are below the incumbent's long run average costs.

In summary, we posit that the average cost (C) of serving a passenger in a given market is determined by the market's distance (DIST), its density (PAX), whether it involves service to a slot constrained airport (NY, CHI, WASH), and whether it is served by a newly certificated airline (NEWC). Costs are also influenced by the quality of service, which, in equilibrium, we assume is related to the time sensitivity of passengers (TS). Algebraically,

$$C = C(\text{DIST, PAX, TS, NEWC, CHI, NYC, WASH}).$$

The ability of carriers to set fares above costs is assumed to be a function of market concentration; the greater is market concentration, the higher the fare relative to costs. The relationship between price (P) and cost is

$$P = M(\text{STRUCTURE}) * C$$

where M is the markup which is a function of the competitive structure of the market.

The Equations Explaining Traffic Volume and Market Concentration

The price equation includes two variable that may be jointly determined with price. The number of passengers in a market clearly depends on the level of fares. Therefore it is appropriate to treat passengers as an endogenous variable in estimating the price equation. As noted in the introduction to this section, there is some question as to whether market structure should be treated as an endogenous or exogenous variable. Therefore we estimate the equation both ways and perform a statistical test to determine which assumption best conforms with the behavior of our sample of markets.

In our simultaneous equations estimates we assume that the equation explaining PAX is as follows:

$$PAX = F(P, DIST, INC, POP, TS),$$

where INC represents a measure of income for the travelers in a market, POP represents a measure of the populations of the cities served by the market which should reflect the scale of the market, and TS is the time sensitivity of travelers in the market. This equation is essentially a demand curve for the market.

As noted earlier, structure will depend in the long run on the volume of traffic in markets, the shape of the average cost curve, and how well the market dovetails with airline networks. Thus we have used the following equation to explain structure when it is treated as an endogenous variable:

$$STRUCTURE = F(PAX, DIST, HUB)$$

Market concentration should decline as PAX increases. We have included DIST in this equation because the optimal aircraft size tends to increase with distance, which would imply that concentration should increase as distance increases. The variable HUB is included to reflect how the concentration of a particular market may depend on airline hubbing and networking strategies. Rather than attempt to obtain detailed information in each market, we have introduced a set of airport dummy variables, one for each of the major hub airports. These dummies capture the specific traits of each airport: some serve more carriers than others, some are used as major connecting point by one or more airlines, and some are used relatively more for local service. For two markets that are otherwise the same, one serving a big hub with many airlines is likely to have a lower concentration than a market serving only minor airports. As we describe in the findings section, this model works reasonably well; however, we believe that further study of the determinants of market structure would be useful, especially in view of the continued evolution of route networks.

The Sample and Variables

We estimated the model for explaining price using a sample of all markets in the *O & D Survey* that had at least ten passengers per day in the second quarter of 1981 (i.e., five passengers per day in each direction). Origin and destination markets include any trips listed on a single flight coupon that happened to be included in the sample. In principle such markets range from those serving a pair of large cities with frequent nonstop service, to very small markets between small towns, in which one or more connections may be required. We excluded markets with fewer than five passengers because these markets have too few passengers to provide meaningful observations. We also excluded markets that had only multistop or interline connecting service. It is often impossible to determine the true origin and destination of trips with multiple connections, and pricing in markets with only interline service were potentially greatly affected by the Board's mandatory joint-fare rule (see chapter 6). Finally, we excluded markets involving intra-Alaskan and intra-Hawaiian service because fares in those markets continue to be influenced by residual state or federal control.[1] Based on these criteria, we obtained a sample of 5,053 markets. These markets account for 92 percent of the passenger trips reported in the Board's *O & D Survey* during the period.

The variables used in analysis are calculated as follows:

Price (P).   We measure price by the average yield (fare divided by nonstop mileage) for non-first-class passengers in the market as reported in the *O & D Survey*. This survey reports the actual ticket price for all local trips in the market sample.

Distance (DIST).   Distance is the nonstop distance between cities, which is reported in the *O & D Survey*. Flights that involve stops or connections typically will actually cover longer distances than the nonstop distance. We introduce a circuity variable (CIRC) to determine whether fares are related to circuity. (For example, if connecting passengers pay the sum of local fares, they are paying for the actual distance flown rather than the nonstop distance.) CIRC is equal to the average distance traveled by all travelers in the market divided by nonstop distance. In calculating CIRC, passengers that travel on a single aircraft are assumed to travel the nonstop distance even if the aircraft makes intermediate stops. (Although direct flights involve some circuity, our data do not allow us to determine how much because the intermediate layover point is not known.) The distance of connecting trips is the sum of the nonstop distances between each of the points on the itinerary.

Density (PAX).   Market density is the number of origin and destination passengers that traveled in the sample period as reported in the Board's *O & D Survey*. All passengers are included, except those reporting multiple connections. As noted earlier the true destination of such passengers is usually not known. Although we excluded markets where only interline connections are available, some fraction of trips in the markets included in the sample involves interline connections. For a number of reasons the average fares in a market will depend on the fraction of trips that is interline. First, not all airlines have specific interline fare agreements, so it is more likely that passengers that make interline connections will pay roughly the sum-of-the-local fares than would a passenger who connects on a single airline. Second, many multistop trips are misclassified as single destination trips in the *O & D Survey*. To account for these effects and attempt to estimate their magnitude, we have also included a variable INT that equals the fraction of travelers in a market who make interline connections. INT is the ratio of interline connecting passengers to total passengers, as reported in the CAB's *O & D Survey*.

Time Sensitivity (TS).   The time sensitivity and the demand for convenient service should increase with income. We therefore include an income variable (INC) which is the product of the per capita incomes of the two cities served by each market. We derived estimates of the per capita income of the communities in our sample from the *Survey of Buying Power* published by *Sales and Marketing Magazine* (1981). The product of the income variables, a "gravity model" specification, has often been used in studies of transportation demand. The second proxy for time sensitivity is based on the assumption that passengers traveling on vacation typically are less time sensitive than passengers traveling for other reasons. (Previously we observed that carriers operating in vacation markets tend to provide service in larger aircraft operated at higher load factors.) Therefore we constructed a tourist-market variable (TOUR), which is set equal to one for markets serving Florida and Hawaii, as well as Las Vegas and Reno, Nevada. (The variable is zero otherwise.) Though a continuous variable measuring the proportion of travel in each market would be preferable (i.e., vacation travel vs. business travel), this variable does reflect the qualitative difference between these predominantly tourist markets and other markets.

Slot Restricted Airports.   To account for the FAA's restrictions on four airports, two of which are in New York, we introduced CHI, WASH, a. ' NYC dummy variables independently set equal to one whenever a market serves one of the cities; they are zero otherwise.[2] For example, CHI would equal one for the Kansas City–Chicago market.

Structure.   We measured market concentration by the Herfindahl index (HERF), the sum of the squares of the shares of each firm in the market. For example, if two firms have equal shares, their Herdindahl would be $0.5 = (0.5)^2 + (0.5)^2$. If a market were a monopoly, the Herfindahl index would be one. If there were many carriers in a market, each with a small share of market output, the Herfindahl index would approach zero. In computing carrier shares, we considered only online traffic. Thus, if only 50 percent of the traffic traveled online, but one airline had all the online traffic, the market was considered a monopoly.[3]

Population (POP).   This variable (POP) is the product of the population of the two cities served by each market. This "gravity-model" specification has often been used in studies of transportation demand. The population of each city comes from the *City-County Data Book* published by the U.S. Census Bureau. We used the population for Standard Metropolitan Statistical Area (SMSA) associated with each city when this data was available; otherwise we used city data. For some small towns only county data was available. To help control for the bias caused by using county data for these small towns, we also introduced a county dummy variable which was included whenever the POP variable is used.

Hub.   HUB is a vector of dummy variables, one each for each of the major hub airports. For example, the Houston dummy takes on a value of one for all markets serving Houston and zero otherwise. When a market serves two major hubs the dummy for each hub will equal one. When a market serves none of the major hubs each of these variables will equal zero.

On average there were only eighty-eight passengers per day traveling in our sample of markets. The average Herfindahl is quite high, 0.77, which is the equivalent to 1.3 airlines per market. (For the means and standard deviations of the variables used in the fare equation, see table 9.1.) The least concentrated market had a Herfindahl of 0.17; only eight markets in the sample had a Herfindahl of less that 0.2.[4] Twenty-two percent of the markets were classified as tourist markets, and 6.5 percent of them were served by a newly certificated airline.

Table 9.1   Description of variables (second quarter 1981)

	Mean	Standard deviation
Distance (DIST)	960	728
Passengers (PAX)	7,910	2,687
Herfindahl (HERF)	0.778	0.246
Tourist (TOUR)	0.224	0.417
Income (INC)	60.55	13.23
Newly Certificated (NEWC)	0.065	0.247
New York City (NYC)	0.029	0.168
Chicago (CHI)	0.042	0.200
Washington (WASH)	0.031	0.173
Interline (INT)	0.170	0.223
Circuity (CIRC)	1.099	0.136

Source: *O & D Survey*.

The Results

Our estimates of the price equation appear in tables 9.2 and 9.3. (The equations are estimated with the variables in logarithms.) We estimated the relationship for each quarter of 1981. The results are quite similar, so the text will describe only the results for the second quarter. The results for the second quarter are presented in equations 1 through 5. To serve as a point of reference, equation 1 provides OLS estimates of the fare equation. Equations 2 and 3 assume PAX is endogenous and HERF exogenous. Both PAX and HERF are endogenous in equations 4 and 5.

In general, the estimated effects of the variables expected to explain costs were of the expected sign and were stable across equations. (The PAX and HERF coefficients do change as described later in this section.) All are statistically significant, indicating that our estimates reflect more than just a random relationship. The average yield per mile falls dramatically with distance. The estimated point elasticity is just under 0.5, which indicates that average fare per mile fell 5 percent for every 10 percent increase in distance.

On average, tourist markets had fares that were between 8 and 10 percent lower than nontourist markets. In markets where incomes were relatively high, fares tended to be higher. Specifically, in markets where INC was one standard deviation below the mean, fares were from 1 to 2 percent lower than fares in cities where INC was one standard deviation above the mean. Both of these findings suggest that average fares do vary depending on the time sensitivity of the travelers in the market.

Compared to similar markets, fares were more than 5 percent higher in markets serving New York and roughly 4 percent higher in markets serving

Table 9.2 Equations explaining the relationship between market structure and fares, 1981 (second quarter)

Equation number	INTERCEPT	LNDIST	LNPAX	$\widehat{LNPAX}$	LNHERF	$\widehat{LNHERF}$	TOUR	LNINC	NEWC	NYC	CHI	WASH	INT	TCIRC	$\bar{R}^2$
OLSQ															
(1)	8.118	−0.491 (0.003)	−0.052 (0.002)		0.037 (0.006)		−0.095 (0.005)	0.071 (0.008)	−0.176 (0.009)	0.090 (0.012)	0.063 (0.012)	0.053			0.883
2 SLSQ: passengers jointly determined with fares															
(2)	8.041	−0.483 (0.003)		−0.021 (0.003)	0.086 (0.008)		−0.096 (0.005)	0.053 (0.008)	−0.212 (0.010)	0.062 (0.013)	0.040 (0.020)	0.041 (0.018)			0.868
(3)	8.176	−0.493 (0.003)		−0.013 (0.003)	0.059 (0.008)		−0.077 (0.005)	0.039 (0.026)	−0.219 (0.010)	0.032 (0.013)	0.048 (0.011)	0.039 (0.012)	0.251 (0.011)	0.057 (0.146)	0.861
2 SLSQ: passengers and Herfindahl jointly determined with fares															
(4)	8.381	−0.497 (0.004)		−0.041 (0.005)		−0.045 (0.029)	−0.104 (0.006)	0.040 (0.009)	−0.213 (0.010)	0.081 (0.014)	0.053 (0.011)	0.045 (0.013)			0.861
(5)	8.477	−0.507 (0.004)		−0.029 (0.005)		−0.055 (0.028)	−0.083 (0.005)	0.027 (0.008)	−0.220 (0.010)	0.047 (0.014)	0.060 (0.011)	0.043 (0.013)	0.268 (0.012)	0.023 (0.146)	0.883

Note: Dependent variable = ln (average fare/mile); there were 5,503 observations. Standard errors are in parentheses. Because estimates were obtained by a two-stage process, the standard errors reported have been adjusted as specified in Maddala (1977, 239).

Table 9.3   Equations explaining the relationship between market structure and fares, 1980–1981

INTER-CEPT	LNDIST	$\widehat{LNPAX}$	LNHERF	NEWCERT	TOUR	LNINC	NYC	CHI	WASH	$\bar{R}^2$
1980, third quarter—5,357 observations										
8.050	−0.481 (0.003)	−0.017 (0.003)	0.080 (0.010)	−0.251 (0.010)	−0.095 (0.006)	0.021 (0.009)	0.055 (0.013)	0.008 (0.011)	0.063 (0.014)	0.889
1980, fourth quarter—5,431 observations										
8.050	−0.463 (0.003)	−0.012 (0.003)	0.078 (0.009)	−0.212 (0.010)	−0.073 (0.005)	0.012 (0.009)	0.046 (0.014)	0.021 (0.011)	0.030 (0.013)	0.870
1981, first quarter—5,042 observations										
7.407	−0.436 (0.003)	−0.003 (0.004)	0.109 (0.010)	−0.205 (0.010)	−0.112 (0.005)	0.060 (0.009)	0.046 (0.014)	0.021 (0.011)	0.030 (0.013)	0.842

Note: Dependent variable = ln (average fare/mile). Standard errors are in parentheses. Because estimates were obtained by a two-stage process, the standard errors reported have been adjusted as specified in Maddala (1977, 239).

Chicago and Washington. Those findings show that the scarcity value of airport slots is reflected in the fares charged by the airlines.

Average fares in markets served by newly certificated carriers were 20 percent lower than in similar markets where they did not serve. Clearly the actual entry by a newly certificated airline has a strong influence on fares. These carriers have lower costs and can make money charging lower fares, whereas the major carriers cannot break even at these fares unless load factors are substantially increased. This result shows that the larger carriers typically wait until actual entry occurs before matching the fares of the new carriers. In general, they have not cut fares to deter entry. This behavior suggests that the established carriers do not view the newly certificated carriers as rivals capable of quickly entering their markets. Indeed, although the new airlines are growing rapidly, they still constitute a relatively small fraction of industry capacity. Therefore they are not in the position to threaten effectively entry into all or even a large share of the major airlines' markets.

It should be emphasized that this finding does not rule out the possibility that contestability among the rival established airlines is working to keep fares equal to the level of their costs. At present there is a two-tiered cost structure with the high cost established airlines comprising one tier and the low cost new entrants comprising the other tier. The established carriers may be trying to retain a set of cost-based fares, which is sustainable when only high cost carriers compete or threaten entry; however, they cannot retain their fares when entry by a low cost carrier occurs. Thus these carriers may not be earning monopoly profits in their markets, even though they usually do cut fares when a new entrant airline enters.

Controlling for the percentage of interline connecting traffic (equation 3 and 5) reduces the estimated effect of both passengers and concentration on average fares. We find that interline passengers pay 25 percent higher fares per mile than online passengers. Since passengers in smaller markets are more likely to use interline service, these higher fares were attributed to both market concentration and density when the interline variable was not included. For example, compare equation 2 with equation 3: when INT is included, the coefficient of PAX falls from -0.021 to -0.013, and the coefficient of HERF falls from 0.086 to 0.059. The interline variable reflects the impact of the Board's joint fare rule and may be a surrogate for the percentage of multidestination itineraries involving the market and the proportion of the time-sensitive passengers.[5] Thus this variable cannot be considered entirely exogenous; to some extent the proportion of passengers making interline connections in a market is related to size and market structure. In interpreting the results of our model therefore, we are inclined to place more reliance on specifications in which the interline variable is excluded (i.e., equations 2 and 4).

As noted already, we have reported the findings for the alternative specifications of HERF (endogenous vs. exogenous). We conducted a specification test to determine which of these assumptions is most consistent with the markets in our sample. Using the test proposed by Hausman (1978), we found that we could not reject the hypothesis that HERF is exogenously determined.[6] The best estimates are those that treat HERF as exogenous; nevertheless, we believe it is useful to present both sets of estimates.

When Herfindahl is entered as an exogenous variable (equation 2), the coefficient is 0.086 and is highly significant. This implies that the fare in a market with two equal-sized competitors (i.e., with a Herfindahl index of 0.5) was 6 percent lower than in a monopoly market. A highly competitive market with four equal-sized airlines (i.e., a Herfindahl of 0.25) is estimated to have an average fare that is about 11 percent below the monopoly fare. (When the interline variable is included, fares are 4 percent lower in a duopoly and 7 percent lower in a market of four equal-sized firms than in a monopoly.) The effect of market density (PAX) is also significant, but the estimated elasticity of −0.021 is relatively small. (Again, it is smaller when the interline variable is included.) This coefficient indicates that fares in a market with 25 passengers per day is about 6.3 percent higher than a market with 500 passengers per day.

The estimates when concentration is included as an endogenous variable are quite different. The main reason for this is that the fitted values of PAX and HERF were very highly correlated. Although the correlation between the raw values of PAX and HERF was −0.27, the fitted values had a correlation of −0.74. This means there was a high degree of collinearity in the equation using the fitted value of HERF (equation 4) that did not exist when the raw value of HERF was used (equation 2). When HERF is endogenous, the coefficient of PAX becomes much larger, and the HERF variable turns negative. Only the coefficient on PAX remains significant, although the endogenous HERF is significant when the interline variable is included. The coefficient of PAX indicates that the fare in a market with 25 passengers per day is 12 percent higher than a market with 500 passengers per day. The HERF coefficient may be negative because of the high degree of multicollinearity with passengers.

In conclusion, estimates of fare difference between very large and very small markets range from about 0 to about 11 percent. Our best estimate is at the high end of the range. This estimate is based on the assumptions that HERF is exogenous and that the interline variable does not exercise an effect on pricing independent of market size and concentration.

The Changing Nature of Market Competition

Prior to deregulation the airlines had strong incentives to compete on the basis of flight frequency and schedules. Average load factors tended to rise as a carrier's share of departures in the market increased; that is, traffic rose faster than capacity. (This relationship was referred to as the S-curve because it implied that a graph of traffic share against departure share would be S-shaped.) The explanation for this finding was that the airline with the most flights tends to be (1) better known by travelers and (2) most likely to have a flight near a traveler's desired flight time, so a traveler can reduce the expected time necessary to arrange a trip by calling the leading carrier first. When fares were regulated, and travelers could assume that all carriers would offer the same fare, this behavior is quite plausible. Since deregulation, however, scheduling rivalry has declined in importance as the airlines have begun to compete on the basis of fares and have adopted systemwide competitive strategies based on the development of interconnecting route networks.

Presumably, the informational advantage from having a large share of flights in a market has not disappeared with deregulation. However, carriers without a large presence in the market can now overcome the informational advantage of the larger carriers by offering lower fares or a more attractive and accessible package of discount fares. There now is a potential trade-off between fare rivalry and schedule rivalry.

In addition the increasing emphasis on networking implies that a carrier's route, pricing, and service decisions in each market are importantly affected by the interrelationship of the market with the other routes in the carrier's network. Although schedule rivalry is important in attracting local travelers, the convenience of connections is more important in attracting nonlocal passengers. Feed from the network provides several additional benefits: First, feed traffic helps support a higher level of service in the local market, thus increasing a carrier's share of available departures and attracting more local traffic; second, by managing the timing of feeder flights to support off-peak flights in major markets, the airlines may be able to smooth the variations in demand on major segments over the day and possibly increase average load factors and average fares; and third, by drawing on passengers from many diverse markets to feed each segment, the airlines may reduce variability in demand and may thus choose a higher target load factor for their flights. In summary, the fact that a market is part of a feeder network may both increase the volume and reduce the variability of traffic. Hence an airline with a feeder network should have more traffic and/or higher fares than an otherwise similarly situated airline without a feeder network.

Networking was important before deregulation, but carriers' added route flexibility has probably increased the importance of competition on the basis of networking convenience relative to schedule rivalry within any given market. To examine these issues, we first determine how departure shares and network-related traffic influence load factors and then consider how these variables affect fares.

Load Factors

To determine how the nature of schedule rivalry has changed, we begin with a comparison of the estimated effect of departure share on load factor for 1976 and 1981 (second quarters). We first consider the relationship between load factor and departure share directly. We then control for differences in market distance and density, as well as the proportion of the carrier's passengers traveling in the markets that are online.[7] The model estimated is

$$COLF = F(DEPSH, DIST, PAX, ONLIN)$$

where COLF is the airlines coach load factor, DEPSH is the carriers share of departures, DIST is market distance, PAX is market service segment passengers, and ONLIN is the share of passengers in the market who connect with another of the carrier's flights.

Sample and Data.   A sample of the 200 top markets is used because these markets will have a sufficient number of flights and airlines to allow us to observe the nature of schedule rivalry.[8] Since the Board did not collect data on intrastate carriers in 1976, we excluded nine intrastate markets in both years. Moreover, we excluded markets of less than 200 miles. In many cases these short-haul markets receive substantial service from commuter airlines not reporting the necessary data to the CAB. Additionally in many short-haul markets carriers offer significant amounts of tag-end service, which serves mainly connecting traffic.

For the 175 remaining markets we collected data on each carrier's load factor (COLF) and each carrier's traffic (PAX) from *Service Segment*

Table 9.4   Estimates of the S-curve (second quarter 1976 and 1981)

Equation	INTERCEPT	LNDEPSH	LNDIST	LNPAX	LNOLIN	R^2
	1976—287 observations					
(1)	−0.495	0.069				0.067
	(0.018)	(0.015)				
(2)	−0.865	0.064	0.042	0.008		0.078
	(0.277)	(0.017)	(0.018)	(0.020)		
(3)	−0.859	0.064	0.046	0.006	0.009	0.077
	(0.277)	(0.017)	(0.019)	(0.020)	(0.012)	
	1981—454 observations					
(4)	−0.500	0.012				0.000
	(0.019)	(0.014)				0.000
(5)	−1.262	0.037	0.032	0.048		0.026
	(0.202)	(0.016)	(0.013)	(0.015)		
(6)	−1.221	0.037	0.040	0.043	0.021	0.035
	(0.202)	(0.016)	(0.014)	(0.015)	(0.009)	

Note: Dependent variable-ln (carrier load factor).

Data. These variables include both local and connecting traffic. We derived carrier nonstop departure shares (DEPSH) from the *Official Airline Guide.* ONLIN is defined as the percentage of passengers on a given nonstop flight who are fed into the flight from a preceding flight or continue their journey beyond the flight on the same airline. We used the *O & D Survey* and *Service Segment Data* to calculate this variable. The fare variable equals the average fare (excluding first-class passengers) paid by the local passengers in each market, as reported in the *O & D Survey.*

Findings.   The estimates are contained in table 9.4. When the effects of distance and density are not controlled (equations 1 and 4), we find that departure share had a significant effect on carrier load factors in the second quarter of 1976 but not during the second quarter of 1981. Our 1976 estimates indicate that in a market with two airlines, one with 70 percent and the other with 30 percent of departures, the bigger carrier would have had a load factor of 59.5 percent versus 56.1 percent for the smaller carrier.

When we control for differences in market distance and density (equations 2 and 5), the estimated effect of departure share on load factor declines slightly for 1976; it increases about threefold for 1981 and becomes significant. The estimated effect, however, is still substantially smaller than for 1976. (We also estimated the relationship using two-stage least squares because of possible simultaneity bias between passengers and load factor. In that case departure share did not have a significant effect on load factor in 1981; it was significant in 1976.)

In addition it should be noted that the actual dispersion of departure shares has declined. In 1976 the mean departure share was 0.53, and the standard deviation was 0.30. In 1981 the mean fell to 0.36, and the standard deviation was 0.20. Thus the variation in load factors across airlines has fallen even more than the regression coefficients alone would imply. The carrier with a relatively high departure share (one standard deviation above the mean) had about a 9 percent higher load factor than a carrier with a relatively low departure share (one standard deviation below the mean) in 1976; it has about a 5 percent higher load factor in 1981. By these estimates the effect of departure share on load factor was at least 75 percent greater in 1976 than in 1981.

To gauge the effect of increased online service, we estimate the load factor equation with a variable measuring the percentage of a carrier's total traffic in the market that was carried online (equations 3 and 6). We find that the amount of online feed had a significant effect on load factors in the second quarter of 1981 but not in 1976. In the second quarter of 1981 a carrier for which ONLIN was 56 percent (one standard deviation above the mean) had approximately 3.5 percent higher load factors (e.g., 60 percent vs. 58 percent) than a carrier for which ONLIN was 10 percent (one standard deviation below the mean).

Fares

To determine the effect of departure share on fares, we estimate a fare equation similar to the one in the first part of this chapter. The differences are that we use carriers as the unit of observation rather than markets, and we include carrier departure shares (DEPSHR) and online feed (ONLIN) as explanatory variables.

Our two-stage least-square estimates produced a positive and statistically significant estimate of the effect of market density on carrier fares, which is contrary to our earlier findings. We therefore also estimated the model without passengers. The coefficients on the remaining variables were not materially affected. (The parameter estimates are contained in table 9.5.)

Even when controlling for market concentration, a carrier's fare is positively related to its departure share. Thus average fares are not only higher in concentrated markets, but within concentrated markets the leading firms have higher fares than smaller firms. These results also suggest that among dense markets, differences in concentration have a greater influence on fares than in the larger sample. For example, a carrier

Table 9.5 Equations explaining schedule rivalry and carrier fares

INTER-CEPT	LNDIST	$\widehat{\text{LNPAX}}$	LNHERF	LNDEPSHR	TOUR	LNINC	LNOLVAR	NEWC	NYC	CHI	WASH	$\bar{R}^2$
2 SLSQ: Passengers Endogenous												
-4.021	-0.442	0.099	0.110	0.102	-0.058	0.225	0.013	-0.165	0.081	0.118	0.084	0.788
(1.590)	(0.017)	(0.036)	(0.33)	(0.016)	(0.026)	(0.081)	(0.010)	(0.030)	(0.033)	(0.026)	(0.043)	
OLSQ												
-3.067	-0.426		0.091	0.100	-0.063	0.213	0.007	-0.110	0.141	0.148	0.105	0.783
(1.362)	(0.014)		(0.29)	(0.014)	(0.023)	(0.070)	(0.009)	(0.020)	(0.023)	(0.216)	(0.367)	
-2.978	-0.441			0.116	-0.057	0.210	0.007	-0.120	0.141	0.137	0.107	0.779
(1.375)	(0.132)			(0.013)	(0.023)	(0.071)	(0.009)	(0.020)	(0.023)	(0.022)	(0.037)	

Note: Dependent Variable = ln (carrier average fare/mile); there were 446 observations. Standard errors are in parenthesis.

with a departure share of 50 percent will charge a fare approximately 7 percent greater than a carrier with a departure share of 25 percent.

The significant positive relationship between a carrier's departure share and its market fare shows that passengers still exhibit a preference for the carrier with the most flights in the market. Smaller carriers in the market apparently offer lower fares or more discounts to overcome the informational advantage of the leading carrier. (This signals the more efficient use of the industry's resources in the deregulated environment as carriers rely more on pricing competition.)

The ONLIN variable is not significant in the fare equation. Thus, although we find that feed increases load factors in a market, it does not influence local market fares.

One implication of this analysis is that for a given level of connecting traffic, the leading carrier in a market will have higher local fares and higher load factors than other carriers. This may reflect cost differences associated with the leading carrier's commitment to provide the highest quality of service in the market. If not, this result implies the dominant carrier would be more profitable. Either way, our finding suggests that schedule rivalry will continue to be an important element in the airlines' competitive strategies.

Our findings also suggest that networking has important competitive advantages in terms of the airlines' ability to maintain high load factors. Hence, even when a carrier does not dominate a particular market, it can successfully serve the market if its flights are well enough supported by network-related traffic. Thus, although the continued importance of scheduling dominance might argue that local markets will become more concentrated, such a trend would be opposed by the governing importance of networks which will allow carriers to compete effectively in local markets they do not dominate.

Conclusion

The theory of contestability suggests that, although airline markets are relatively concentrated, the ability of airlines to enter and exit easily should prevent fares from exceeding the cost of service. Our analysis has indicated that the contestability benchmark does not fully hold sway in the first years after deregulation. Carriers in concentrated markets have the ability to price above cost. The degree of this market power is relatively small. Even if some degree of such power should persist in the long run, it would be preferable to the cumbersome and inefficient regulatory mechanism that would be needed to prevent it.

Other economic theories of the aviation industry, especially those of monopolistic competition, appear to offer equally valid insights into current practices. Schedule rivalry remains and is important, albeit less so than under regulation. Today the advantage of a large presence in a market is reflected in terms of both fares and load factors. Whether this means that the dominant carrier is more profitable depends on the relative costs of the airlines in the market. Certainly networking now contributes to higher load factors, which makes this an important dimension of the airlines' competitive strategies.

Chapter 10

Antitrust Interventions

In addition to rate and route regulation, the Federal Aviation Act empowered the Board with other economic regulatory functions, most of which have continued under deregulation. The most significant of these are the responsibility to oversee mergers and acquisitions. In this chapter we describe how the Board's antitrust responsibilities have evolved since deregulation. Specifically, we argue that the Board has been quite aggressive in interpreting the act's standards as permitting it to adopt a policy of relying on potential competition in evaluating proposed mergers. Hence the Board approved mergers even when carriers were competitors on some routes.

Another major area of antitrust activities relates to the Board's ability to grant antitrust immunity to carrier agreements. Important carrier agreements that affect domestic air transportation include those by which airlines apportion scarce landing rights at congested airports and those relating to the distribution of airline tickets through travel agents. The chapter concludes with a discussion of two areas of continuing concern—airport access and access to computer reservation systems.

Airline Mergers and Acquisitions

The ADA made significant changes in the section of the Federal Aviation Act that applied to mergers and acquisitions. Congress directed the Board to analyze mergers in a manner that placed more emphasis on the legal standards of Section 7 of the Clayton Act, which applies to mergers in most sectors of the U.S. economy. These standards are intended to prevent combinations that will substantially lessen competition or tend to create a monopoly. Congress required airlines to seek prior approval before consummating a merger or acquisition. Consequently antitrust review procedures for airline mergers or acquisitions differs from those in other industries. Indeed, there is a special provision of the act that allows anticompetitive mergers to be approved if the Board finds that a merger meets a significant transportation need that cannot be met by a less anticompetitive alternative.

Traditional Merger Policy

The Board's policy toward mergers changed several times in the years between 1938 and 1978. In the first decade of its regulation, the Board denied all proposed mergers between trunk carriers.[1] It did, however, allow trunks to absorb three minor carriers. For a few years in the mid-1950s the Board swung to the other extreme and encouraged and approved mergers on public interest grounds even when they had an anticompetitive effect.[2] From 1956 to 1970 the Board reverted to its earlier posture of resisting trunkline merger attempts, approving only one (United-Capital), and that on grounds of rescuing a failing firm (Capital). This policy held despite much carrier enthusiasm for mergers in the early 1960s.[3] In the early 1970s the Board became somewhat more permissive, approving a merger between Northwest and Northeast (which was never consummated), another between Allegheny and Mohawk (two local service carriers), and a third between Delta and Northeast. It did, however, disapprove a merger between American and Western, and a related defensive merger between Northwest and National was thereafter also dismissed.

Throughout this period the airlines' chief incentive for mergers was to acquire new routes a carrier could otherwise hope to obtain only through long and tortuous route award procedures, if then. For example, in the Northwest-Northeast case in 1970, Northwest had the option of backing out of the merger in the event the Board failed to approve the transfer of Northeast's lucrative Miami–Los Angeles route. When the Board disapproved this transfer, Northwest exercised its option, and the agreement was terminated.[4]

The statutory standards required the Board to approve proposed mergers unless it found they would not be consistent with the public interest. For example, the Board was not to approve a merger it it would create a monopoly or if it would jeopardize a carrier not a party to the merger. The Board interpreted this criterion as enabling it to disapprove a merger that would cause diversion of traffic and revenue from competing carriers.[5] Potential networking efficiency gains from mergers were thus often considered a reason for disapproval. The use of mergers to avoid bankruptcies of carriers also relied on the value of route rights. Through merger, the valuable route rights of the failing carrier were acquired by a stronger carrier who would continue.[6]

Mergers under the ADA

The merger guidelines under the ADA took a large step toward the Clayton Act standards that govern most unregulated industries. The act changed the Board's antitrust authority by directing the CAB to disapprove an application if it would result in a monopoly in any region of the United States (the Sherman Act test) or if the effect of the transaction may be substantially to lessen competition or to tend to create a monopoly (the Clayton Act test). However, the act also included a savings clause for anticompetitive mergers if the transaction serves "significant transportation conveniences and needs of the public" and those needs "may not be satisfied by a reasonably available alternative having materially less anti-competitive effects." [7] The act also required the Board to make its findings within six months of an application. Originally authority over domestic mergers was to transfer to the Department of Justice on January 1, 1983. This was later extended to January 1, 1985.

After passage of the Airline Deregulation Act, a carrier could obtain almost any route in the United States after only a few months delay by simply applying for it. With increased route freedom a carrier's ability to expand quickly was limited mainly by its ability to acquire aircraft and personnel, airport gate space, or landing rights. High factor mobility combined with route freedom meant that in a deregulated environment there would be ease of potential entry and exit in most markets. Thus, although the Board was aware that in even the least concentrated origin-destination markets, carriers' market shares were in excess of the level that the Department of Justice considered to be consistent with competition, it deemed that market shares would not be an adequate indicator of the effectiveness of competition in the new regime. In practice, the Board focused on those structural characteristics of the markets at issue that are most likely to determine the ability of actual and potential competitors to check the exercise of monopoly power over prices. These structural characteristics include the number of actual competitors, the presence of a suffcient number of potential entrants situated to enter easily, the likelihood of new entry, traffic density, and the magnitude of entry barriers, such as those caused by the inability to gain access to an airport.

At the time of passage of the ADA, the Board had several merger cases already pending before it and had begun to focus on developing overall merger policy for a deregulated environment. [8] In the series of merger and acquisition applications that came before it after 1978, the Board attempted, as a conscious policy move to treat the airline industry according to the competitive standards of the Clayton Act whenever possible. The Board did not give weight to traditional arguments based on claims that the applicant carriers' managements were making unwise choices or that there was a negative profit effect on a competing carrier. Overall, the Board's policy with respect to mergers, like its policies toward routes and rates, has been that airlines should not be treated differently from other industries.

To ensure continuation of this policy, in 1982 the Board suggested that Congress eliminate antitrust provisions that apply exclusively to the airline industry and, instead, let the Clayton, Sherman and Federal Trade Commission standards prevail.[9] With the transfer of the authority to the Department of Justice, there would be judiciary review of each and every transaction. Repeal of the authority would enable the agencies to challenge a particular merger in court, but only if there were a competitive problem. Similarly the savings clause that allows otherwise anticompetitive transactions would be eliminated. This provision of the act has not been invoked by the Board since the deregulation act passed. In 1984 the Board changed its position and recommended that antitrust authority be transferred to the Department of Transportation rather than the Department of Justice.

Table 10.1 displays the merger and acquisition applications decided by the Board from 1979 to 1983. Specific aspects of Board policy in these cases are outlined next.

Market Performance Standards

The Board has based its assessment of a merger's likely effect on competition on two related findings: (1) that concentration ratios alone are not an accurate gauge of competitive performance in city-pair markets, and (2) that potential competition has a disciplining effect on market performance.

The Board's reliance on these standards is illustrated in the proposed merger between Texas International and National. In this case sixteen city-pair markets were analyzed in which the carriers were considered to be potential entrants in one another's markets. The Board noted that there were other potential entrants that could readily enter these markets and so did not bar the merger on grounds of concentration.

The Board's administrative law judge and the Department of Justice argued that actual competition between these two carriers in the Houston-New Orleans market was substantial and that therefore the merger should not be approved. In the Houston–New Orleans market, for the twelve months ending June 30, 1978, National had 27 percent of the traffic and Texas International had 24 percent. The share of the two leading firms before the merger was 51 percent and would be almost 75 percent after the combination. The market was more concentrated than mergers declared unlawful by the Supreme Court and greater than Justice Department guidelines for merger approval.

Table 10.1 Chronology of airline merger and acquisition decisions since deregulation

Date	Title	Item ID	Description
10-24-79	Texas International-National acquisition case	Order 79-12-163/164/165	Law Judge found acquisition to be anticompetitive using traditional market share and concentration ratio analysis. Board approved the acquisition, focusing on potential entry and lack of entry barriers. The proposed acquisition was never consummated, however.
10-24-79	Pan American acquisition of National	Order 79-12-163/164/165	Approval of end-to-end merger conditioned upon divestiture of Miami–London route where restrictive international agreement limited the United States to one carrier. Condition withdrawn after negotiation with the United Kingdom.
12-13-79	Eastern-National acquisition	Order 79-12-74	Law Judge found acquisition to be anticompetitive because of extensive overlap of the two carriers' systems and because of significant barriers to entry at airports. Eastern withdrew its application before final Board decision.
9-27-79	Continental-Western Merger case	Order 79-9-185	Concerns about airport constraints as barriers to entry and carrier dominance at hubs led to rejection of merger.
5-15-79	North Central-Southern	Order 79-6-7/8	End-to-end merger. Approved upon a finding of no anticompetitive effect.
5-14-80	Tiger International-Seaboard acquisition case	Order 80-7-20/21	Approval of domestic overlap merger of two all-cargo carriers.
9-12-80	Republic-Hughes Air West	Order 80-9-65	End-to-end acquisition. Approved.
3-31-81	Continental-Western Merger case	Order 81-6-1/2	Approval upon showing that airport constraints had not proved major barrier and that western United States no longer had commercial significance as a geographic market. However, the merger was not consummated because of acquisition of Continental by TXI.
9-3-81	Texas International-Continental acquisition	Order 81-9-37	Approval of hostile takeover. The two airlines integrated their operation under the name Continental.
1-29-82	Air Florida-Western acquisition case	Order 82-1-148	End-to-end acquisition. Approved but never consummated.
7-29-82 10-15-82	Bergt-AIA-Western-Wein acquisition and control case	Orders 82-7-121 and 72-10-94	Approval conditioned on Mr. Bergt being insulated from control over AIA for 18 months. Insulation required because state imposed regulatory ban on entry and airport terminal unavailability restricted potential entry in intrastate Alaskan markets. The acquisition of Wein by Western was not consummated.

Upon review of the administrative law judge's decision, the CAB reasoned that concentration ratios were not instructive in this case; since the passage of the ADA, entry even by small carriers was relatively easy. Specifically, in the Houston–New Orleans market there were eleven carriers with stations and functioning facilities already in place at both ends of this market. Therefore the CAB reasoned there was ample potential competition and approved the merger. Indeed, by the time the CAB order was written, a small regional carrier, Southwest Airlines, had entered the market with a low-fare, turnaround service and was offering over 24 percent of the capacity in the market. (Despite the approval the merger was never consummated.)

In contrast, the Board had been concerned about situations in which sunk costs or barriers to entry might confer at least transitory monopoly power to a merged or acquired carrier. In the first Continental-Western case the Board announced its intention to disapprove the merger. Its decision was based in large measure on the possibility that barriers to entry might exist in the short run because of direct constraints on airport entry. The combined carriers would use Denver as their hub, with major operations at San Diego, Los Angeles, and San Francisco. The Denver airport was near capacity, and the three California airports were dealing with serious noise problems. The Board was uncertain about whether airport authorities would adopt procompetitive policies at these environmentally constrained airports. The Board was also uncertain about the ability of actual and potential entry to discipline a variety of markets in the western region of the United States. Thus it was unwilling to approve the merger until time had passed, and it had more experience with deregulation.

In retrospect the Board's fears did not seem justified. The barriers to entry at many of the airports in fact proved to be less severe than the Board had felt could be possible, and the airport authorities by and large displayed a willingness to encourage competitive practices. Moreover entry into the major hubs in the western regions of the United States proceeded at a healthy pace. Thus the Board reversed itself a year later and approved the merger when it was again proposed. The merger was not however consummated. In the interim Texas Air Corporation (the parent of Texas International) purchased a large block of Continental stock and received Board permission to acquire it.

In other decisions the Board conditioned its approval of mergers. The reasoning relied on the need to intervene because of entry barriers. In the Pan American-National merger the Board conditioned its approval on the willingness of the merged carrier to relinquish its right to National's

Miami–London route so that the Board could decide whether a different carrier should serve it. The air agreement between the United States and United Kingdom only permitted one carrier to serve that route, and Pan American's strength in other U.S.-U.K. markets led the Board to be concerned that the merger might substantially lessen competition among gateways on the North Atlantic. However, the U.S. government was able to renegotiate this provision of the U.S.-U.K. bilateral agreement and open the route to a second U.S. carrier.[10] The restriction on the merger was then removed by the Board.

Consequences of Airline Mergers

The merger activity immediately following passage of the ADA was at first feared to be a wave that would decrease the number of firms in the industry and increase their size. Yet, as we discussed in chapter 3, the trend has instead been shrinkage of the largest carriers relative to the smaller carriers. The limited economic gains to the carriers that have merged have done little to encourage other carriers to grow in this manner.[11]

Pan American spent over $300 million in acquiring National and then suffered serious problems in trying to consolidate the labor forces and route schedules of the two carriers. The consolidation of North Central, Southern, and Hughes Air West into Republic has not been immediately successful financially, since it too incurred large indebtedness and major interest expenses.

There seem to be few incentives at present for domestic mergers. Not only has the scarcity value of domestic routes declined to zero, but also the melding of labor forces has proved difficult. Moreover aircraft of all types are available from active second hand and lease markets, so this incentive to merge is not strong. International authority, which continues to have scarcity value because of the policies of many foreign countries, is more likely to attract merger partners or other creative transfer or lease arrangements. The proposed sale/lease of Braniff's South American Route system, first to Pan American and then ultimately to Eastern, provides an important example.[12]

In sum, the post-ADA merger wave did not serve carriers' interests nearly as well as it was hoped it would, and thus activity in this area has declined.

Carrier Agreements

Effective collusive behavior between competitors in an industry can lead to higher profits. Such behavior can consist of agreements that control prices, agreements on rules for marketing the product, agreements that restrain capacity, and so forth. Under the Federal Aviation Act an air carrier has the option to file for CAB approval of agreements, contracts, or requests for authority to discuss possible cooperative arrangements. Many such discussions and agreements are clearly anticompetitive. Yet before deregulation the CAB approved and even sponsored such actions. The Board, by statute, was required to grant immunity from the antitrust laws to all agreements it approved.

History of Major Grants of Immunity

Under the Federal Aviation Act the CAB could approve a wide variety of multicarrier agreements which it did not find to be adverse to the public interest. There have typically been literally thousands of such agreements on file at any one time. Many were innocuous, such as agreements that permit one carrier to subcontract maintenance on its aircraft to another. Many, however, were not.

The capacity reduction agreements that were approved in the early 1970s and discussed in chapter 2 raised substantial concerns. Initially the Board had approved the transcontinental capacity reduction agreement but had tailored its approval to a one-year period, hoping that the financial picture would improve and it could then withdraw its approval. However, succeeding Board policy in 1973 had appeared to signal a willingness to institutionalize capacity limitation agreements, which would have been a major anticompetitive step.[13] A Department of Justice suit and the Kennedy oversight hearings did much to prevent the continuation of this type of agreement.

There were also mutual aid pacts among carriers. These were approved in the 1950s after labor unions appeared to have the ability to use strikes as an instrument to whipsaw the industry into granting favorable settlements. Carriers responded by coming up with an agreement to divide revenues between the nonstruck carriers (who would receive windfall gains from a strike) and the struck carrier. The CAB approved such agreements as not being adverse to the public interest. Mutual aid pacts were eliminated by Congress in the Airline Deregulation Act.

A number of other Board approved agreements continue to have a substantial effect on scheduled air service. One such agreement allows carriers in certain congested airports to form airline scheduling committees in order to allocate among themselves the limited number of landing and takeoff rights, or slots.

Another group of agreements were those establishing a travel agency program under which persons who operate in accordance with prescribed procedures are designated exclusive agents for the sale of airline tickets. The agreements concerning slot allocations and travel agents continue to influence scheduled domestic air transportation. We will discuss both in more detail subsequently.

International agreements were also approved, the most important of these being International Air Transport Association agreements establishing a traffic conference mechanism under which air carriers coordinate rates and practices in international air transportation.

As in the case of mergers Congress in the ADA continued to give the Board a savings clause permitting it to approve agreements that would otherwise violate basic antitrust principles. The test permits Board approval if transportation needs or international comity or foreign policy reasons require it and if there are no alternatives available to achieve those benefits that are materially less anticompetitive. The new law specified that the Board may grant such immunity only after finding it is in the public interest and only to the extent necessary to secure the sought-after public benefit.

As part of the transition in deregulating the industry, the CAB began a systematic review of all such agreements. Given that there would no longer be regulation of rates and routes, it seemed appropriate to open the industry to the same exposure under the antitrust laws as any other industry. Thus the antitrust laws would provide the check and balance on industry behavior substituting for direct regulatory oversight. In theory this was the goal. In practice by 1982 and 1983 a rather altered Board was tending to use public interest reasons to extend at least transitional immunity in a number of instances.

Scheduling Committee Agreements

In the late 1960s airport congestion became a serious problem, with aircraft stacked and circling over major airports for one or more hours prior to landing. Amid the controversy the FAA imposed a quota on takeoffs and landings, and the CAB authorized carriers to discuss how they might rationalize their flights into these airports.[14] It is not surprising that carriers would react to such a scarce resource by using the opportunity to come up with a scheme that transferred the excess rents to themselves.

Scheduling committee agreements, rather than a fee or auction system of allocation, were thus devised by the carriers and approved by the CAB. Committee rules required that agreements be unanimously approved by participating carriers. [15] Under the statute then in effect, Board approval automatically conveyed an antitrust exemption.

The issue of whether to continue to approve and confer antitrust immunity on these agreements was reviewed after deregulation. The CAB and the Department of Transportation jointly commissioned a study by Polinomics Research Laboratories to evaluate the economic properties of the given system and to suggest more efficient methods for allocating the scarce slots, should any exist and appear practical. The agencies were thus seeking the best way to ensure that landing rights were distributed equitably and with the least anticompetitive effect.

The Polinomics report (see Grether, Isaac, and Plott 1979) was a model study from the point of view of economic tools, both pure and applied. The report reflected the view that the congestion problem arises because a scarce resource, airspace, had no price put on it. Instead, the FAA allocated such slots administratively among different user classes. Within each user class the current committee process was evaluated as the core of a cooperative unanimity voting game without side payments. However, the authors concluded this did not represent the most efficient allocation of the scarce resource. Rather, they contended that an auction mechanism would ensure that the slots would go to the highest value users. To allow adjustments for changed circumstances, mistakes, and unfilled expectations, the study recommended an after market.

In practical terms, this market system had a predictable outcome. A large plane carrying many passengers would be likely to outbid a small plane carrying few passengers. It was estimated that a slot at Washington's National Airport would cost $1,000 during peak periods. Although it is easy to imagine that 100 passengers arriving in a B-727 aircraft might be willing to pay an additional $10 each to land at the convenient in-town airport, it is less likely that ten passengers in a commuter would be willing to pay an additional $100 each.[16] Thus large planes were most likely to present winning bids for slots. Similarly planes covering longer hauls, where a given dollar amount per passenger amounted to a smaller percentage of the ticket price, might be able to outbid shorter-haul flights. Thus the solution proposed by the economic study might have altered the character of the airport radically.

Once the implications of the recommended policy change became clear, it became nearly impossible to adopt the Polinomics plan. This might have been regrettable from the point of view of efficiency except for one critical consideration: the study had addressed itself to the apparent rather than the real underlying constraint. At National Airport the basis for the high-density rule—airside congestion—no longer applied. By the late 1970s technological improvements had substantially increased the airport's capacity. Actual operations substantially exceeded the supposed maximum almost every day, including in the worst weather conditions. Slots had become a device used to constrain takeoffs and landings of commercial carriers, but private aircraft had achieved virtually unconstrained access to the airport.

The FAA, as proprietor of the airport, was limiting operations of scheduled aircraft to deal with a number of other concerns about the use of the airport. These included the need to limit aircraft noise, to relieve ground-side congestion, and to coordinate the use of Washington National and Dulles International Airports. If economists had designed an efficient solution under these constraints, it would have been quite different. The winning bidders would now most often be planes that carried few rather than many people and were turboprop rather than noisy jet aircraft. Even among jets preference would be given to the DC-9's flown from less dense proximate communities rather than to the B-727 aircraft flown from more dense cities. The reasons would be both the smaller number of passengers and the fact that a B-727 contributes about three times as much to the cumulative noise level (which is the source of annoyance) as a DC-9. The noisy large jets would tend to serve the outlying airports such as Dulles or Baltimore-Washington. Economists would still recommend a price system, but fees would be determined by the noise the aircraft generates, the time of landing, and the number of passengers on the plane, so as to balance the total demands on the airport at any given time with the available airport capacity.[17] This case, in which an economic analysis with a given analytic structure can yield very different policy recommendations, indicates how sensitive such a calculation can be to a change in the pertinent constraints.

The PATCO job action and the FAA restrictions on aircraft operations superceded the concern with the scheduling committees for a period of time. However, deregulation has placed substantial pressure on the existing methods of restricting airport activity and the methods of allocating access. Since the passage of the Airline Deregulation Act the scheduling committees have been able to accommodate a small number of the new entrants such as Midway, Air Florida, and New York Air. However, with continued growth in demand, it will become increasingly difficult for the carriers to reach a consensus. A price system still seems the most efficient approach, but it will be difficult to devise one given the politization of the issue in the Washington area.

Competitive Marketing Case

The Air Traffic Conference (ATC) agreements, first filed with the Board in the 1940s, established a single screening body that member air carriers would use in selecting their agents.[18] Over time these agreements were revised through the process of repeated amendment. The system of rules in place at the time of the ADA was an extensive one, governing most facets of the travel agent–air carrier relationship.

Some of the provisions related to common appointments or accreditation. Under these provisions the airlines delegated the responsibility of screening applicants, monitoring their activities, and taking enforcement action to their trade associations. Carriers thus eliminated duplication in the creation and oversight of their ticket distribution networks and shared the cost of administering the system. Carrier entry and exit into new markets was made less costly by the system because air carriers did not have to bear the cost of establishing a new distribution network when they entered a new town or city. Travel agents in turn were in a position to sell the service of more than one or two air carriers, and the public was assured that agents could present them with a complete menu of the available travel options.

There is little doubt that this agency system had an important role in facilitating the marketing of air transportation by smaller carriers. Nevertheless, many of the agreement provisions were designed to provide benefits to the travel agents rather than to the public. One provision prevented air carriers from using and compensating persons other than agents accredited by their trade association for selling air transportation. Thus unlike other areas of our economy, in which competition in marketing services often produces a variety of distribution systems, there could be no rivalry in air carrier ticket distribution. However, airlines were permitted to determine jointly agent commission rates, although the Board reviewed proposed changes in the rates the airlines agreed on.

Under terms of the agreement an airline would have to convince the carriers participating in the conference that a marketing innovation was useful before it could be instituted. In addition travel agents' representatives were consulted prior to any deviation from the existing arrangements. These procedures impeded innovation in the distribution of airline services. Essentially the Board granted antitrust immunity for airlines to decide collectively that only accredited travel agents and the carriers could sell air transportation. For example, the Air Traffic Conference effectively prevented business travel departments from obtaining agency status, even though they performed many of the same tasks as travel agents. Agent status was precluded by rules that prohibited an agent from doing more than 20 percent of its business with itself and by rules that established location and personnel standards. The airlines rationalized this decision by claiming that travel agents promoted the use of air transportation whereas business travelers merely needed ticket and reservation services. The effect of preventing business travel departments from becoming agents was to limit competition with travel agents as well as to reduce carrier commission expenses. Similarly travel agents were not permitted to locate their agencies at airports or in hotel lobbies, where agents might be in competition with airline ticket offices.

A major review of this system was started in 1978. The Board decided to disapprove agreements fixing commissions, even though entry by competing distribution systems was blocked.[19] A decision on opening the distribution system to new entry was to be delayed until an administrative law judge held an oral evidentiary hearing and issued a decision. In retrospect, the decision to end regulation of the prices travel agents paid while continuing to block the development of alternative distribution channels may have had unintended consequences.

The effect of the Board's decision was a transfer of economic rents to travel agents. The basic domestic commission rate increased from 7 to 10 percent. Carriers competed by offering higher rates to agents that exceeded certain sales goals. Also rising fuel prices led to a sharp escalation of air fares, further increasing agents' compensation.[20] But the percentage of tickets that travel agents issued increased. In 1977 they accounted for 38 percent of ticket sales; this increased to 53 percent in 1979 and has increased further since. The larger role of travel agents was due in part to the more complex fare structure that has evolved under deregulation.

Four years after opening up the commission rate structure, the Board finally addressed the full panoply of issues concerning the government's role in the distribution and sale of travel agents' tickets. In its decision in the *Competitive Marketing Investigation*, the Board eliminated the exclusivity provisions that prevented air carriers' compensating persons other than agents accredited by the trade association. It also required that the Area Settlement Plan, a mechanism by which travel agents and carriers settle their accounts, be available to nonaccredited agents. Further the Board decided that antitrust immunity be removed from all Air Traffic Conference activity in December 1984.

The travel agents, after enjoying the benefits of higher commissions for a number of years, tried to reverse the decision to effect the quid pro quo of open entries. Yet the Board's intent in its decision in the *Competitive Marketing Investigation* was not to displace the travel agency network.[21] The Board recognized that the existing system was in many respects quite efficient. Rather, the Board decided to allow the development of competing distribution channels. Individual carriers would not be required to act any differently, but now a carrier's choice of distribution channel would reflect that carrier's independent judgment rather than the consensus of competitors.

As with antitrust immunity the Board's decision with respect to exclusivity was also phased out. Online sales were opened to new distribution channels immediately. However, a two-year transition period was permitted before interline transportation was fully opened to competitive distribution. The carriers had negotiated a variety of bilateral and multilateral arrangements that governed the sale of interline travel. The transition period was designed to give carriers ample opportunity to renegotiate their agreements in the new environment. Similarly, even though the rules that prohibited business travel departments from becoming their own travel agents were found to be anticompetitive, they continued to be approved for two years under the Board's decision to continue the transitional antitrust exemption.

As we have already noted, a substantial portion of airline tickets are sold through travel agents, and for a considerable period of time this will remain unchanged by the *Competitive Marketing Investigation*. Since on most trips passengers have a choice between two or more equally acceptable airlines, travel agents have substantial ability to influence a significant proportion of passengers' carrier selection. Consequently any carrier that upsets its relationship with its travel agents, either by reducing commission rates or by establishing an alternative distribution channel, is vulnerable to reduced travel-agent bookings. This is not the result of a conspiracy or a cartel but rather the product of each travel agent operating in his best interest. Given the low marginal cost of accommodating the passengers, even a relatively small negative response by travel agents to a carrier's initiative can have a substantial impact on a carrier's profitability.

Without the Board's regulation it is doubtful that the present agent system would have evolved as it did. Before ATC-appointed agents became such an important segment in the distribution of airline tickets, carriers would undoubtedly have used their opportunities to use alternative methods of sale. In fact the strong incentive for the establishment of competing distribution systems is what prompted the Board to approve the marketing agreement in the first place.

Access Issues

Access issues are perhaps the greatest remaining challenge for the Board and its successor in guaranteeing the success of deregulation. One of these, which we have already considered in part, is airport access. Another is access to computer reservation systems. The ability of airlines to obtain fair and equal access to these facilities is an important and growing concern of the Board and the aviation community.

Computer Reservations Systems
A particular challenge for the Board and its successor agency has arisen in the question of access to computerized reservation systems.[22] Several airlines have developed, at considerable expense, systems that automate the travel agents' ticketing, reservation, and accounting systems. American's Sabre and United's Apollo are the two predominant systems, although a number of other airlines and at least one nonairline company offer competing systems. The use of the computer technology is beneficial in that it is easier for travel agents to obtain schedule and fare information. The use of carrier-controlled computer reservation systems may, however, have anti-competitive effects on smaller carriers.

As we have already noted, travel agents apparently have a significant role in influencing a passenger's choice of airlines. It has been alleged that several of the airlines have designed their systems so that agents are more apt to ticket passengers on their flights. One example is the so-called display bias in the reservation system. If an agent were to ask for flights at a particular time in a given market, the flights of the carrier that sponsors the reservation system are listed before competing airline's flights that are nearer to the requested time. In particular, United has a two-hour "look-back" advantage for its flights. If an agent asks for a 3:00 P.M. flight, a 1:00 P.M. United flight would be displayed before a 3:00 P.M. flight of its competitor. American Airlines ranks flights on the basis of elapsed time and certain service features, and in addition adds penalty minutes to other carriers such that an American flight is most likely to be displayed first.

Carriers that sponsor computer reservation systems, as well as those that do not, believe that such biases have a significant impact on travel-agent booking practices. Agents are most apt to book on the flights listed first or on the flights listed on the first few screens (about 90 percent of all ticket

		SABRE					APOLLO					
	A/L	FLT NBR	CITY PAIR	DEPT	ARRV	STP	A/L	FLT NBR	CITY PAIR	DEPT	ARRV	STP
SCREEN #1	1 FL	403	DTWDEN	730A	833A	0	1 UA	221	DTWDEN	820A	915A	0
	2 UA	221	DTWDEN	820A	915A	0	2 UA	825	DTWDEN	450P	545P	0
	3 AA	181	DTWORD	820A	820A	0	3 FL	27	DTWDEN	606P	708P	0
	4 AA	379	DEN	900A	1026A	0	4 7NW	732	DTWMKE	800A	752A	0
	5 DL	239	DTWCVG	822A	914A	0	5 RC	55	DEN	835A	959A	0
	6 DL	721	DEN	957A	1045A	0	6 UA	533	DTWORD	745A	742A	0
							7 AA	379	DEN	900A	1028A	0
SCREEN #2	1 AA	527	DTWDFW	845A	1021A	0	1 UA	955	DTWORD	900A	900A	0
	2 AA	333	DEN	1120A	1214P	0	2 CO	15	DEN	1005A	1127A	0
	3 UA	955	DTWORD	900A	900A	0	3 UA	955	DTWORD	900A	900A	0
	4 CO	15	DEN	1005A	1127A	0	4 UA	263	DEN	1015A	1143A	0
	5 AA	527	DTWDFW	845A	1021A	0	5 RC	589	DTWMSP	1010A	1130A	1
	6 FL	362	DEN	1115A	1211P	0	6 RC	573	DEN	1205P	100P	0
							7 RC	589	DTWMKE	1010A	1002A	0
							8 UA	661	DEN	1140A	102P	0
SCREEN #3	1 AA	291	DTWORD	1044A	1045A	0	1 7RC	563	DTWMSP	1015A	1045A	0
	2 AA	579	DEN	1135A	101P	0	2 UA	663	DEN	1158A	1250P	0
	3 RC	563	DTWMSP	1015A	1045A	0	3 7RC	563	DTWMSP	1015A	1045A	0
	4 RC	573	DEN	1205P	100P	0	4 RC	573	DEN	1205P	100P	0
	5 NW	55	DTWMSP	945A	1022A	0	5 TW	293	DTWSTL	1030A	1101A	0
	6 NW	503	DEN	1205P	100P	0	6 TW	561	DEN	1220P	128P	0
							7 7RC	563	DTWMSP	1015A	1045A	0
							8 NW	503	DEN	1205P	100P	0

Figure 10.1 Comparison of flight information displayed by various computer reservations systems. (This is the schedule information a travel agent will see when requesting information on flights between Detroit and Denver on July 15th leaving at 7 A.M.)

sales). So a carrier whose flights do not show up at all or are listed on later screens may have difficulty achieving viable load factors. Figure 10.1 displays the information on the first three screens of United's Appllo system and American's Sabre system. The Frontier Airlines flight, for example, listed by the American Airlines Sabre system as the most conveniently timed flight for a passenger desiring early morning service between Detroit and Denver, does not show up in the first three screens of United's Apollo system. Frontier of course is a major competitor to United at Denver.

In addition, when listing connecting flights between particular city pairs, the systems do not necessarily display all the available connecting service; only the routings over preselected cities are displayed. It has been alleged that the connecting points the sponsoring carrier chooses to list are influenced by competitive considerations. For example, a competitor's more convenient flight over a different hub may be deliberately excluded by such a strategy.

American and United have been very aggressive in selling their reservation systems to travel agents in cities where they compete. In Dallas–Ft. Worth where American is the major carrier, its Sabre system is far and away the most popular system. Similarly United's Apollo dominates the Denver and Cleveland markets where it is the major carrier. Apparently both carriers offered attractive long-term deals to travel agents leasing their equipment in their primary cities and areas. In addition there are a number of advantages to travel agents booking flights on the sponsoring carrier's computer reservations system. In the first place the schedule information and seat availability is presumably more up to date for the host's flights. Second, the host's system issues boarding passes for its flights, although recently the sponsoring carriers have begun to make this option available to other carriers as well. Finally, it is alleged that sponsoring carriers pay greater commission rates to agents that book above specified percentages of its passengers in a given market on the sponsoring carrier's flights. Such a commission structure is not viable for rival carriers because the only information they receive relates to reservations on their flights.

For these reasons travel agents may be booking a disproportionate number of passengers on the sponsoring carrier's computer reservation system. If this is true, then at least in cities where the airline has a major presence, it can charge a price for its computer reservation system below that at which rival marketers of reservation systems can earn a competitive rate of return. The dominant carrier in turn will extract the rents from its dominant position in the reservation system market through increased sales of airline service. A new entrant that is integrated in computer reservation systems would need to enter at an enormous scale to overcome such advantages.

Additionally the sponsoring carriers apparently employ a highly differentiated price structure for carriers to display their flights on their reservation system. Large established carriers tend to pay relatively low rates; the ability to book passengers on these carriers' flights is needed to market effectively the reservation system to travel agents. New entrants, however, often pay booking fees several times the cost paid by these larger carriers.

Nevertheless, the long-term competitive effect of these computer reservation systems is not entirely clear. If agents at particular cities face financial incentives to use the reservation systems of the largest carrier, and that carrier can achieve higher load factors because of the system, then the competitive advantage may be skewed toward the larger carrier. However, competing carriers may be able to use increased advertising or revised commission structures effectively to overcome the advantage of the reservation systems. With the rapid developments in data processing, alternative systems would allow, among other things, reservation to be made with personal computers.

The Department of Justice began a formal investigation into the use of computer reservation systems in early 1983. The Civil Aeronautics Board began a rule making in the summer of 1983 to consider whether restrictions on the use of computer reservation systems were needed, and in March 1984 it proposed a rule the would prohibit system owners from biasing displays to give better displays to flights of any particular airline. It also proposed to ban as unjustly discriminatory the ability to exclude airlines that wish to have their flights listed on the computer systems. The proposed rule would also require the system's owners to make available for a fee any marketing information the reservations systems generate.

Airport Access
A variety of access problems can arise at airports. For some time airports have grappled with operating constraints stemming from environmental and safety concerns, and airport terminal and ground congestion. Capacity constraints have been exacerbated by the consequences of the PATCO job action. Congress, CAB, and DOT have been concerned that restrictions on airport access can undermine the freedom of entry and exit instituted in the Airline Deregulation Act of 1978. Thus Congress in P.L. 97-248 directed the secretary of transportation to appoint an Airport Access Task Force, headed by the chairman of the Civil Aeronautics Board, to study the allocation of scarce airport facilities and airspace.

Airports are characterized by dedicated use, large capital costs, and long lead times for expansion and new construction. The level of airport access may be constrained by airspace, airfield, terminal, or ground capacity. Access to the physical terminal and ground facilities are controlled by the airport operator. Access to airspace is controlled by the FAA.

Restrictions on aircraft operations at many airports are now recognized as inevitable. Local airport proprietors are having to limit operations and impose curfews in order to reduce the level of noise affecting nearby residents. Some airports are becoming more congested as carriers exercise their new opportunities to enter markets where previous regulatory constraints had denied them access. FAA restricts hourly operations when demand for airspace access is more than existing systems can safely accommodate. These restrictions have been particularly severe during the two-year period following the PATCO job action. Expansion is slowed or even stopped by environmental objections to new facilities or facility expansion.

The concern of public policy in a deregulated environment is with the manner in which airport access and slots are allocated among the airlines. To achieve efficiency, entry by new carriers and changes in service by existing carriers must be permitted to the maximum extent possible. Carriers should be given an opportunity to compete at the airport, even under circumstances in which they might not be able to start or add as many new flights as they might prefer. Thus rules should be developed that make facilities available to carriers on reasonably competitive terms.[23]

Noise and Environmental Constraints

Aircraft noise is an unfortunate by-product of airline service. While quieter new technology is being incorporated into carriers' fleets, local airports often impose use restrictions in order to mollify communities or to meet state laws. These restrictions are sometimes, but not always, consistent with the judgments inherent in the federal standards which allow higher noise levels to be made by larger aircraft.[24] To give an idea of the magnitude of the problem, noise-related restrictions on existing capacity have been imposed at not less than nineteen of the thirty-five largest passenger-handling airports during the past decade, and virtually none of the prior restrictions were removed. During the same period, noise concerns inhibited expansion at about twelve of these airports.[25]

State regulations are beginning to be added to federal law. For example, the state of Washington has granted large airport operators authority to control noise impact by monitoring, land acquisition, sound proofing, and the provision of mortgage insurance to properties affected by noise. In California a number of airports are being forced to limit access to their facilities because of state environmental laws that prohibit them from allowing the noise in surrounding areas from increasing. Airport authorities have at times proposed to apply stricter standards on entrants than on incumbents. San Francisco Airport once proposed to apply harsher noise standards on new entrants; San Diego initially imposed a condition on new entrants subjecting them to diffferent curfew and noise standards; Orange County's John Wayne Airport proposed a rule that would freeze access to the airport at the status quo, thus favoring incumbent airlines over new entrants.[26]

The CAB and FAA mounted a concerted effort to convince these airport authorities to adopt less anticompetitive rules. It was somewhat successful at San Francisco and San Diego. However, Orange County did not change plans, even though independently Pacific Southwest Airlines fought the airport authority in court seeking to obtain an equal opportunity to use the airport.[27] The court held the rule to be nondiscriminatory and within the airport authority's power. The court focused not on the prohibition against unjust discrimination in terms of promotion of competition but rather on a narrower issue of assurance of equal access to interstate and intrastate flights.

Airport Facilities Constraints

A second type of access constraint at airports has evolved from the traditonal pattern of long-term leases for terminal facilities. Historically airport operators required airline tenants to enter into long-term leases and sometimes even to build their own terminals on airport property. This was done in order to support revenue bond financing of airport facilities. In turn the carriers were given full control of their leased properties whether actually used by them or not.

This can conceivably give incumbent carriers power to set the price and conditions of entry of actual and potential competitors. The problem was illustrated by Laker Airways' search for gate and terminal space at JFK Airport in 1977 and 1978. Because the international terminal, which is owned by the New York Port Authority, was full, Laker contacted various airlines. He had no success despite the fact that at least one terminal—National's—had unused space throughout this period. Similar difficulties have been encountered domestically. Eastern Airlines, for example, undertook extended and difficult negotiations with TWA, in order to sublease TWA space at Los Angeles. TWA was of course not enthusiastic about offering attractive terms to a possible major new competitor in the New York–Los Angeles market.[28]

Other contractual difficulties that continue from the prederegulation period are majority-in-interest clauses that grant the majority of airlines at an airport the power to veto new capital improvements or expansion at the airport. These provisions originated in the regulated era when entry of new airlines into airports was limited and the airport administrators demanded long-term leases to facilitate the raising of capital to ensure a stable financial environment. In addition the majority-in-interest clauses allow existing carriers at an airport to curb expansion at the airport. Since the carriers with long-term leases at the airport have a major financial stake, the ability to curb airport expansion may have been acceptable. Although many of these arrangements may have been justified in a regulated regime, they may serve to limit airlines' ability to expand in the deregulated environment. Consequently negotiating arrangements between incumbent carriers and airports on budget, planning, and operations may also have antitrust ramifications.

A number of airports are renegotiating with carriers to include in their new leases provisions allowing the airport to buy back underutilized gates and reassign the areas to other carriers with greater demand. This approach does not preclude the use of long-term leases but does prevent these leases from becoming a competitive weapon. Other airports are beginning to rely on the underlying strength of the air traffic market at that location rather than on particular incumbent carriers as the underpinning for the sale of airport bonds. These are certainly beneficial moves, which some observers feel should be codified into the law. They believe it should clearly be the duty of airport operators to make airport access available on fair and reasonable terms that give all carriers an equal opportunity to compete and confirm the rights of private citizens to enforce these duties.[29]

Conclusion

Rate and route deregulations were justified on economic grounds. But economic theory did not say that total economic deregulation of air transport was appropriate. Rather, government intervention through the antitrust laws should continue to govern airline merger and acquisition policy. Moreover extensive review of antitrust immunity conferred for intercarrier agreements should be undertaken to assess its appropriateness in a deregulated regime.

Chapter 11

Concluding Remarks

Dramatic technological advances in aerospace coupled with the rapid growth in air travel obscured the economic distortions that airline regulation had spawned. With the conversion to jet aircraft complete, the airline industry was no longer immune from the inflationary pressures in the economy. Political events combined with the changing economics of the industry to force a reevaluation of the regulatory framework.

In the mid-1970s Congress, the industry, the academe, and the Civil Aeronautics Board simultaneously studied and debated the effects of regulation on the airline industry. These analyses not only considered the Board policies but also analyzed the experiences of the intrastate markets in California and Texas which operated in a much less restrictive regulatory climate. There was virtual unanimity that the existing regulatory framework had to be changed.

Beginning late in 1976, the Board began relaxing its regulatory hold, and the results were extremely positive. This confirmed the experience of the intrastate markets. Two years later Congress passed the Airline Deregulation Act.

Despite the extensive analysis that proceeded the passage of the act, despite the experiences of the intrastate markets, and despite the industry's performance under a more flexible regulatory policy, no clear prediction had developed about all of the consequences of airline deregulation. Moreover there was no anticipation of the adverse effects caused by simultaneous fuel price shocks and an economic recession. At the time the Airline Deregulation Act passed, few, if any, of the analysts accurately foresaw the full extent of the multitude of changes that deregulation would bring.

Regulatory Fairness versus Market Efficiency

In retrospect the failure to predict the precise effects of injecting competition into the airline industry is not surprising. Determining the full consequence of any regulation is virtually an impossible task. For that reason economists have long argued that the competitive marketplace is the only truly effective regulator of economic activity. Through a process of trial and error the market determines the most efficient way for producers to provide goods and services to consumers. The developments in the deregulated airline industry vividly demonstrate this view. A number of trends under deregulation, especially the growth of hub-and-spoke operations, were not fully anticipated but in retrospect are readily explained.

Regulation, by definition, substitutes the judgment of the regulator for that of the marketplace. Just as analysts were unable to forecast fully how the deregulated airline industry would perform, the regulator cannot know what the full effect of its regulations will be. Moreover the regulator is dictated by concerns of fairness and equity in developing its policies. But in so doing, it dictates a structure and a way of doing business that ultimately is not in the best interests of either regulated firms or consumers.

This notion of fairness is readily apparent in the Board's route and rate decisions. The CAB granted the large trunk carriers the rights to the densest routes, whereas small local service carriers were granted regional monopolies of thin routes which were subsidized. The local carriers had the advantage of monopolies, as well as a subsidy, but were locked out of larger markets. Although the trunks often faced competition, they were guaranteed the feed of the local carriers and were protected from wholly new entry.

It seemed fair that it should cost more to go a longer distance, but somehow it was less fair that passengers on heavily traveled routes should pay less than those on less traveled routes. Thus distance-based, but not density-based, formulas were used to set prices. Also it was not fair, or at least not necessary, to pay more to travel on Friday afternoon than to travel on Sunday morning. Therefore peak-load pricing was not encouraged,

Deregulation has shown that the well-intentioned and orderly views of the regulators caused enormous distortions in productivity and in service. Although passengers prefer frequent nonstop service, such service can be quite costly. There are economies of aircraft size, whereas the costs of accomodating a passenger in an otherwise empty seat are quite small. Since a large proportion of city-pair markets cannot support convenient nonstop service, hub-and-spoke operations have proved to be the dominant networking strategy of air carriers since deregulation. There has been a significant shift away from the regulatory vision of linear systems and toward sunbursts of routes. The delivery of air services has become far more productive as all carriers are able, through route flexibility, to achieve economies of scope in their operations. It is significant that air carriers of all sizes and types—trunks, locals, new entrants, and commuters—are expanding their hub-and-spoke operations. Air carriers are selecting one or two hubs at which to focus their operations, and this new focus is benefiting both them and their customers. Whereas before deregulation only a few carriers enjoyed such operations, now all carriers are enjoying their benefits. Deregulating the route network has permitted carriers to expand and to tailor their route networks to match traffic flows. As a result a greater share of connecting trips are now made online. Moreover carriers are diversifying the markets they serve, adding vacation markets if they had primarily served business markets and adding north–south markets if they had been restricted to east–west markets. Such strategies enhance equipment utilization.

Other Changes since Deregulation

Since deregulation many new jet entrants have arrived on the scene. Despite a very low initial market share these carriers have had high leverage in lowering prices in airline markets. Moreover they have been an important spur to increased carrier concern in reducing costs. It is now clear that inflexible work rules and higher than competitive pay flourished during regulation. Airline employees appear to have benefited substantially from CAB's protective regulation. With deregulation a productivity gap between the newer and older airlines has loomed in importance. The current coexistence of high and low cost airlines has created a competitive disequilibrium that will undoubtedly influence the development of the airline industry for many years. In the short run profits for the high cost carriers have been severely eroded. In the long run these carriers cannot compete successfully unless their cost structures are brought into line with those of the lower cost airlines. Thus there is considerable pressure on the older certificated airlines to move toward competitive pay levels and more flexible work rules. This is enhancing productivity and efficiency throughout the industry.

Most observers of the industry predicted that deregulation would lower average fares and bring with them higher load factors. However, the advantages of restricted discount fares were not foreseen. The practice of mixing discretionary and time-sensitive passengers on a single flight appears to be beneficial to all parties. The low-fare passenger attains greater flexibility of itinerary; the high-fare passenger attains more frequent and better-timed service (albeit at the cost of less empty seats nearby on which a briefcase can be laid); and the carrier is using equipment more economically.

The regulatory boundary between charter and scheduled flights has eroded. Deregulation has shown that once trunk carriers had the choice of offering capacity-controlled deep discount fares, they chose to combine both business and vacation travelers on the same flight. They could use vacation traffic to fill otherwise empty seats on off-peak flights, while limiting availability of deep discount seats during peak business travel times.

In addition prices are moving closer to costs in all markets. There is some difficulty convincing people that fares closer to costs are "fair." The perception is that smaller communities pay too much under deregulation, since prices on their routes have begun to reflect costs and hence become more expensive relative to those on thicker routes of similar mileage. Through much of the period under deregulation, prices have been particularly low on the densest long-haul routes, reflecting the excessive amount of wide-bodied equipment that was accumulated during regulation. Yet these same small community travelers now pay less to their vacation destinations than they do in their primarily business markets. This lower price occurs, in part, because tourist markets can be served with a higher load factor and, in part, because aircraft can serve these markets during off-peak hours when demand by time-sensitive business travelers is relatively low.

Regulators seemed to have chosen a somewhat smaller average number of carriers per market than that which has resulted from the free play of competitive forces. The names of the serving carriers on many of the routes are now different, and about half a carrier more serves the denser markets. The average trip time has remained about the same. The freedom of choice of frequencies that was permitted carriers in the regulated era has meant that postderegulation timing choices have not been too different. There has been about a 7 percent improvement of service convenience to small-hub cities, largely attributable to the larger emphasis on the hub-and-spoke method of delivery.

The deregulated period has still been characterized by high concentration in its markets compared with markets in other industries. Although regulation clearly contributed to the market structure, in most markets, economies of aircraft size still limit the extent of deconcentration. Nevertheless, carriers have limited market power. Convenient connecting service is often available by carriers who do not provide nonstop service. This constrains the fares of the nonstop carriers. At the same time carriers offer competitive connecting service, particularly in long-haul markets. In thin short-haul markets, where competitive services are not widely available, carrier pricing is constrained by surface competition as well as the threat of entry.

Fares are somewhat higher in more concentrated markets, even when adjusted for cost differences. However, the market power is not large— fares are in general only about 5 to 10 percent higher in concentrated than in nonconcentrated markets. Thus the degree of market power in terms of prices for the general public is sufficiently small that market forces rather than regulatory actions are being used as the mechanism to erode it.

In the regulated era commuter airlines were well on their way to replacing jet operators in many thin short-haul markets. This trend has continued after deregulation. Small communities where commuters have replaced jet operators have had a 25 percent increase in flights on average and a corresponding increase in convenience. Those communities retaining jet operators have had a small net deterioration of service. The essential air service program, enacted to protect the smallest communities from the loss of all air service, has worked. Less than 150 communities require subsidy now in contrast to about 400 communities prederegulation, whereas taxpayer costs for the new subsidy program have been far lower. Even the smallest nonhubs have had improvements in their connecting opportunities to large nearby cities, as commuters chose to arrange their routing patterns favoring more hub-and-spoke operations and less linear route patterns. These figures do reflect averages. Since worsening of service gets much press, and improvements in service do not, the general public may still perceive the overall convenience has declined, though on average it has improved.

Many of the formerly regulated carriers have had some difficulty in adjusting to the new deregulatory regime and have seen their share of the industry decline. The aircraft mix that carriers acquired differs from the mix they would have puchased had the industry never been regulated. Moreover regulators' contributions to noncompetitive carriers' pay scales and work rules will persist for sometime. Nevertheless, a number of these carriers have been successful in adjusting to competition. Some airlines inherited route systems, cost structures, and aircraft mixes that were better suited for a more competitive environment. The former local service carriers, for example, had fleets of two-engine jet aircraft and route systems that were readily expanded into hub-and-spoke operations.

Although initial endowments are certainly important in predicting a carrier's relative success, they are by no means dispositive. There is ample evidence that managements have a critical role in determining the success of any particular airline. Some carriers have been able to negotiate more flexible labor contracts with their employees, and others have secured efficient aircraft on favorable terms. Others have started new hubs that are highly successful. Still others have developed successful programs such as the marketing of computer reservation systems and the introduction of frequent flyer programs.

Toward a Long-Run Equilibrium

This book has not attempted to develop an equilibrium model of the industry. Given the current situation of the industry, it would be difficult to test any such model. Instead, our approach has been to consider various aspects of the industry's performance to determine whether the industry is behaving efficiently. Thus we have considered pricing, productivity, and route realignments separately. Yet in the course of this analysis we have highlighted a number of factors that appear critical to the operation of airline markets.

These factors tempt us to predict in at least general terms the long-run impact of deregulation on the performance of the industry. We recognize that in attempting such a prediction, we may well be falling into the trap of those who attempted to guide structure in the regulated era. It is not at all possible to predict accurately efficient outcomes, particularly in a world subject to all sorts of technological and other exogenous changes. Yet certain trends in the development of the industry do seem susceptible to longer-run generalization.

Some of these relate to hub-and-spoke operation. Since a large portion of city-pair markets cannot support convenient nonstop service, hub-and-spoke operations should continue to be a major networking strategy of air carriers. At any airport only a few carriers will be able to develop a hub-and-spoke operation, and therefore most nonstop markets, even dense ones, will tend to be concentrated. Moreover the size of a carrier's operation at any hub will be limited because service convenience is inversely related to size of the hub. Airport capacity constraints may also limit a carrier's ability to establish a significant new hub at airports that already serve as a main hub to another carrier. Many airports do not have substantial room for expansion; citizen groups often object to the increased noise and traffic that may accompany such an expansion.

Despite the concentration in airline markets, carriers will, for the most part, be unable to earn above a competitive rate of return. Thus some version of the theory of contestable markets may eventually be demonstrable. Entry is relatively easy, and competitive connecting service is available in many markets. In some less dense, short-haul markets surface transportation may be the major competitive constraint on fares; hence carriers may have some price setting power in these markets. The monopolistic competition view of aviation markets may also offer valuable insights, with schedule rivalry still remaining an important phenomenon.

The ability to use peak-load pricing, as well as restricted discount fares, means that average load factors will be substantially higher than they were in a regulated environment. Also, since a significant segment of passengers value time savings highly, carriers will tend to price-discriminate between time-sensitive and discretionary passengers. In addition discretionary passenger demand is more elastic; thus restricted discount fares, as well as fares in leisure markets, will vary more with changes in demand than do unrestricted coach fares.

We also speculate that carriers may increasingly specialize in serving certain types of passengers such as business travelers or travelers who are willing to suffer some service inconvenience for very low fares. Economies of aircraft size, however, will limit the degree of specialization.

Finally, it appears that the prospective equilibrium toward which the industry will head is one in which the larger carriers will cut their costs to enable them to meet the increased competitive pressures of new carriers with lower costs. To the extent this takes a long time or is only partially successful, the low cost airlines will continue to grow in importance in the industry. During the interim period a variety of creative schemes are being tried to close the productivity gap between the older and newer airlines. Incentive schemes involving profit sharing and stock ownership have improved the benefit packages for some of the newer airlines, and these and other risk-sharing packages are being considered by the employees of the older airlines as well. It seems to make sense in an industry as affected by the business cycle as aviation, for there to be extra wage benefits in good times and a lesser benefit package in bad times.

We will be in a much better position to judge the long-term effects of deregulation on productivity as the current economy recovery continues. Load factors will undoubtedly reach levels approaching those in the late 1970s. In addition the productivity changes due to other factors will continue apace.

Though we believe our analysis supports these conclusions, our study has not focused on the long run. Rather, we have examined the initial changes that have occurred without the intrusive hand of the Civil Aeronautics Board. Although the industry is still very much in transition and despite the financial difficulties of a number of carriers, the changes we have observed indicate the industry is using its resources more rationally. As we have noted, it will be many more years before regulation's effect on the trunks' and locals' costs and equipment mix completely disappears. Thus the conclusions in our book are tentative. Nevertheless, the changes that we have observed indicate that the industry is using its resources better; deregulation is leading to a substantially more efficient airline system.

Appendix

Appendix Table A Domestic trunks' selected traffic and financial data, 1945–1983

	Scheduled revenue passenger service							All services		
Calendar year	RPM (000)	ASM (000)	Load factor (percent)	Average on-flight trip (miles)[a]	Passenger revenue per RPM (¢) current	Consumer price index (1980 = 100)	Operating expenditure per ASM (¢) current $	Operating revenue less subsidy per RTM (¢)	Operating expenditure per RTM (¢)	Operating profit margin (percent)
1945	3,336,278	3,784,532	88.2	523	4.93	21.8	4.69	b	43.55	15.8
1946	5,903,111	7,490,387	78.8	496	4.62	23.7	4.23	b	48.78	(1.7)
1947	6,016,257	9,152,389	65.7	490	5.04	27.1	4.08	b	54.18	(5.9)
1948	5,840,211	9,980,163	58.5	474	5.73	29.2	4.12	b	58.24	0.5
1949	6,570,726	11,117,703	59.1	469	5.75	28.9	3.91		53.79	5.4
1950	7,766,008	12,385,635	62.7	486	5.54	29.2	3.73	b	47.91	11.9
1951	10,210,726	14,671,982	69.6	495	5.59	31.5	3.77	b	45.87	16.1
1952	12,120,789	18,068,123	67.1	533	5.54	32.2	3.72	b	47.61	12.4
1953	14,297,581	22,114,772	64.7	547	5.43	32.4	3.57	b	48.07	10.1
1954	16,234,638	25,623,314	63.4	553	5.37	32.6	3.43	52.43	47.28	10.2
1955	19,205,675	29,978,597	64.1	557	5.32	32.5	3.37	51.58	46.11	10.8
1956	21,643,140	33,752,551	64.1	576	5.28	33.0	3.73	51.39	47.39	8.0
1957	24,499,510	39,838,165	61.5	608	5.25	34.1	3.46	52.15	50.64	3.0
1958	24,435,657	40,695,035	60.0	618	5.58	35.1	3.48	54.92	51.55	6.3
1959	28,127,216	45,793,218	61.4	632	5.80	35.3	3.70	56.80	53.47	5.9
1960	29,233,199	49,153,265	59.5	647	6.01	35.9	3.88	58.29	57.25	1.8
1961	29,534,792	52,525,014	56.2	661	6.19	36.3	3.88	58.99	59.31	(0.6)
1962	31,827,840	59,736,760	53.3	681	6.35	36.7	3.64	59.67	57.68	3.3
1963	36,383,756	67,601,302	53.8	682	6.07	37.1	3.44	57.57	54.55	5.3
1964	41,658,368	75,242,408	55.4	688	6.01	37.6	3.31	56.55	50.60	10.6
1965	48,986,972	88,731,152	55.2	701	5.94	38.3	3.21	54.48	47.59	12.8
1966	56,802,788	97,174,719	58.5	716	5.69	39.4	3.30	51.66	45.28	12.4

Year										
1967	70,990,141	124,141,624	57.2	730	5.50	40.5	3.23	49.24	44.70	9.3
1968	81,611,832	153,864,640	53.0	749	5.45	42.2	3.06	48.83	45.72	6.4
1969a,c	95,657,705	190,064,198	50.3	737	5.59	44.5	3.05	48.51	45.78	5.6
1970	95,899,744	194,461,931	49.3	781	5.77	47.1	3.22	49.83	49.59	0.3
1971	97,756,113	202,509,471	48.3	786	6.09	49.1	3.22	52.73	50.94	3.4
1972	108,189,968	206,617,921	52.4	792	6.16	50.7	3.42	53.47	50.38	5.8
1973	115,352,180	222,446,581	51.9	797	6.38	53.9	3.50	56.26	53.48	4.9
1974	117,616,261	210,997,105	55.7	795	7.24	59.8	3.87	65.95	61.44	6.8
1975	119,445,956	217,855,445	54.8	810	7.35	65.3	4.58	67.85	67.30	0.8
1976	131,424,511	235,538,771	55.8	819	7.79	69.0	4.70	70.95	68.14	4.0
1977	141,276,272	252,567,993	55.9	820	8.24	73.5	4.99	75.10	72.22	3.8
1978	164,150,171	268,190,511	61.2	837	8.08	79.1	5.39	76.01	71.86	5.5
1979	180,717,936	285,962,923	63.2	854	8.50	88.0	6.13	81.14	81.45	(0.4)
1980	168,224,205	288,315,986	58.3	884	10.96	100.0	7.30	103.56	104.71	(1.1)
1981	159,188,061	277,840,827	57.3	909	12.37	110.2	8.14	114.89	117.31	(2.2)
1982d	167,776,366	285,286,830	58.8	935	11.60	117.1	7.27	110.20	114.60	(4.0)
1983	173,796,691	288,201,186	60.3	1,922	11.61	120.8	7.31	109.95	113.04	(2.8)

a. Effective with 1969, "on-flight passenger trip length" has been substituted in place of "online passenger stage." Data are based on passenger enplanements rather than originations, which were no longer reported after 1968. Year ago percentage comparisons for 1968 were based on "on-flight" concepts.

b. Separation of service mail pay and subsidy not required on *Form 41* prior to 1954.

c. Data before 1969 was on a fourty-eight state basis. Data for 1969 and after based on a fifty state concept. Year ago percentage comparison for 1969 was based on a fourty-eight state concept.

d. Texas International merged with Continental in November 1982. Data for Texas International were included with the majors.

Appendix Table B Local service carriers' selected traffic and financial data, 1945–1983

	Scheduled revenue passenger service							All services			Subsidy as percent of Total operating revenue
Calendar year	RPM (000)	ASM (000)	Load factor (percent)	Average on-flight trip (miles)[a]	Passenger revenue per RPM (¢) current	Consumer price index (1980 = 100)	Operating expenditure per ASM (¢) current $	Operating revenue less subsidy per RPM (¢)	Operating expenditure per RPM (¢)	Operating profit margin (percent)	
1945	1,312	2,486	52.8	328	4.95	21.8	9.13	b	178.74	(57.6)	b
1946	6,812	17,964	37.9	272	4.62	23.7	6.70	b	188.85	(12.5)	b
1947	46,418	155,507	29.8	197	4.91	27.1	5.14	b	171.22	(7.4)	b
1948	87,928	323,942	27.1	206	5.31	29.2	4.48	b	160.72	2.9	b
1949	134,742	477,991	28.2	199	5.46	28.9	4.58	b	152.43	(2.1)	b
1950	188,782	599,159	31.5	195	5.46	29.2	4.52	b	129.63	2.1	b
1951	289,644	774,713	37.4	196	5.61	31.5	4.64	b	113.76	2.1	b
1952	339,644	905,796	37.5	196	5.82	32.2	4.80	b	120.42	(2.6)	b
1953	390,854	1,013,729	38.6	192	5.96	32.4	5.02	b	124.91	(3.1)	b
1954	461,175	1,092,906	42.2	190	6.15	32.6	4.96	65.81	112.14	2.9	43.0
1955	534,788	1,184,100	45.2	182	6.27	32.5	4.88	66.37	102.92	1.2	36.3
1956	633,228	1,382,543	45.8	183	6.34	33.0	4.94	67.16	103.07	(0.9)	34.3
1957	747,288	1,652,132	45.2	189	6.35	34.1	5.02	66.85	105.59	(0.9)	36.1
1958	820,192	1,793,463	45.7	192	6.89	35.1	5.20	71.88	107.79	1.7	34.5
1959	1,024,336	2,309,162	44.4	197	7.14	35.3	5.29	74.11	112.28	0.5	34.3
1960	1,141,593	2,724,666	41.9	204	7.32	35.9	5.30	76.23	119.11	1.5	37.0
1961	1,343,761	3,228,491	41.6	208	7.71	36.3	5.19	80.12	117.74	5.3	35.5
1962	1,607,673	3,797,465	42.3	210	7.80	36.7	5.08	81.11	113.15	6.5	33.0
1963	1,868,988	4,266,886	43.8	211	7.66	37.1	5.02	79.71	107.90	5.3	30.0
1964	2,244,488	4,836,305	46.4	214	7.54	37.6	4.90	78.48	98.86	6.7	25.9
1965	2,621,201	5,545,691	47.3	213	7.76	38.3	4.82	80.20	95.12	8.3	22.7
1966	3,467,510	6,908,077	50.2	223	7.64	39.4	4.70	79.07	87.54	6.7	15.8
1967	4,114,304	8,862,400	46.4	227	7.63	40.5	4.50	78.83	90.19	0.2	12.7
1968	5,489,224	12,153,586	45.2	248	7.56	42.2	4.20	77.55	86.00	(1.8)	8.2

1969[a,c]	6,312,630	14,722,390	42.9	257	8.25	44.5	4.27	82.97	90.49	(2.9)	5.7
1970	7,430,666	17,024,403	43.6	281	8.44	47.1	4.38	81.89	87.56	(1.2)	5.5
1971	7,851,515	17,335,816	45.3	286	8.77	49.1	4.61	85.92	89.27	3.5	7.1
1972	8,899,388	18,074,128	49.2	292	8.87	50.7	4.88	85.98	87.15	5.6	6.9
1973	9,829,603	20,178,505	48.7	303	9.05	53.9	4.85	88.86	88.94	6.0	6.1
1974	10,808,141	20,513,800	52.7	307	10.10	59.8	5.74	101.60	98.97	7.7	5.3
1975	10,683,528	20,680,683	51.7	314	10.82	65.3	6.25	108.62	111.53	2.3	4.2
1976	12,127,464	22,907,196	52.9	320	11.44	69.0	6.47	113.10	111.62	5.6	4.3
1977	13,541,668	25,129,836	53.9	324	11.93	73.5	6.71	118.14	114.13	6.9	3.6
1978	16,477,664	28,130,174	58.6	339	11.90	79.1	7.17	117.72	113.12	6.3	2.6
1979	19,904,145	33,904,420	58.7	386	12.38	88.0	7.90	124.33	121.69	4.6	2.6
1980	21,601,526	39,404,649	54.8	420	15.35	100.0	8.91	154.46	150.18	4.4	1.6
1981	23,707,260	42,726,879	55.5	459	16.83	110.2	9.79	168.36	163.41	4.8	1.9
1982[d]	24,846,145	43,966,926	56.5	472	16.34	117.1	8.96	165.13	159.00	3.7	0.8
1983	28,529,392	50,716,171	56.3	514	15.58	120.8	8.58	156.39	151.92	2.9	1.0

a. Effective with 1969, "on-flight passenger trip length" has been substituted in place of "online passenger stage length. "Data are based on passenger enplanements rather than originations, which were no longer reported after 1968. Year ago percentage comparisons for 1968 were based on "on-flight" concepts.

b. Separation of service mail pay and subsidy not required on *Form 41* prior to 1954.

c. Data before 1969 was on a fourty-eight state basis. Data for 1969 and after based on a fifty state concept. Year ago percentage comparison for 1969 was based on a fourty-eight state concept.

d. Texas International merged with Continental in November 1982. Data for Texas International for 1982 were included with Continental.

Appendix Table C   Traffic, load factors, and profitability by carrier, 1970–1983

| Year | Scheduled service | | | Operating profit margin (operating profit as percent of operating revenue) |
	Revenue passenger miles (millions)	Revenue passenger load factor (percent)	On-flight passenger trip length (miles)	
American Airlines (trunk) domestic operations				
1970	16,238	50.9	860.2	(1.8)
1971	16,037	49.8	875.5	2.0
1972	17,192	52.8	908.9	2.5
1973	18,339	52.6	930.4	(3.3)
1974	18,183	57.4	953.6	1.9
1975	18,379	56.5	965.6	(2.5)
1976	20,044	58.1	968.2	3.1
1977	21,432	58.3	972.5	2.8
1978	25,200	63.1	995.7	3.1
1979	29,036	67.4	1,039.8	(0.3)
1980	24,264	59.7	1,054.4	(3.5)
1981	25,615	61.3	1,103.8	1.2
1982	28,509	63.7	1,092.7	(0.6)
1983	31,276	64.6	1,051.8	5.9
Braniff International (trunk) domestic operations				
1970	3,375	46.4	592.1	0.7
1971	3,320	47.9	611.4	5.7
1972	3,725	49.2	619.2	5.4
1973	4,232	50.3	624.1	7.3
1974	4,693	49.2	628.1	9.5
1975	5,003	50.4	642.0	8.6
1976	5,535	51.9	661.9	8.1
1977	5,957	50.3	670.7	8.9
1978	7,173	52.5	694.5	6.2
1979	9,489	55.0	745.8	2.3
1980	7,336	56.1	704.5	(5.7)
1981	6,257	55.8	684.7	(9.3)
1982	3,146	53.6	804.0	(18.7)
Continental Airlines (trunk) domestic operations				
1970	4,434	51.2	874.5	7.0
1971	4,712	49.3	852.1	8.6
1972	5,190	51.3	879.4	9.7
1973	5,576	48.5	887.8	4.4
1974	5,572	53.9	858.6	10.8
1975	6,270	54.0	888.2	6.6
1976	6,121	56.0	890.5	6.9
1977	7,093	55.6	879.7	7.3
1978	8,411	59.4	916.6	5.9
1979	8,838	60.6	927.2	0.2
1980	7,305	57.4	907.8	(5.2)
1981	6,934	57.7	888.8	(5.0)
1982	10,106	57.8	919.3	(4.5)
1983	7,894	60.0	858.3	(18.5)

Note: Braniff ceased operations May 12, 1982.
Note: Texas International merged with Continental in November 1982. Data for Texas International for 1982 were included with Continental.

Appendix Table C (*Cont.*)

Year	Scheduled service			Operating profit margin (operating profit as percent of operating revenue)
	Revenue passenger miles (millions)	Revenue passenger load factor (percent)	On-flight passenger trip length (miles)	
Delta Airlines (trunk) domestic operations				
1970	11,437	48.1	609.1	9.3
1971	11,831	47.2	609.1	11.0
1972	13,536	50.5	607.9	6.6
1973	15,022	51.2	610.5	11.0
1974	15,662	56.9	602.2	12.1
1975	16,056	55.9	614.0	4.8
1976	17,191	55.6	618.9	7.7
1977	18,655	56.9	618.5	9.3
1978	22,401	62.0	627.3	9.6
1979	24,602	62.4	623.0	4.9
1980	24,209	58.4	642.2	5.4
1981	22,834	52.5	668.6	2.4
1982	22,892	51.9	693.6	(2.7)
1983	25,250	53.3	699.3	(2.1)
Eastern Airlines (trunk) domestic operations				
1970	11,649	53.0	589.3	3.3
1971	11,725	51.9	590.4	4.4
1972	13,252	57.6	593.3	5.4
1973	13,430	54.9	585.2	0.3
1974	13,958	59.6	586.6	6.4
1975	14,501	56.8	603.8	1.0
1976	15,679	56.0	604.7	4.6
1977	16,782	55.6	602.8	2.0
1978	20,750	66.1	622.3	3.7
1979	24,028	68.6	635.0	4.4
1980	23,586	60.6	675.4	0.5
1981	24,198	55.8	727.6	(0.8)
1982	23,837	57.2	731.9	(0.6)
1983	25,278	59.3	745.7	(2.0)
Frontier Airlines (local) domestic operations				
1970	1,023	43.8	377.9	0.5
1971	1,040	45.8	379.8	1.6
1972	1,100	51.9	374.7	10.4
1973	1,308	52.9	387.5	7.1
1974	1,389	55.8	384.4	11.7
1975	1,455	55.6	389.8	6.9
1976	1,680	56.9	395.0	10.3
1977	1,887	58.3	400.6	11.1
1978	2,378	63.2	429.9	4.6
1979	2,989	60.5	457.1	8.5
1980	2,945	58.8	489.4	7.4
1981	3,475	61.6	552.9	9.2
1982	3,546	60.6	606.1	1.3
1983	3,902	59.5	608.5	(3.9)

Note: Northeast merged with Delta on August 1, 1972. Data for the two carries have been combined.

Appendix Table C (*Cont.*)

Year	Scheduled service Revenue passenger miles (millions)	Revenue passenger load factor (percent)	On-flight passenger trip length (miles)	Operating profit margin (operating profit as percent of operating revenue)
Northwest Airlines (trunk) domestic operations				
1970	3,415	44.0	760.6	11.6
1971	4,385	37.7	776.3	3.3
1972	3,658	37.1	759.1	4.8
1973	5,926	39.8	818.3	8.1
1974	6,780	44.8	834.6	12.3
1975	6,934	43.7	868.7	6.1
1976	7,920	47.2	899.8	12.4
1977	8,168	47.1	874.7	11.1
1978	4,902	47.1	834.6	9.0
1979	8,853	54.8	862.4	5.0
1980	8,443	52.7	849.9	2.1
1981	8,217	53.3	877.2	0.3
1982	8,528	55.4	914.3	(2.4)
1983	9,426	55.7	907.7	2.3
Pan American World Airways (trunk) domestic operations				
1970	4,509	45.6	1,109.0	(3.5)
1971	6,165	46.5	998.2	4.7
1972	7,413	54.2	1,017.7	7.7
1973	7,511	52.1	990.0	6.7
1974	5,528	51.4	1,013.9	3.3
1975	5,261	51.5	1,078.7	0.9
1976	6,731	48.6	1,086.9	0.4
1977	7,488	48.2	1,083.6	(1.6)
1978	8.833	56.8	1,117.1	(0.9)
1979	9,210	58.0	1,234.3	(6.6)
1980	8,916	56.6	1,264.3	(9.0)
1981	7,591	56.6	1,317.9	(28.4)
1982	7,126	54.7	1,405.9	(35.3)
1983	7,424	61.2	1,208.8	(24.8)
Ozark Airlines (local) domestic operations				
1970	653	43.4	270.4	2.2
1971	743	47.1	273.0	10.1
1972	820	49.1	274.6	6.9
1973	617	47.6	272.7	3.1
1974	866	50.4	269.4	6.8
1975	936	49.0	279.7	2.6
1976	1,105	51.3	295.6	8.1
1977	1,221	51.1	301.2	7.7
1978	1,488	55.1	324.4	8.8
1979	1,553	58.4	384.9	(1.4)
1980	1,572	52.8	408.7	(0.4)
1981	1,865	55.1	448.4	8.9
1982	2,156	54.5	503.0	4.4
1983	2,621	56.0	541.2	0.6

Note: Beginning January 1980, National was merged with Pan American. Data for the two carriers have been combined.

Appendix Table C (*Cont.*)

Year	Scheduled service Revenue passenger miles (millions)	Revenue passenger load factor (percent)	On-flight passenger trip length (miles)	Operating profit margin (operating profit as percent of operating revenue)
Piedmont Airlines (local) domestic operations				
1970	745	44.8	276.3	2.4
1971	785	47.6	276.0	7.1
1972	877	50.1	277.1	10.0
1973	994	50.0	282.0	8.7
1974	1,097	52.9	287.1	11.6
1975	1,061	49.6	294.4	1.8
1976	1,157	51.1	299.8	6.2
1977	1,261	51.8	302.6	6.0
1978	1,434	54.8	313.1	2.8
1979	1,932	55.6	352.5	6.7
1980	2,363	51.8	414.0	6.5
1981	3,234	58.1	445.1	9.8
1982	3,894	55.7	456.9	3.3
1983	5,130	53.8	438.4	6.8
Republic Airlines (local) domestic operations				
1970	2,101	43.2	248.7	(6.3)
1971	2,229	44.4	261.3	1.8
1972	2,464	48.3	271.8	6.2
1973	2,937	47.8	284.8	5.8
1974	3,291	52.3	288.8	8.8
1975	3,379	50.5	295.4	2.9
1976	3,742	50.9	300.5	4.3
1977	4,362	51.4	310.6	6.1
1978	5,533	56.9	323.8	6.9
1979	6,196	54.1	362.8	1.3
1980	7,004	50.2	403.4	0.6
1981	7,555	50.3	450.5	1.1
1982	9,173	55.6	508.9	2.4
1983	9.632	54.4	542.7	(2.0)
Texas International Airlines (local) domestic operations				
1970	660	43.0	297.3	(5.6)
1971	706	47.2	297.5	(1.9)
1972	686	49.9	301.5	2.5
1973	682	45.9	317.1	4.3
1974	759	50.4	336.8	2.8
1975	580	49.7	354.6	(3.7)
1976	947	53.6	362.3	4.3
1977	1,167	57.7	361.8	8.2
1978	1,561	60.0	391.4	9.2
1979	2,186	62.1	492.3	6.0
1980	2,242	57.5	515.8	2.7
1981	2,154	57.6	572.5	(2.5)

Note: On July 1, 1979, North Central merged with Southern Airways to form a new carrier, Republic Airlines. Effective October 1980, Hughes Air West was merged into Republic. Data for all three carrier have been combined.

Note: Texas International merged with Continental in November 1982. Data for 1982 were included with Continental.

Appendix Table C (*Cont.*)

Year	Scheduled service		On-flight passenger trip length (miles)	Operating profit margin (operating profit as percent of operating revenue)
	Revenue passenger miles (millions)	Revenue passenger load factor (percent)		
Trans World Airlines (trunk) domestic operations				
1970	12,396	45.7	1,038.0	(11.9)
1971	12,515	46.9	1,047.4	(1.8)
1972	13,581	52.2	1,044.0	6.3
1973	12,457	50.9	1,056.6	4.3
1974	13,837	53.0	1,028.8	1.8
1975	14,388	53.4	1,038.9	(5.9)
1976	15,282	55.8	1,035.4	(0.6)
1977	16,113	56.5	1,035.1	(1.8)
1978	17,635	60.6	1,033.4	0.1
1979	20,521	62.6	1,045.5	(2.5)
1980	18,418	60.9	1,039.1	(1.9)
1981	15,966	59.4	1,039.9	(2.4)
1982	15,630	61.0	1,038.4	(10.2)
1983	15,991	61.0	1,024.2	(13.2)
United Air Lines (trunk) domestic operations				
1970	23,768	50.5	845.7	(1.4)
1971	22,339	48.9	875.5	2.3
1972	25,194	53.5	873.7	4.4
1973	27,029	54.7	893.5	7.7
1974	27,333	58.9	893.5	8.0
1975	26,226	57.1	904.3	(0.2)
1976	29,789	59.4	909.4	1.3
1977	31,744	59.9	923.2	2.7
1978	39,399	63.6	967.3	8.2
1979	36,826	66.0	1,041.0	(7.3)
1980	37,893	57.8	1,171.0	(1.6)
1981	34,341	59.3	1,196.9	(3.3)
1982	38,483	62.7	1,174.0	(1.5)
1983	42,484	64.4	1,125.3	3.4
USAir (local) domestic operations				
1970	2,249	43.9	272.8	2.4
1971	2,350	44.2	285.6	4.2
1972	2,952	48.7	293.0	2.1
1973	3,291	48.4	304.0	6.1
1974	3,405	52.9	312.3	5.0
1975	3,272	53.1	318.6	0.9
1976	3,497	54.5	317.0	4.1
1977	3,643	55.5	312.6	5.2
1978	4,083	60.8	318.0	6.0
1979	5,049	64.3	359.1	7.1
1980	5,476	60.9	385.2	9.4
1981	5,424	57.8	404.6	5.3
1982	6,078	57.0	415.1	6.2
1983	7,245	59.2	446.4	9.0

Note: Mohawk merged with Allegheny on April 12, 1972. Data for both carriers were combined. Allegheny changed its name to USAir on October 28, 1979.

Appendix Table C (*Cont.*)

Year	Scheduled service			Operating profit margin (operating profit as percent of operating revenue)
	Revenue passenger miles (millions)	Revenue passenger load factor (percent)	On-flight passenger trip length (miles)	
Western Air Lines (trunk) domestic operations				
1970	4,679	51.7	747.9	2.0
1971	4,722	52.8	745.8	3.2
1972	5,449	57.1	763.6	5.1
1973	5,830	56.7	770.1	8.7
1974	6,070	60.1	802.8	7.4
1975	6,427	60.6	837.3	1.6
1976	7,132	57.7	858.5	4.8
1977	7,843	56.8	866.2	3.9
1978	9,446	64.3	887.6	6.7
1979	9,317	62.0	822.6	2.5
1980	7,853	56.4	848.7	(3.6)
1981	7,232	58.2	853.4	(4.7)
1982	8,326	59.4	865.2	(2.4)
1983	8,774	56.4	816.3	(4.7)

Appendix Table D Changes in route networks of the trunk and local airlines, 1978 and 1981, second quarter

Mileage blocks	Departures		Revenue passenger miles		Percent of departures		Percent of RPMs	
	1978	1981	1978 (100,000)	1981 (100,000)	1978	1981	1978	1981
Trunks								
001–200	153,996	86,446	11,704	7,159	22.90	14.97	3.39	2.13
201–500	230,781	199,014	58,683	49,190	34.32	34.46	17.00	14.64
501–1,000	178,752	176,900	109,627	104,480	26.58	30.63	31.76	31.09
1,001–1,500	65,246	72,872	69,060	74,743	9.70	12.62	20.01	22.24
1,501–2,000	28,223	28,876	53,165	53,815	4.20	5.00	15.40	16.01
2,001–over	15,359	13,387	42,900	46,660	2.28	2.32	12.43	13.88
Total	672,357	577,495	345,139	336,055	100.00	100.00	100.00	100.00
Locals								
001–200	193,715	125,406	9,155	6,484	60.29	42.69	24.81	12.04
201–500	106,380	116,650	19,414	21,676	33.11	39.71	52.61	40.26
501–1,000	21,215	45,015	8,330	19,806	6.60	15.32	22.58	36.79
1,001–1,500		6,309		5,337		2.15		9.91
1,501–2,000		362		535		0.12		1.00
2,001–over								
Total	321,310	293,742	36,899	53,838	100.00	100.00	100.00	100.00

Source: Service Segment Data for the second quarter of 1978 and 1981.

Appendix Table E   Departure concentration and percentage of traffic making connections at large hubs, 1978 and 1981

City	1978 Concentration two firms[a]	Percent connecting	1981 Concentration two firms[a]	Percent connecting	1982 Concentration two firms[a]
Atlanta	73.05	64.61	79.15	64.03	79.85
Boston	39.45	25.74	34.41	26.09	32.21
Chicago O'Hare	30.67	42.35	35.56	37.74	36.65
Dallas–Ft. Worth (DFW)	53.97	47.07	54.83	47.13	62.48
Denver	44.28	47.42	48.18	47.66	47.23
Detroit	44.81	31.09	49.68	35.31	48.03
Houston-International	40.56	34.55	34.09	34.71	40.00
Las Vegas	54.29	29.30	29.41	30.19	35.66
Los Angeles-International	32.09	29.99	28.02	25.48	27.75
Miami-International	49.84	24.25	45.28	22.55	45.30
Minneapolis-St. Paul	56.06	40.82	66.27	40.63	65.16
New Orleans	47.71	40.45	43.58	36.51	47.28
New York-La Guardia	40.94	15.95	36.69	16.46	28.41
Orlando	63.08	38.65	46.92	33.10	42.84
Philadelphia	55.57	35.87	65.52	34.29	56.32
Phoenix	40.68	35.49	30.99	32.87	28.14
Pittsburgh	73.68	44.49	73.99	47.72	75.83
St. Louis	55.61	43.09	56.01	47.73	64.40
San Francisco	41.47	33.19	37.52	27.74	39.24
Seattle	43.82	39.10	38.78	35.99	35.71
Tampa	55.84	38.28	46.09	33.03	41.44
Washington-National	41.16	28.61	35.99	25.53	34.20

Source: Concentration ratios are calculated from the *Official Airline Guide* for flight listings for March of each year. Connecting traffic data come from the *O & D Survey* for the second quarter. These data were not yet available for 1982. In some cases they include traffic from other airports in the metropolitan area.

a. The two firm concentration ratio is the percentage of total departures at an airport performed by the two largest carriers.

Appendix Table F   Revenue passenger miles and industry share by carrier and by carrier group, 1978 and 1981

Carriers	1978 RPM (all services)	Percent total	1981 RPM (all services)	Percent total
Trunks				
United	41,435,613	21.5	35,262,510	17.7
American	25,498,652	13.2	25,654,581	12.9
Delta	22,850,092	11.9	22,842,787	11.4
Eastern	20,769,570	10.8	24,277,388	12.1
Trans World	17,959,644	9.3	15,970,189	8.0
Western	9,872,438	5.1	7,246,917	3.6
Pan American	8,952,189	4.7	7,703,724	3.9
Continental	8,556,698	4.4	6,936,021	3.5
Northwest	5,025,371	2.6	8,272,040	4.1
Braniff	7,301,340	3.8	6,282,443	3.2
Total	168,221,607	87.3	160,398,600	80.4
Locals				
Republic	6,085,278	3.2	7,641,170	3.8
USAir	4,243,425	2.2	5,520,380	2.8
Frontier	2,381,516	1.2	3,476,279	1.8
Texas International	1,688,223	0.9	2,251,758	1.1
Ozark	1,634,800	0.8	1,982,711	1.0
Piedmont	1,469,263	0.8	3,270,207	1.6
Total	17,502,505	9.1	24,142,505	12.1
Charters				
World	274,255	0.1	2,753,848	1.4
Capitol	372,382	0.2	1,493,529	0.7
Others	588,074	0.3	217,443	0.1
Total	1,234,711	0.6	4,464,820	2.2
Intrastates				
PSA	2,477,876	1.3	2,238,608	1.1
Southwest	1,048,624	0.6	2,310,951	1.2
Air California	812,949	0.4	1,393,403	0.7
Air Florida	263,629	0.1	1,362,279	0.7
Total	4,603,078	2.4	7,305,241	3.7
New Carriers				
New York Air			460,863	0.2
Midway			377,711	0.2
Muse			42,839	a
People Express			403,993	0.2
Total			1,285,406	0.6
Commuters				
Total	1,116,931	0.6	1,952,515	1.0
Grand total	192,678,832	100.0	199,549,087	100.0

Sources: CAB, *Air Carrier Traffic Statistics*; CAB, *Commuter Air Carrier Traffic Statistics*; CAB, *Air Carrier Industry Scheduled Service Traffic Statistics, Medium Regional Air Carrier Details*; CAB, *Tabulation, Form 298C, Schedule A-1, 4 Quarters Ending December 1981*, (unpublished); Carrier annual reports.
a. Less than 0.1 percent.

Appendix Table G   Distribution of samples of nonstop and origin and destination markets by distance and density, 1981, second quarter

Market distance (miles)	Market size (O & D passengers per day)				
	10–50	51–200	201–500	501 +	Total
Markets receiving nonstop service by large aircraft[a]					
1–200	147	60	19	15	241
201–500	150	209	81	60	500
501–1,500	52	213	140	76	481
1,501 +	5	31	35	29	100
Total	354	513	275	180	1,322
Origin and destination markets[b]					
1–200	230	75	19	16	340
201–500	1,023	254	90	66	1,433
501–1,500	2,357	463	148	76	3,044
1,501 +	893	181	53	32	1,159
Total	4,503	973	310	190	5,970

a. Source: Service Segment Data.
b. Source: O & D Survey. Includes markets that received online service and had at least ten passengers per day.

Appendix Table H   Cost and yield indexes, 1971–1982

	Trunks				Locals			
	Input cost	Yield per RTM	Cost per RTM	Cost per ATM	Input cost	Yield per RTM	Cost per RTM	Cost per ATM
2Q71	49.0	72.2	65.5	53.9	50.5	75.7	69.9	59.1
4Q71	49.9	71.1	64.4	54.8	51.9	75.6	72.0	62.4
2Q72	52.5	72.1	65.3	57.0	53.5	75.8	72.1	66.1
4Q72	53.4	73.1	66.5	58.9	55.6	75.7	70.3	65.2
2Q73	55.6	75.2	67.6	60.2	57.6	78.9	71.8	66.6
4Q73	58.4	78.4	72.2	66.5	60.3	78.6	72.8	68.9
2Q74	66.2	85.7	74.8	74.4	66.7	86.6	76.5	78.8
4Q74	70.8	88.6	86.7	75.0	70.5	90.1	89.4	79.9
2Q75	73.1	87.4	85.2	78.2	75.3	93.5	91.2	85.0
4Q75	78.7	87.4	88.1	86.0	78.6	92.1	87.7	86.7
1Q76	81.8	89.6	92.7	86.1	83.3	93.5	95.7	89.3
2Q76	82.3	91.2	85.3	84.4	84.0	96.3	90.1	89.0
3Q76	83.9	92.2	85.6	84.2	85.8	97.3	89.7	88.9
4Q76	85.5	96.3	94.2	89.7	87.5	98.9	94.9	91.5
1Q77	88.7	97.4	98.4	91.5	90.5	98.4	99.5	92.3
2Q77	92.3	97.8	94.2	92.0	92.6	99.7	94.5	92.6
3Q77	94.2	95.9	91.3	91.6	95.0	100.1	92.8	93.3
4Q77	97.3	101.0	99.5	97.8	97.0	107.7	97.0	96.2
1Q78	100.0	100.0	100.0	100.0	100.0	100.0	100.0	100.0
2Q78	100.3	98.6	93.1	102.1	100.3	102.2	92.2	100.6
3Q78	102.5	96.4	88.8	99.7	102.3	99.9	90.3	99.3
4Q78	104.4	99.9	101.4	102.9	102.4	101.0	96.6	98.3
1Q79	108.4	98.2	102.3	107.1	106.9	97.6	98.4	100.9
2Q79	116.4	102.5	101.7	122.2	110.2	99.2	89.3	104.9
3Q79	124.7	103.9	108.9	118.9	118.6	108.8	104.7	112.7
4Q79	132.1	118.6	128.1	128.4	125.5	121.8	124.4	120.3
1Q80	143.1	129.0	140.6	137.6	134.5	119.5	122.4	121.0
2Q80	148.0	131.0	139.9	141.3	138.6	128.4	124.7	125.4
3Q80	152.0	134.3	138.8	142.0	142.4	138.3	131.1	127.1
4Q80	157.2	146.9	152.1	151.7	145.9	143.8	134.1	130.7
1Q81	166.5	155.1	164.4	157.2	161.3	142.4	139.0	137.3
2Q81	171.6	150.4	156.5	161.2	164.7	145.5	137.2	139.0
3Q81	173.1	146.6	154.3	162.9	166.1	144.4	141.0	142.2
4Q81	175.0	148.0	166.2	166.1	168.3	145.6	142.8	136.7
1Q82	175.0	141.3	162.4	166.1	168.0	139.8	141.7	136.6
2Q82	175.6	142.3	150.1	161.7	168.0	136.9	123.6	135.9
3Q82	175.2	144.5	149.9	157.0	169.5	138.3	129.3	133.2
4Q82	176.0	140.8	158.9	162.3	174.0	134.7	138.3	130.8

Appendix Table I   Expenditure percentages for domestic trunk, local, and aggregate indexes, 1978 and 1981

Class of expenditure	Trunk		Local		Aggregate	
	1978	1981	1978	1981	1978	1981
Labor	47.0	40.0	47.3	39.1	47.1	39.8
Personnel expenses	2.1	1.9	2.0	1.8	2.1	1.9
Fuel and oil	22.2	32.4	19.3	29.9	21.8	32.0
Maintenance, excludes labor	4.1	2.8	6.4	4.2	4.4	3.0
Passenger food	4.2	3.3	2.3	2.4	3.9	3.2
Landing fees	2.2	1.5	2.4	1.8	2.2	1.6
Advertising	1.7	1.8	1.1	1.1	1.6	1.7
Commissions	4.6	6.1	3.7	6.0	4.5	6.1
Miscellaneous	11.9	10.2	15.4	13.7	12.4	10.8
Total	100.0	100.0	100.0	100.0	100.0	100.0

Notes

Introduction

1. Thus we do not treat international aviation policy or air cargo deregulation or the Civil Aeronautics Board's consumer-oriented rules. Federal Aviation Administration rules are discussed only when they have particular consequences for economic efficiency.

2. The material is discussed more comprehensively in the cited sources.

3. See Baumol, Panzar, and Willig (1982).

4. See Kahn (1979).

5. Policymakers will no longer have to worry about a mismatch between regulatory tools and the circumstance of the industry (see Breyer 1982).

Chapter 1

1. For a more thorough discussion, see CAB Staff Report on Routes (1974).

2. Between 1950 and 1974 the CAB blocked entry by seventy-nine applicants desiring to create newly certificated airlines. See U.S. Congress (1975).

3. See MacAvoy and Show (1977).

4. Unlike the Interstate Commerce Commission (ICC) which condones the purchase and sale of route rights between carriers, the 1938 act did not permit such market transactions in airline routes.

5. See Bailey (1981). For example, in 1970, a year of exceptionally high activity, the Board awarded fifty-six new route certificates and eliminated restrictions on nineteen others.

6. Rarely did the Board authorize more than three airlines on a particular route. These policies may well have been adopted in response to the view offered by Gill and Bates (1949) that air carriers' financial difficulties were due to "extensive competition" that had already been authorized under the 1938 Act or by the CAB.

7. One well-known example was when Northeast Airlines was granted Florida route authority in the early 1970s in the hope of aiding the financially troubled airline. See CAB Staff Report on Routes (1974).

8. The agreements were met with protest by other carriers who feared that the capacity removed from transcontinental routes would be used to compete in markets they served.

9. The courts sustained some of these decisions on appeal but turned down a more permanent agreement in 1975. For example, Air Line Pilots International v. CAB, 475 F. 2d 900 (D.D. Cir. 1973), cert. denied, 420 U.S. 972 (1975) was sustained whereas U.S. v. CAB, 511 R. 2d, 1315 (D.C. Cir. 1975) was overturned.

10. At first the Board was reluctant to approve coach service because of the industry's poor profitability following World War II. By 1952 the improvement in industry profits and the pressure from the large irregulars combined to get the Board, in fact, to advocate the expansion of coach service by certificated carriers. (See Caves 1962, 144–146.)

11. Discounts were allowed for families, children, and military travelers. In addition transcontinental excursion discounts were introduced. See Jordan (1970, 60 and table 8-1).

12. See Douglas and Miller (1974, 96).

13. At various time beginning in 1952, the Board allowed carriers to increase fares by one dollar per ticket, thereby increasing short-haul fares by a proportionately greater amount than long-haul fares.

14. Douglas and Miller (1974) documented the distortions caused by the Board's fare policies. For example, in 1969 they found industry load factors declined with distance, whereas according to economic analysis, we should expect load factors to increase with distance. For a more detailed discussion of Douglas and Miller's study and evidence on how the relationships between distance and load factor has changed since 1969, see chapter 8.

15. See chapter 5.

16. For an excellent description of these and other instances, see Jordan (1970).

17. For example, in the *States-Alaska Fare Case*, 21 CAB 354 (1955), the CAB did not permit Alaska Airlines to charge a lower price in older DC-4 equipment than was being charged by Pan American using newer DC-6 equipment.

18. The new fare structure was designed to adjust prices so that they were more in line with costs. Consequently American's formula increased fares substantially in short-haul markets; in some long-haul markets fares declined somewhat.

19. See John E. Moss v. CAB, 430 F. 2d 891 (1970).

20. See Douglas and Miller (1974, ch. 4).

21. See Phase 9 of the *DPFI*. In 1969, just prior to instituting the *DPFI*, the Board also adjusted the fare taper. See Order 69-9-68.

22. In part, the decision in the *DPFI* was based on Federal Court of Appeals decisions which found standby fares (Transcontinental Bus System, Inc. v. CAB, 393 F.2d 466) and family fares (Trailways to New England v. CAB, 412 F.2d 926) to be discriminatory. The courts ruled that the Board could approve fares that were based on the costs of transportation. It was prohibited, however, from approving fares based solely on the status of passenger. Although the *DPFI* mandated a reduction in discounts, carriers had already begun limiting the size and availability of them. Discover America fares for markets under 1,500 miles were canceled in 1970 and were phased out entirely in 1974. Carriers were free to extend the Discover America fare, with justification, but no carrier tried to do so.

23. Low season winter fares can be considered an example of off-peak fares that were permitted, but these were on a seasonal rather than a daily or weekly basis.

24. See *DPFI*, Phase 9.

25. The profit impact test required that the fare generate "sufficient additional traffic to more than offset (1) the diversion of full-fare traffic; and (2) the added non-capacity costs associated with the generated traffic, less any savings in cost attributable to the nature of the service provided to the discount traffic."

26. For example, one-way group fares proposed by Hughes Air Corp. (Order 76-1-49) and by Frontier (Order 76-12-10).

27. For example, extension of peak and off-peak fares for Delta (Order 76-12-76) and of capacity-controlled economy excursion fares for Continental (Order 76-12-109).

28. See MacAvoy and Snow (1977).

29. The 1976 DOT study concludes: "... certificated service has been lost by small communities and the quality of service (measured either in terms of frequency or markets served) has been reduced at many of the small communities still served by certificated carriers. This long-term trend shows no sign of slackening and, if anything, is increasing in speed."

30. The Board could suspend a point without a hearing, but deletions required a hearing if it

was contested by the affected community. Generally, the Board promptly approved uncontested deletions, but contested deletions could be held up several years (see Pulsifer 1975, 55–57). For an account of changes in certificated service levels, see MacAvoy and Snow (1977, 31–106).

31. U.S. Department of Transportation (1976, 28–29). Small cities are defined to be those with populations of less than 100,000.

32. There is evidence cited by Caves (1962) and Keeler (1972) that the airline industry earned a return on investment about the same, on average, as the return in the corporate sector. Such a comparison is the appropriate reference point for comparison for an opportunity cost of capital.

Chapter 2

1. For a more detailed description of this early history, see Levine (1965).

2. For a discussion, see Kelleher (1978).

3. It is interesting to note that PSA moved away from the entrepreneurial qualities that had brought its initial success. By 1965 PSA was able to obtain legislation within the State of California which empowered the California Public Service Commission to regulate entry. Thereafter intrastate prices, though below CAB-mandated levels of routes of similar distance, began to increase substantially. Also new carriers, with the exception of Air California, were kept from the market. Moreover, until the mid-1970s, there was a policy of dividing routes between PSA and Air California, rather than the freer policy of permitting either or both of the carriers to enter a market as conditions dictated. Thus the low-fare carrier, once it had established itself as a substantial force in the marketplace, asked for the sort of protection against entry that, had it existed earlier, would have prevented this entrant from ever having established itself.

4. Aside from Alfred Kahn, the other three consistent reform votes would be supplied by G. Joseph Minetti and Lee West, and a new appointee and economist, Elizabeth E. Bailey.

5. The air cargo carriers sought freedom to restructure routes to obtain greater pricing flexibility. An air cargo deregulation bill was enacted in October 1977, one year earlier than passenger deregulation. The deregulation in pricing, route entry, and equipment for incumbent carriers was immediate, with new carriers permitted into the industry only after a year. Deregulation of pricing before entry caused some perverse incentives, but these were swamped by the rapid growth in service (see Carron 1980). The case for this bill was made by the industry. Federal Express, a rapidly growing overnight small package delivery service, was exempted from CAB regulation because it operated small commuter aircraft. Its request to operate larger aircraft, though still outside of the Board's route and rate authority, was denied by the Board. Federal Express turned to Congress for help, and Flying Tiger, the largest all-cargo carrier, supported its effort. With industry support and little active opposition by others, the bill moved swiftly in Congress.

6. Airline Deregulation Act of 1978. Public Law 95-504, 95th Congress, S. 2493.

Chapter 3

1. See Douglas and Miller (1974).

2. Order 77-3-80, p. 4.

3. The early warning system was also used a few months later in international fare policy where much the same issues were arising. Specifically, scheduled carriers were reducing their Super Apex fare in September 1977, clearly in response to the great expansion of charters and the entry of Freddie Laker's Skytrain. The Board at first suspended the Super Apex fares on

the grounds that proposed fares appeared predatory, and if Laker were driven from the market, it might take many years before another new entrant could gain permission to enter. President Carter overruled the Board after obtaining a side letter with the United Kingdom that permitted intervention if it appeared Laker would go bankrupt. The Board used its Early Warning System to study the situation. It found that U.S.–U.K. scheduled traffic was up 61.2 percent from July to September 1978 over the similar period in 1977, with Laker gaining a healthy share of the market. Charter traffic was down 35.8 percent over the same period, with the bulk of the loss being in charter seats of the scheduled carriers. The net traffic increase was 25.1 percent. Because Laker prospered during this period, Board concerns about the potential for predation under deregulation eased.

4. For a wide ranging discussion of his view of this dilemna, see Alfred E. Kahn (1977).

5. After the CAB indicated to the certificated carriers that it would no longer adhere to its formerly rigid attitude about the relative prices of first-class and coach fares, it took about two weeks for the carriers to settle on a level approximately 130 percent of coach (as contrasted to the old 160 percent of coach), and within a few months this was reduced further to 120 percent of coach. The percentage remained in the 120 to 130 percent range until 1983, when it began to increase.

6. A problem with the Board's regulatory policies was illustrated by its decision to hold fares in California below SIFL, where state regulatory policies had kept fares below interstate level. Opportunities to serve interstate markets at higher fares were attractive to the intrastate carriers, and the trunks were restructuring their routes and fleet configurations. Since exit was easier under the act, some at the Board felt that these relatively low fares prompted United to leave Bakersfield and other carrier withdrawals from California communities. At the disparately low fares, set by the Board to increase only gradually in a transition process, carriers found that other entry opportunities dominated those in California. The communities would have preferred higher prices and continued service to CAB "help" in pricing. See Robert Frank (1979). It would seem that the strategy of non-intervention would clearly have been superior here, and the Board was reminded again how difficult it is to try to regulate perfectly.

7. These percentages are based on the Air Transport Association's "Monthly Discount Report." The standard coach fare includes all standard coach Y fares. However, it classified unrestricted low fares like the Y5 and the Y28 as discounts. The percentage of Y fares are as follows: 1977 = 61.5 percent; 1978 = 52.1 percent; 1979 = 49.2 percent; 1980 = 40.0 percent; 1981 = 34.3 percent; 1982 (six months) = 24.7 percent.

8. It should be noted that at the time the ADA passed fares were still largely based on the *DPFI* formula. The ADA mandated fare ceilings; because of a number of technical changes, the new formula became known as the Standard Industry Fare Level (SIFL). In projecting costs under this formula, the Board ensured that historic rates of cost increases would continue. Consequently, when fuel prices leveled off in 1981, the SIFL rose substantially above actual costs.

9. Management and advertising are not generally considered to be fixed expenses: as the size of an enterprise is reduced, the number of managers as well as the amount of advertising can be adjusted accordingly. In discussing pricing in particular markets, however, each can be considered a fixed cost. Additions or deletions of flights will not have an appreciable effect on the demand for management service or on advertising.

10. We also have comparable data for three former intrastate carriers. The structure of cost is comparable for each class of carrier. For a detailed discussion of the new entrants cost structure, see chapter 5.

11. See, for example, White (1979) or Keeler (1978).

12. Since the smaller aircraft is less efficient, its price on the used aircraft market is substan-

tially less. Therefore the differences in the costs of operating the two aircraft, though quite substantial, is smaller than this discussion indicates.

13. Some of the later model DC-8s are being reequipped with more fuel-efficient engines. These aircraft will undoubtedly remain in service for quite some time. The price of fuel will have a strong effect on the phaseout speed of different models of aircraft. With the decline in fuel prices since 1981, the service life of older generation aircraft has been extended.

14. Studies have generally found that the frequency elasticity of demand is less than one (i.e., the percentage increase in demand from an additional flight is less than the percentage increase in the number of flights). See, for example, Devany (1975).

15. The data in tables 3.5, 3.6, and 3.7 are weighted averages derived from service segment data. The weights are based on O & D passengers. The sample of 1,322 markets includes all those receiving nonstop service and for which service segment and O & D fare data was available. The number of markets in each distance-density category is shown in appendix G. Connecting, as well as local origin and destination passengers, travel on nonstop segments. Thus it is quite plausible that, as indicated, markets with ten to fifty O & D passengers per day average forty-four passengers per flight.

16. At a 55 percent load factor, the Board deliberately set the *DPFI* fares below costs in the short-haul markets. Consequently the actual loss incurred in serving these markets was higher than the Board estimated.

17. Ideally, we would like to compare the actual fares before and after deregulation. Unfortunately reliable market fare data are available only since late 1979. Average fares exclude first-class fares but include all coach and discount fares. The *DPFI* formula reflects cost adjustments made through May 1981.

18. In general, fares relative to the *DPFI* tend to decrease as distance and density increase, but there are some notable exceptions. For example, in the long-haul markets average fares do not vary substantially with market density. Low fares in the densest long-haul markets, where airlines are trying to fill up their wide bodies, have apparently put downward pressure on fares in the thinner long-haul markets as well.

Medium distance (501 to 1,500 miles) high-density (501 + passengers) markets tend to have higher fares than shorter-haul markets. In part, this is due to a relatively large proportion of the markets in this cell involving service to FAA slot restricted airports at New York, Chicago, and Washington, D.C.

19. For an early discussion of the efficiencies associated with capacity-controlled discount fares, see Salop (1978).

20. The discussed change in regulations are in CAB Order 80-2-23 and CAB Regulation ER-1246.

21. See the *Competitive Marketing Investigation*, Order 82-12-85.

22. For a discussion of this issue, see Frank (1983). Frank argues that the time sensitivity of some passengers and the economies of scale of aircraft encourage airlines to differentiate prices among consumers. He maintains that instead of operating small aircraft to satisfy time-sensitive passengers' demand for frequent service, carriers operate large equipment. The lower marginal cost of operating the bigger equipment allows carriers to charge lower fares for discretionary passengers. The advance purchase and minimum stay requirements are effective means of distinguishing between passengers who value highly frequent flights and those passengers who do not.

23. For a discussion of the welfare implications of monopolistic competition, see Spence (1976) or Schmalensee (1977). In 1983, to take account of the changing competitive environ-

ment, the Board redefined the circumstances under which it might make a finding of price discrimination, (see ER-93). In chapter 9 we show that the dominant carrier achieves high load factors and sets higher fares. Thus, in practice, entry may not completely eliminate excess profits.

24. Thus far the evidence indicates that carriers are more likely to employ unrestricted off-peak fares in large markets than in small markets. Keeler (1981) found that in a sample of ninety large markets over 60 percent had an unrestricted fare that was at least 15 percent below the cost-adjusted *DPFI* formula. In a sample of sixty-two markets that were not among the largest 100, but had nonstop service, we found that only 14 percent had unrestricted coach fares below the fare formula in June 1981. An additional 14 percent had capacity-controlled discounts that were below the fare formula but did not have advance purchase or minimum stay requirements.

25. The higher cost of developing and administering a restricted discount pricing system may explain why new entrants tend to select a more simplified fare structure.

Chapter 4

1. For example, Allegheny Route Realignment (Order 73-10-24) and Western Route Realignment (Order 77-11-74).

2. For an excellent discussion of policy planning at this time, see the speech of Alfred E. Kahn before the New York Society of Security Analysts, February 2, 1978.

3. Public Charter Rule, PR-149, August 15, 1978.

4. Carlton, Landes, and Posner (1980) estimate the value in 1978 of an airline connection to be as much as $17 on a connecting trip with a fare of $117.

5. Prior to deregulation, USAir established a network of commuter airlines, termed Allegheny Commuters, which shares gate and reservation facilities with USAir (formerly Allegheny Airlines). In the *Origin and Destination Survey*, passengers who connect between USAir and an Allegheny Commuter are considered to be traveling online.

6. United's initial decision to sell its B-737 was undoubtedly influenced by uncompetitive pilot work rules. See chapter 5.

7. For a detailed examination of changes in firm shares of industry traffic between 1978 and 1981, see appendix F.

8. A large hub is defined as a city that accounts for a least 1.00 percent of all domestic enplanements. Medium hubs are those with 0.25 to 0.99 percent. Small hubs have 0.05 to 0.024 percent. Nonhubs have less than 0.05 percent.

9. The *O & D Survey* does not distinguish between voluntary layovers from connections that are required to complete a trip. For example, if a passenger stops at a city for business while enroute to another city, the stop may be counted as a connection. Thus connections will be greater than zero even in the biggest markets. Those trips on flights that make one or more stops are not considered connections.

10. As we discuss in the chapter 3, the economies of aircraft size become quite pronounced in long-haul markets, so there are strong incentives to develop feed for such markets.

Chapter 5

1. Braniff ceased operation in May 1982, and Muse began in July 1981. Both are included.

2. In the fall of 1981 United renegotiated a new labor contract with its pilots which allowed it to begin using a two-man crew. At the same time it reconfigured its B-737 to increase the number of seats substantially.

3. For more on this, see chapter 8.

4. This was mitigated by a Mutual Aid Pact agreed on by the carriers and approved by the Board. Essentially, the agreement required a struck carrier to be compensated for part of its profit shortfalls by the operating carriers. This agreement was terminated by the Airline Deregulation Act.

5. The discussion in this section is based on Baitsell (1966), M. L. Kahn (1971), and Pulsifer et al. (1975).

6. Before the Civil Aeronautics Board was formed in 1938, the industry was essentially regulated by the Post Office and then the Interstate Commerce Commission.

7. Under the Decision #83 rates, the mileage pay component accounted for only a small part of total pilot earnings; its relative significance has increased over time. During the 1930s the Decision #83 rates set the pay scale standard for the entire airline industry. The first air carrier labor agreement with ALPA used those rates in 1939.

8. For a more detailed analysis of the later negotiations and the ensuing changes, see Baitsell (1966).

9. For additional discussion of pilot compensation, see chapter 8.

10. One study of labor relations in that time period found that over 16 percent of the total pilot work force in 1961 could attribute their employment to work rules. Similarly a 1960 ALPA report concluded that a return-to-work rule prevailing in 1950 would have permitted most airlines to furlough up to 20 percent of their pilots. M. L. Kahn (1971). If each pilot works fewer hours, air carriers must employ larger pilot work forces to cover the same flight schedules.

11. Pulsifer et al. (1975, 146).

12. Pulsifer (1975, 147–148) notes that flights attendant overtime pay begins with 65 to 71 hours per month. We also show that the productivity of flight attendants has not increased significantly since 1977 (see table 8.6).

13. Airline productivity and wage numbers were obtained from Form 41. Data for the manufacturing sector were obtained from the Bureau of Labor Statistics.

14. Airline earnings data are based on U.S. Bureau of Labor Statistics 1980 prepublished data on occupational earnings. Unless otherwise noted, data for other industries are based on U.S. Bureau of Labor Statistics publication, *Occupational Earnings in All Metropolitan Areas*, July 1980.

15. Blue-collar supervisor earnings are based on U.S. Bureau of Labor Statistics data from the unpublished 1981 Current Population Survey. Since wages generally increased between 1980 and 1981, the wage differential is probably understated.

16. School teachers earnings are based on U.S. Bureau of Labor Statistics publication, *Current Wage Developments*, January 1981.

17. Wage data for nurses are based on the U.S. Bureau of Labor Statistics *Industry Wage Survey of Hospitals in the Washington, D.C. Metropolitan Area*, October 1981.

18. Data for military pilots' earnings are based on 1981 approximations by the U.S. Navy Compensation Policy Branch. Commercial pilot earnings are based on "B/CA Survey: Pilot and Mechanic Salaries," *Business and Commercial Aviation*, 35 : 56–63, September 1974, from Pulsifer et al. (1975). The Pulsifer report noted that airline captains enjoyed annual earnings of 59 percent above those of the company captain. While jet equipment in business aviation is much smaller than trunk carrier jets, the necessary level of skill differs little between company pilots of heavy jets and airline pilots of some aircraft types.

19. For more on this, see our discussion of the S-curve in chapter 9.

20. For a period of time after deregulation some new entrants adopted the strategy of precommiting itself to remaining small by limiting its available capacity and setting a low price. In this way it minimized its ability to injure the incumbent, and its low price made retaliation expensive. Therefore it gave incumbents an incentive to accommodate its entry.

Chapter 6

1. See Eads (1972).

2. See Douglas and Miller (1974, 91).

3. U.S. Senate Report (1975, 65–68).

4. The report was published in MacAvoy and Snow (1977, 141–159).

5. Eads (1972, 133); See Order E-8758, November 1954.

6. Eads (1972, 135).

7. Eads (1972, 143).

8. MacAvoy and Snow (1977, 84).

9. Eads (1972, 119).

10. Eads (1972, 152).

11. Eads (1972, 181).

12. Pulsifer (1975, 91).

13. Association of Local Transport Airlines (1977).

14. U.S. Civil Aeronautics Board (1978).

15. Consumers would pay a through fare based on distance on itineraries that involved connection to a commuter flight. This through fare would normally be less than the sum of the local fares. For an analysis of the anticipated versus actual effects of this rule, see Kaplan (1980).

16. Testimony of Patrick V. Murphy, Jr., Acting Associate Director of Subsidy Policy and Programs, before the Joint Economic Committee, Subcommittee on Economic Goals and Intergovernmental Policy, June 21, 1982.

17. A flight is defined somewhat differently from a departure. If a plane travels from A to B to C along a linear route, there will be two flights from point A—one of them a nonstop to point B and the other a one-stop to point C. But there is only one departure from A. If point B were dropped, the number of flights from A would decrease by 1, but the number of departures would remain the same.

18. A nonhub is defined to have less than 0.05 percent of domestic enplanements.

Chapter 7

1. For definition of hub sizes, see chapter 4, note 8.

Chapter 8

1. A rigorous examination of the behavior of airlines under CAB fare regulation can be found in Schmalensee (1977).

2. Since the equations are estimated in log form, the changes are calculated using a given percentage change in concentration. For the number of airlines variable the change is $(2 - 1)/1.5 = 0.666$, and $0.666 \times -0.146 = -0.097$. (Note the midpoint of the range is used

to calculate the percentage change.) For 1976 the calculation is $(0.5 - 1)0.75 = -0.666$, and $-0.666 \times 0.126 = -0.084$. Similarly in 1981 the result is $-0.666 \times 0.061 = -0.041$.

3. We consider efficient aircraft to be the wide-bodied aircraft as well as the B-727-200, DC-9-30, and B-737. The locals utilization rate is based on their use of the B-737 and DC-9-30. To control for changes in fleet composition, we compute the average utilization weighted by the share of ASMs supplied by each aircraft type in 1978.

4. The development of a hub-and-spoke operation appears to inhibit increases in productivity as measured by utilization. However, such a conclusion may be based on too narrow a view. A hub-and-spoke operation reduces travel times by providing more frequent and well-timed flights in a large number of markets. Also, as we show in chapter 9, carriers that provide significant amounts of online feed onto a flight segment tend to operate at higher load factors.

5. Despite the decrease in the number of B-727-100s in their fleets between 1978 and 1981, the utilization of this aircraft and the larger and more efficient version, B-727-200, fell by comparable percentage amounts. Given the relative inefficiency of the smaller B-727-100, we would expect its utilization rate to have fallen faster.

6. The locals underwent a rather distinct jump in average seating density in 1979 and 1980. Prior to that time average seating densities had remained essentially unchanged throughout the 1970s. In 1980 seating densities were about 7 percent higher than in 1977.

7. At most airlines a pilot is guaranteed a minimum flight-hour credit for time on duty, even when he is not operating the aircraft. Some of the airlines have negotiated contracts that change the rates at which pilots are compensated for time they are not flying. For example, a pilot often is guaranteed one hour of flight pay for every three hours of duty time, whether or not he actually flies for an hour. Thus, if a pilot is away from base for twenty-four hours he is guaranteed at least eight hours of flight pay, regardless of whether he flies eight hours, six hours, or even less. In some cases the credit for layover time has been reduced so that now three and a quarter hours of duty time is required for each hour of guaranteed flight time.

Also a pilot is generally paid for a minimum number of flight hours per month, regardless of his actual service time. Historically, if he flew more, he banked those extra hours against another month's service. Recently several airlines have renegotiated contracts to increase the guaranteed number of credit hours. The industry standard has been seventy-five hours; it seems to be increasing to eighty hours. Also several airlines have negotiated contracts so that pilots with flight hours above the minimum in one month are not credited for flight time in subsequent months but instead received supplemental pay. For a discussion of recent labor relation developments, see Northrup (1984).

8. If one factor price increases more rapidly than another, firms will tend to substitute away from the higher cost factor. Thus, even with no productivity improvement, average cost will not increase as rapidly as the average input price. For example, the increase in fuel prices during 1979 and 1980 led to some factor substitution by airlines. They reduced cruising speeds to conserve fuel, substituting capital and labor for fuel.

9. The input index is contained in appendix H. The input index contains eight elements plus a miscellaneous category. The categories for the domestic trunks index and their weights appear in appendix I. For a description of the methodology used in developing the index, see Sobin (1981).

10. These relationships are derived from the simple algebraic equation for average airline costs:

$$AC = \frac{C}{Q} = \frac{P * X}{Q},$$

where

C = total cost,
P = a vector of input prices,
X = a vector of inputs,
Q = output.

Taking logs and differentiating yields

$$\frac{dAC}{AC} - \frac{dP}{P} = \frac{d(X/Q)}{X/Q}.$$

We define the ratio of inputs per unit of output as our measure of productivity. Hence the equation shows that the percentage change in productivity is equal to the difference between the percentage change in average cost and the percentage change in input prices. The equations in the text essentially repeat this equation, with the notation applicable to the data used for the calculations.

11. Caves, Christensen, and Tretheway estimate total factor productivity growth over the period 1970 to 1980. Their estimates include capital and cover a slightly different time period than the estimates reported in the text, so there are several differences. Our estimate of productivity growth for the trunks was substantially higher in the 1970 to 1975 period: 4.7 percent per year versus 2.6 percent for Caves et al. This may be due to the fact that the introduction of wide bodies substituted capital for other inputs, and our index would capture only the savings in noncapital costs but not the increase in capital costs.

Since the estimates we reported in the text for the post 1975 period include 1981, we recalculated our index for the 1975 to 1980 period to make a comparison with Caves et al. Our index for the 1975 to 1980 period indicates productivity growth was 5.5 percent for the trunks (vs. 4.9 percent for Caves et al.) and 8.1 percent for the locals (vs. 6.3 percent); both of these estimates are substantially higher than the estimates including 1981. The difference between the two estimates is smaller in the second half of the decade. This probably reflects the fact that substitution of capital for labor and fuel due to the introduction of wide-bodied aircraft slowed substantially in the middle of the decade.

Qualitatively, the main difference in the results is that for the trunk airlines Caves et al. finds a substantially higher productivity growth after 1975 than before 1975, whereas we find that productivity growth was only slightly higher after deregulation (5.5 percent in 1975 to 1980 vs. 4.7 percent in 1971 to 1975). When 1981 is included, we find that productivity growth (4.5 percent per year for 1975 to 1981) is actually somewhat lower after 1975 than before.

Chapter 9

1. In Alaska charter operations are still under the control of the state. Charter operations are an important part of the scheduled carriers' operations. Fares in intra-Hawaiian markets are undoubtedly affected by the Board's common fare rule, which was in effect until June 1982.

2. Operations at the four slot-controlled airports have been restricted since 1966 and are unrelated to the PATCO strike which occurred after the period considered in this analysis. Service to New York City includes service to Newark International Airport, which is not slot constrained. The *O & D Survey*, the source of our fare and traffic data, does not distinguish service among the New York City airports, and thus, neither do we. Service to Washington National is restricted for the most part to cities that are less than 650 miles away. Nevertheless, many long-haul markets receive substantial amounts of one-stop or connecting service from National Airport in addition to nonstop service to other airports in the metropolitan area. We therefore do not distinguish between cities that are served nonstop from National and those that are not.

3. As we noted earlier, we also provide estimates of the effect of concentration on fares after adjusting for the amount of interline traffic.

4. It is noteworthy that the Department of Justice's recently published merger guidelines define a market to be competitive if it has a Herfindahl of less than 0.1.

5. In general, carriers are more likely to offer a discount fare on an online service than an interline service. Consequently interline passengers are more likely to be time sensitive and to be traveling on an unrestricted fare. Thus in some markets the interline variable may be a surrogate for the proportion of passengers who are time sensitive. Also some interline trips may be misclassified in our sample. Thus, if a passenger's itinerary took him from Washington, D.C., to Chicago and then to Los Angeles and finally back to Washington, the *O & D Survey* would classify him as traveling round trip between Washington and Los Angeles. In fact the itinerary should be classified as three trips—Washington–Chicago, Chicago–Los Angeles, Los Angeles–Washington. Such complex itineraries are more likely to include more than one carrier.

Finally, the CAB's mandatory joint fare rule may have led to higher interline fares. This rule expired with the Board's regulatory authority over fares on January 1, 1983. The Board stipulated that unrestricted fares for interline connecting trips could not exceed the sum of the local fares minus a terminal charge and that revenues were to be shared according to a CAB-determined formula. Carriers could negotiate alternative agreements, but short-haul carriers usually did not do so because they were favored under the joint fare rules. With the lapsing of the rule, the premium paid by interline passengers will probably decline. Nevertheless, since there are costs in negotiating joint fare agreements and since the cost of handling interline connecting passengers is greater than online connecting passengers, the premium cannot be expected to disappear.

6. For a discussion of the test see Hausman (1978). Nakamura and Nakamura (1981) have shown that Hausman's test is equivalent to Wu's T2 test. See Wu (1973, 1974).

7. Our estimate of the S-curve is slightly different from that employed by Douglas and Miller (1974) and discussed by Schmalensee (1977). Their estimation technique assumes the number of flights in the market remains constant as carriers' departure shares change. However, we would expect the total number of flights to increase as the concentration of the market declines. Our equation allows this and therefore is a somewhat better specification for estimating the effects of market share on load factors.

8. These markets were classified as the two hundred largest in terms of local passengers in the Board's *O & D Survey* for the year ending June 1978. Six of the markets did not receive nonstop service.

Chapter 10

1. It denied a proposed United-Western merger in 1940, a proposed American–Mid-Continent merger in 1946, and a Capital-Northeast merger in 1947. It also blocked a proposed Braniff-Frontier merger in 1946.

2. Braniff absorbed Mid-Continent in 1952, Western absorbed Inland also in 1959, Delta absorbed Chicago and Southern in 1953, Continental absorbed Pioneer in 1955, and Eastern absorbed Colonial in 1956. A proposed Eastern-Colonial-National merger was denied in 1954, and a Delta-Northeast merger was withdrawn in 1955.

3. A proposed Continental-National merger was withdrawn in 1962, a Pan American–TWA merger was withdrawn in 1963, and an American-Eastern merger was disapproved in 1963.

4. CAB Orders 70-12-162 and 70-12-163 (December 22, 1970).

5. See, for example, American-Western merger application, June 13, 1972, CAB Orders 72-7-92.

6. See, for example, Delta-Northeast Case, April 27, 1972, CAB Orders 72-5-73 and 73-5-74.

7. Section 408(b)(1)(13) of the Airline Deregulation Act of 1978, P. L. No. 95-504.

8. The Board's Office of Economic Analysis had sponsored a series of Airline Industry Merger Policy Seminars in the late fall of 1978. These seminars helped the Board to frame issues in a broadly consistent fashion.

9. For a detailed discussion of this recommendation and of post-ADA CAB merger policy, see Jollie and Sibley (1982). See also Wentz (1982).

10. It is sometimes possible to avoid being boxed in by a constraint by enlarging the set of options currently available, in this case through the process of renegotiation. This is an important principle for policymakers.

11. See *The Consequence of Airline Mergers Since Deregulation*, Report of Civil Aeronautics Board Staff, April 1982.

12. Order 82-4-144 gave Eastern an exemption to replace Braniff's service and granted *pendente lite* approval to the transactions contemplated by the "Interim Operating and Joint Service Agreement." Order 82-9-81 instituted the Braniff–South American route Transfer Case. The six-year agreement was approved but not granted antitrust immunity, by Order 83-6-74.

13. See, for example, CAB Order 73-4-98 (April 24, 1973), pp. 1–2.

14. The high-density rule went into effect in 1968. Included in the rule were Washington National, Chicago O'Hare, and New York's Kennedy and La Guardia Airports. Newark Airport was initially included but later dropped.

15. The certificated carrier approval was first granted in Order 68-12-11, December 3, 1968, and the commuter carriers in Order 69-2-52, February 12, 1969.

16. Since carriers undoubtedly earn rents by serving a limited access market, the impact on fares could be significantly less.

17. For a discussion of one method of implementing such a system, see Graham, Kaplan, and Sharp (1980). The staff of the CAB supported such an approach in comments before the FAA. See comments of the CAB staff to DOT's rule-making proposal for National Airport, January 26, 1981.

18. A parallel screening organization by the International Air Transportation Association was approved for international air transportation.

19. Order 78-8-87, August 17, 1978, and Order 80-2-23, February 5, 1980.

20. Since carriers as well as their agents were required to sell tickets at the posted tariff prices, agents could not legally rebate any of their increased compensation to passengers. In 1980 the Board adopted the maximum tariff rule (CAB Regulation ER-1246), which allowed carriers' fares to deviate from airline tariffs as long as the fares did not exceed the ceiling. The Board's decision meant that the relationship between airline prices and posted tariffs was a contractual matter between the carriers and their agents.

21. See Order 82-12-85.

22. Since one of the authors is at the CAB and the issue is still pending, we have been constrained to give a rather superficial treatment that avoids taking any policy stand. Our material is thus confined to that given in U.S. CAB Report to Congress on Computer Reservation Systems, May 1983. In March 1984, the CAB proposed a rule to deal with a number of the alleged problems with computer reservation systems. (Docket 41686).

23 Rules should not, for example, favor one group of carriers, say incumbents, over another group, say new entrants. Market-based rules, such as those put forward in the Polinomics

Study, offer an efficient approach but one that is being strongly resisted by air carriers. They fear that such fees will cause an erosion of profits.

24. The FAA's chief regulations to reduce aircraft noise are known as "FAR 36 Standards." FAA, Noise Standards: Aircraft Type and Airworthiness Certificate, 14 CFR, No. 36.1 (1978).

25 See Report and Recommendations of the Airport Access Task Force, Pursuant to PL 97-248, March 1983.

26. Specifically, on May 5, 1981, the Board of Supervisors rejected criticism and suggestions of other parties and approved a final airport access plan which (1) grandfathers its 41 slots to incumbent carriers—Air California 23–1/2, Republic 11–1/2, Frontier 2, Western 2, and PSA 2; (2) freezes that allocation for three years with no new entrants permitted to acquire slots; (3) adds additional slots during the three-year period only if noise reduction goals are exceeded by the incumbents, at which time the new slots become available to the incumbents with the least number of slots; (4) retains a 500-mile perimeter rule; (5) retains a 95,000 pound gross weight limitation (with an exception for DC-9-80 aircraft); and (6) requires conversion to "Stage III or equivalent" aircraft within two years.

27. Pacific Southwest Airlines vs. County of Orange, et al., CA-81-3248 (C.D. Gal.).

28. The Airport Access Task Force Report (1983) concludes that Air Transport Association members have not always received the precise facilities they desired, or as quickly as they had hoped, but access was obtained in all instances. Members of the Regional Airline Association, in contrast, reported problems with airport signing, less than desirable space, operating restrictions on terminal ramps, and restrictions on their ability to service their own aircraft.

29. See, for example, Marvin S. Cohen, "The Antitrust Implications of Airline Deregulation," January 13, 1983.

Bibliography

Airline Pilots Association. *Report of the Wage and Working Conditions Policy Committee.* Washington, D.C.: Airline Pilots Association, August 1966.

Air Transportation Association. *Consequences of Deregulation of the Scheduled Air Transport Industry: An Analytical Approach.* Washington, D.C.: Air Transport Association, 1975, 29 pp.

Air Transportation Association. "Monthly Discount Reports." Washington, D.C.: Air Transport Association, 1980.

Association of Local Transport Airlines. "Five Myths about Subsidized Airline Service to Small Cities." December 1977.

Anderson, J. E., and M. Kraus. "Quality of Service and the Demand for Air Travel." *Review of Economics and Statistics*, November 1981, pp. 533–540.

Bailey, E. E. "Reform from Within: Civil Aeronautics Board Policy, 1977–1978." *Problems in Public Utility Economics and Regulation*, Michael Crew, ed. Lexington, Mass.: Lexington Books, 1979.

Bailey, E. E. "Deregulation and Regulatory Reform of U.S. Air Transportation Policy." *Regulated Industries and Public Enterprise*, Bridger Mitchell and Paul Kleindorfer, eds. Lexington, Mass.: Lexington Books, 1980.

Bailey, E. E. "Contestability and the Design of Regulatory and Antitrust Policy." *American Economic Review 71*, May 1981, pp. 178–183.

Bailey, E. E., and J. C. Panzar, Jr. "The Contestability of Airline Markets during the Transition to Deregulation." *Law and Contemporary Problems*, Winter 1981, pp. 125–145.

Baumol, W. J., J. C. Panzer, and R. D. Willig. *Contestable Markets and the Theory of Industry Structure.* New York: Harcourt, Brace, Jovanovich, Inc., 1982.

Baitsell, J. M. *Airline Industry Industrial Relations: Pilots and Flight Engineers.* Cambridge, Mass.: Harvard University Press, 1966.

Brenner, M. A. "Deregulation Spawns Self-Destruct Pricing." *Airline Executive*, February 1982, pp. 14–15.

Brenner, M. A. "Need for Continued Economic Regulation of Air Transport." *Journal of Air Law and Commerce*, Autumn 1975, pp. 793–813.

Breyer, S. *Regulation and Its Reform.* Cambridge, Mass.: Harvard University Press, 1982, 472 pp.

Breyer, S., and L. Stein. "Airline Deregulation: The Anatomy of Reform Instead of Regulation." *Alternatives to Federal Regulatory Agencies*, Robert Poole, Jr., ed. Lexington, Mass.: Lexington Books, 1981, pp. 1–41.

Brown, S. R. L. "Regulatory Reform at the Civil Aeronautics Board to 1977." Washington, D.C.: Civil Aeronautics Board, November 1980, 47 pp.

Carlton, D., W. Landes, and R. Posner. "Benefits and Costs of Airline Mergers: A Case Study (Market Share Due to Single-Carrier Service in North Central–Southern Merger)." *Bell Journal of Economics*, Spring 1980, pp. 65–83.

Carron, A. S. *Transition to a Free Market: Deregulation of the Air Cargo Industry,* Washington, D.C.: Brookings Institution, 1981, 45 pp.

Caves, D. W., L. R. Christensen, and M. W. Thretheway. "Airline Productivity under Deregulation." *Regulation*, November–December 1982, pp. 25–28.

Caves, D. W., L. R. Christensen, and M. W. Thretheway. "Productivity Performance of U.S. Trunk and Local Service Airlines in the Era of Deregulation," *Economic Inquiry 21*, July 1983, pp. 312–334.

Caves, R. *Air Transport and Its Regulators: An Industry Study*. Cambridge, Mass.: Harvard University Press, 1962.

Cohen, Marvin S. "New Air Service and Deregulation: A Study in Transportation." *Journal of Air Law and Commerce 44* (4), 1979, pp. 695–703.

Cohen, Marvin S. "The Antitrust Implication of Airline Deregulation." January 13, 1983.

Daughety, A. F., and F. S. Inaba. "An Analysis of Regulatory Change in the Transportation Industry." *Review of Economic Statistics*, May 1981, pp. 246–255.

Demsetz, H. "Industry Structure, Market Rivalry and Public Policy." *Journal of Law and Economics 16*, April 1973, pp. 1–10.

DeVany, A. S. "The Effect of Price and Entry Regulation on Airline Output, Capacity and Efficiency." *Bell Journal of Economics*, Spring 1975, pp. 327–345.

Dorman, G. J. "Air Service to Small Communities After Airline Deregulation." New York: National Economic Research Associates, Inc., NERA Topics, 1982, 7 pp.

Dorman, G. J. "A Model of Unregulated Airline Markets," *Research in Transportation Economics*. Vol. 1. Greenwich, Conn.: JAI Press, Inc., 1983, pp. 131–148.

Douglas, G. W., and J. C. Miller III. *Economic Regulation of Domestic Air Transport: Theory and Policy*, Washington, D.C.: Brookings Institution, 1974.

Eads, G. C. "Competition in the Domestic Trunk Airline Industry: Too Much or Too Little." *Promoting Competition in Regulated Markets*, A. Phillips, ed. Washington, D.C.: Brookings Institution, 1975, pp. 13–54.

Eads, G. C. *The Local Service Airline Experiment*. Washington, D.C.: Brookings Institution, 1972.

Ellison, A. P. "The Structural Change of the Airline Industry Following Deregulation." *Transportation Journal*, Spring 1982, pp. 58–69.

Forsyth, P. J. "U.S. Airline Deregulation: An Interim Assessment." Working Paper. University of New South Wales, Australia, July 1981.

Frank, R. H. "What Should Board Policy Be with Respect to Intra-California Fares." Washington, D.C.: Civil Aeronautics Board Staff Memo, December 11, 1979.

Frank, R. H. "When are Price Differentials Discriminatory?" *Journal of Policy Analysis and Management 2*, Winter 1983.

Fruhan, W. E., Jr. *The Fight for Competitive Advantage: A Study of the United States Domestic Trunk Carriers*. Boston, Mass.: Harvard University Graduate School of Business Administration, 1972, 200 pp.

Gaskins, D. W., Jr., and J. M. Voytko. "Managing the Transition to Deregulation." *Law and Contemporary Problems*, Winter 1981, pp. 9–32.

Gill, F. W., and G. L. Bates. *Airline Competition*, Cambridge, Mass.: Harvard University Press, 1949.

Graham, D. R., D. P. Kaplan, and K. L. Sharp. "A Proposal to Adopt Noise and Congestion Fees at Washington National Airport." Office of Economic Analysis Staff Report. Washington, D.C.: Civil Aeronautics Board, January 1981.

Graham, D. R., and D. P. Kaplan. "Airline Deregulation Is Working." *Regulation*, May–June 1982, pp. 26–32.

Graham, D. R., and D. P. Kaplan. "Competition and the Airlines: An Evaluation of Deregulation." Office of Economic Analysis Staff Report. Washington, D.C.: Civil Aeronautics Board, December 1982.

Graham, D., D. P. Kaplan, and D. Sibley. "Efficiency and Competition in the Airline Industry." *Bell Journal of Economics 14*(1), Spring 1983, pp. 118–138.

Grether, D. M., R. M. Isaac, and C. R. Plott. "Alternative Methods of Allocating Airport Slots: Performance and Evaluation." Pasadena, Calif.: Polinomics Research Laboratories Inc., August 1979, 136 pp.

Grether, D. M., R. M. Isaac, and C. R. Plott. "The Allocation of Landing Rights by Unanimity among Competitors." *American Economic Review 71*(2), May 1981, pp. 166–171.

Hausman, J. A. "Specification Tests in Econometrics." *Econometrica 46*, November 1978, pp. 1251–1271.

Havens, A., and D. Heymsfeld, "Small Community Air Service under the Airline Deregulation Act of 1978." *Journal of Air Law and Commerce*, Spring 1981, pp. 641–686.

Hendricks, W. P., F. Szerszen, and C. Szerszen. "Regulation, Deregulation and Collective Bargaining in Airlines." *Industrial Labor Relations Review*, October 1980, pp. 67–81.

Ippolito, R. A. "Estimating Airline Demand with Quality of Service Variables." *Journal of Transport Economics and Policy*, January 1981, pp. 7–15.

James, G. W., ed. *Airline Economics*. Lexington, Mass.: Lexington Books, 1982.

Johnson, L. "Route Exit and Regulation under the Airline Deregulation Act: The Impact of Fuel Cost and Availability." *Journal of Air Law and Commerce*, Summer 1980.

Johnson, R. L. *Entry conditions in the Domestic Commercial Airline Industry under Deregulation*. Ph.D. Dissertation. Washington, D.C.: The George Washington University, 1982.

Jordan, W. A. *Airline Regulation in America: Effects and Imperfections*. Baltimore: The Johns Hopkins University Press, 1970.

Kahn, A. E. "Applications of Economics to an Imperfect World." *American Economic Review 69*, May 1979, pp. 1–13.

Kahn, A. E. "Talk to the New York Society of Security Analysts." New York City, February 2, 1978.

Kahn, A. E. "Regulatory Reform or How Do We Get from Here to There." Aero Club Speech, October 25, 1977.

Kahn, A. E. "The Airline Industry: Is It Time to Regulate?" New York: National Economic Research Associates, Inc., April 28, 1982.

Kahn, A. E. "Deregulation and Vested Interests: The Case of Airlines." *The Political Economy of Deregulation*, Roger B. Noll and Bruce M. Owen, eds. Washington, D.C.: American Enterprise Institute, 1983, pp. 132–151.

Kahn, M. L. "Collective Bargaining on the Airline Flight Deck." *Collective Bargaining and Technological Change in American Transportation*, H. Levinson, L. M. Rehmur, J. P. Goldberg, and M. L. Kahn eds. Evanston, Il.: Northwestern University, 1971.

Kaplan, D. P. "The Effects of the Mandatory Joint Fare Program on Commuter Airlines." Washington, D.C.: Civil Aeronautics Board Staff Memo, February 1980.

Keeler, T. "Airline Regulation and Market Performance." *Bell Journal of Economics*, Autumn 1972, pp. 399–424.

Keeler, T. "The Effect of Deregulation of Airfares: An Update." Unpublished, September 1981.

Keeler, T. "The Revolution in Airline Regulation." *Case Studies in Regulation: Revolution and Reform*. L. Weiss and M. Klass, eds., Boston and Toronto: Little, Brown and Company, 1981.

Keeler, T., and M. Abrahams. "Market Structure, Pricing, and Service Quality in the Airline Industry under Deregulation." *Applications of Economics Principles in Public Utilities Industries*, W. Sichel and T. Gies, eds. Ann Arbor: University of Michigan Press, 1981.

Kelleher, H. D. "Deregulation and the Practicing Attorney," *Journal of Air Law and Commerce 44*, 1978, pp. 261–296.

Keyes, L. S. *Federal Control of Entry into Air Transportation*. Cambridge, Mass.: Harvard University Press, 1951.

Levine, M. "Is Regulation Necessary? California Air Transportation and National Regulatory Policy." *Yale Law Journal 74*, July 1965, pp. 1416–1447.

Levine, M. "Revisionism Revised: Airline Deregulation and the Public Interest." *Law and Contemporary Problems*, Winter 1981, pp. 179–195.

MacAvoy, P. W., and J. Snow. *Regulation of Passenger Fares and Competition among the Airlines*. Washington, D.C.: American Enterprise Institute, 1977.

Maddala, G. S. *Econometrics*. New York: McGraw-Hill, 1977.

McMullen, B. S. "Truck Airline Financial Requirements and Economic Performance." *Research in Transportation Economics*, forthcoming 1984.

Meyer, J., and C. V. Oster, Jr. *Airline Deregulation: The Early Experience*. Boston, Mass.: Auburn House Publishing Company, 1981.

Morrison, S. A. "Estimation of Long-Run Prices and Investment Levels for Airport Runways." *Research in Transportation Economics*. Vol. 1. Greenwich, Conn.: JAI Press, Inc., 1983, pp. 103–148.

Nakamura, A., and Nakamura, M. "On the Relationships among Several Specification Error Tests Presented by Durgin, Wu, and Hausman." *Econometrica 49*, November 1981, pp. 1583–1588.

Nixon, S. "A Capsule History: ALPA's 50 Years." *Airline Pilot*, July 1981, pp. 7–23.

Northrup, H. R. "The New Employee-Relations Climate in Airlines." *Industrial and Labor Relations Review 36*, January 1983.

Olson, C. V., and J. M. Trapani. "Who Has Benefited from Regulation of the Airline Industry." *Journal of Law and Economics*, April 1981, pp. 75–93.

Panzar, J. C. *Regulation, Service Quality, and Market Performance: A Model of Airline Rivalry*. New York: Garland Publishing Inc., 1979.

Panzar, J. C. "Equilibrium and Welfare in Unregulated Airline Markets." *American Economic Review 69*, May 1979, pp. 92–95 (1979a).

Panzar, J. C. "Regulation, Deregulation and Economic Efficiency: The Case of the CAB." *American Economic Review*, May 1980, pp. 311–315.

Peltzman, S. "The Gains and Losses from Industrial Concentration." *Journal of Law and Economics 20*, October 1977, pp. 229–263.

Phillips, A., ed., *Promoting Competition in Regulated Markets*. Washington, D.C.: Brookings Institution, 1975, 397 pp.

Pulsifer, R., L. S. Keyes, J. A. McMahon, P. Eldridge, and W. L. Demory. *Regulatory Reform, Report of the CAB Special Staff*. Washington, D.C.: Civil Aeronautics Board, 1975.

Pustay, M. W. "Airline Regulation and Service to Small Communities." *Land Economics*, May 1979.

Revankar, N. S. "Asymptotic Relative Efficiency Analysis of Certain Tests of Independence in Structural Systems." *International Economic Review 19*, February 1978, pp. 165–179.

Revankar, N.S., and Hartley, M. J. "An Independence Test and Conditional Unbiased Predictions in the Context of Simultaneous Equation Systems. *International Economic Review 14*, October 1973, pp. 615–631.

Salop, S. "Alternative Reservations Contracts." Office of Economic Analysis Staff Memo. Washington, D.C.: Civil Aeronautics Board, 1978.

Schmalensee, R. "Comparative Static Properties of Regulated Airline Oligopolies." *Bell Journal of Economics*, Autumn 1977, pp. 565–576.

Scherer, F. M. *Industrial Market Structure and Economic Performance*, 2nd ed. Chicago: Rand McNally, 1980.

Sobin, B. "An Index of Input Costs for Domestic Trunk and Local Carriers." Washington, D.C.: Civil Aeronautics Board, September 1981.

Spence, M. "Product Differentiation and Welfare." *American Economic Review*, May 1976, pp. 407–414.

Spiller, P. T. "The Differential Impact of Airline Regulation in Individual Firms and Markets: An Empirical Analysis." *Journal of Law and Economics 26*, October 1983, pp. 655–689.

Stein, H. "What Economists Do." *The American Enterprise Institute Economist*, January 1984.

Stephenson, F., and F. Beier. "The Effects of Airline Deregulation on Air Service to Small Communities." *Transportation Journal*, Summer 1981, pp. 54–62.

Taneja, N. K. *Airlines in Transition*. Lexington, Mass.: Lexington Books, 1981.

U.S. Airport Access Task Force. Report and Recommendations, March 10, 1983.

U.S. Bureau of the Census. *Department of Commerce County and City Data Book, 1972. A Statistical Abstract Supplement*. Washington, D.C.: U.S. Government Printing Office, 1973.

U.S. Bureau of the Census. *Department of Commerce County and Data Book, 1977: A Statistical Abstract Supplement*. Washington, D.C.: U.S. Government Printing Office, 1978.

U.S. Civil Aeronautics Board. *Domestic Route System: Analysis and Policy Recommendations*. Washington, D.C.: Civil Aeronautics Board, October 1974.

U.S. Civil Aeronautics Board. *Domestic Passenger Fare Investigation: January 1970 to December 1974*. Washington, D.C.: U.S. Government Printing Office, 1976, 976 pp.

U.S. Civil Aeronautics Board. *Five Truths about Subsidized Small Community Air Service*. Testimony submitted to the Aviation Subcommittee of the House Public Works and Transportation Committee, March 6, 1978.

U.S. Civil Aeronautics Board. *Bibliography of Important Civil Aeronautics Board Regulatory Actions, 1975–1979*. Washington, D.C.: Civil Aeronautics Board, December 1979.

U.S. Civil Aeronautics Board. *Study of Competition and Other Factors Affecting Trunkline Load Factor and Profitability*. Washington, D.C.: Civil Aeronautics Board, January 1980.

U.S. Civil Aeronautics Board. *Consequences of Airline Mergers since Deregulation*. Washington, D.C.: Civil Aeronautics Board, April 1982.

U.S. Civil Aeronautic Board. The Impact of PATCO Job Action: November through March 1981. Office of Economic Analysis Memorandum. Washington, D.C.: Civil Aeronautics Board, July 16, 1982.

U.S. Civil Aeronautics Board. *Antitrust Policy for the Aviation Industry.* Washington, D.C.: Civil Aeronautics Board, 1982.

U.S. Civil Aeronautics Board. *Report to Congress on Airline Computer Reservation Systems,* Washington, D.C.: Civil Aeronautics Board, 1983.

U.S. Civil Aeronautics Board. *Report to Congress on Implementation of the Provisions of the Airline Deregulation Act of 1978.* Washington, D.C.: Civil Aeronautics Board, January 31, 1984.

U.S. Civil Aeronautics Board. "Employment, Productivity and Unit Cost, System Majors 1978–1984." Office of Economic Analysis Report. Washington, D.C.: Civil Aeronautics Board, April 2, 1984 (1984a).

U.S. Congress, Senate. *Committee on the Judiciary Oversight of Civil Aeronautics Board Practices and Procedures.* Washington, D.C.: U.S. Government Printing Office, 1975.

U.S. Department of Transportation. *Air Service to Small Communities.* Washington, D.C.: Department of Transportation, 1976.

Wentz, W. H. "Mobility Factors in Antitrust Cases: Assessing Market Power in Light of Conditions Affecting Entry and Fringe Expansion." *Michigan Law Review 80*(8), August 1982, pp. 1545–1613.

White, L. J. "Economics of Scale and the Question of Natural Monopoly in the Airline Industry." *The Journal of Air Law and Commerce 44*, November 3, 1979, pp. 545–573.

Wu, D. M. "Alternative Tests of Independence between Stochatic Regressions and Disturbances." *Econometrica 41*, July 1973, pp. 733–750.

Wu, D. M. "Alternative Tests of Independence between Stochastic Regressors and Disturbances: Finite Sample Results." *Econometrica 42*, May 1974, pp. 529–546.

Wyckoff, D. D., and D. H. Maister. *The Domestic Airline Industry.* Lexington, Mass.: Lexington Books, 1977, p. 191.

Index